IMAGES
of Rail

AMADOR CENTRAL RAILROAD

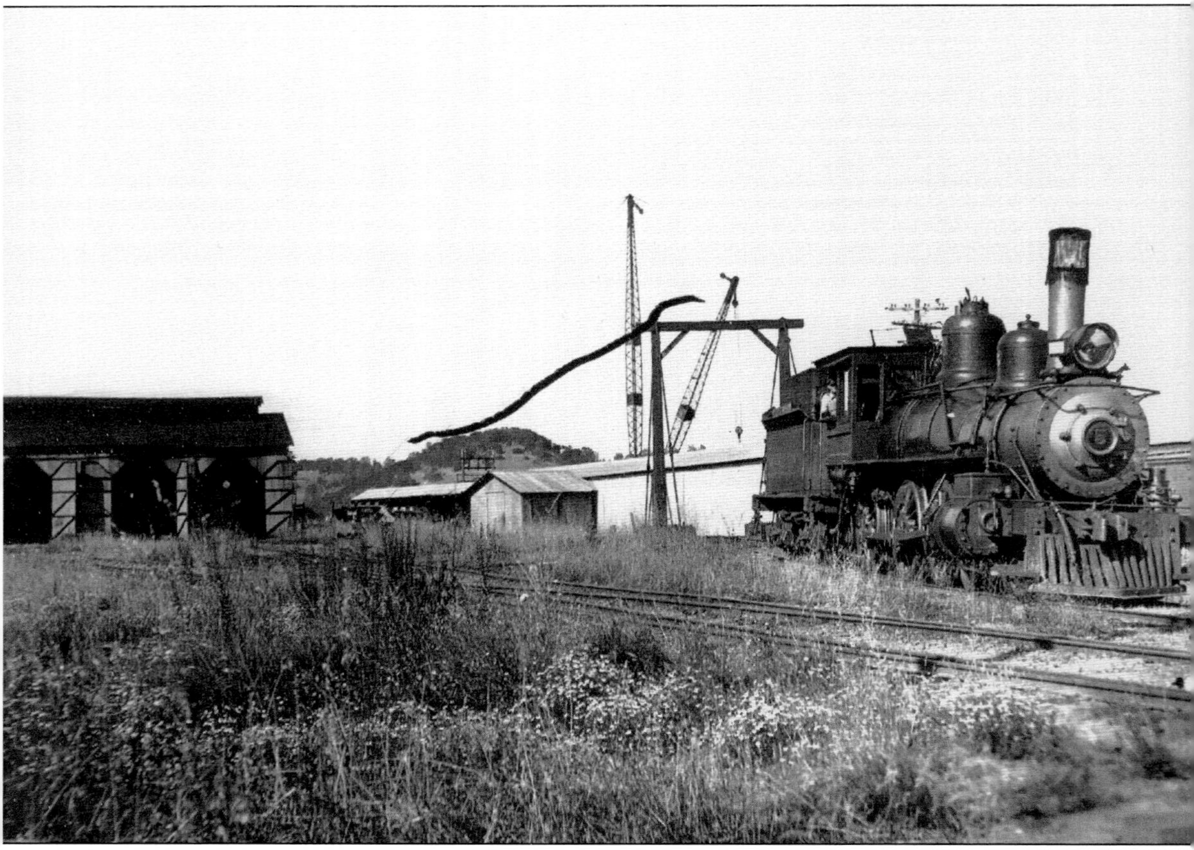

ON THE COVER: Pictured here and on the cover is Amador Central engine No. 5, parked at the Martell depot, the eastern terminus of the railroad. This Schenectady 4-6-0 locomotive was manufactured in 1875 for the Central Pacific Railroad, where it served as engine No. 189. It was then employed on the Southern Pacific Railroad as engine No. 1554 and later served as No. 2023. It ran on the line as No. 5 until 1945, when it was scrapped.

IMAGES
of Rail

AMADOR CENTRAL RAILROAD

Deborah Coleen Cook

ARCADIA
PUBLISHING

ISBN 978-0-7385-7550-6

Published by Arcadia Publishing
Charleston, South Carolina

Printed in the United States of America

Library of Congress Control Number: 2011920700

For all general information, please contact Arcadia Publishing:
Telephone 843-853-2070
Fax 843-853-0044
E-mail sales@arcadiapublishing.com
For customer service and orders:
Toll-Free 1-888-313-2665

Visit us on the Internet at www.arcadiapublishing.com

This book is dedicated to all those who worked to build and sustain the Amador Central Railroad through its many lives, to Sierra Pacific Industries for their generosity, and to those who have devoted themselves to preserving it for future generations.

Contents

ACKNOWLEDGMENTS

This book is a labor of love—for I have always loved the sound of the whistle and the clacking of the train. However, this story would not have become what it is without the help and support of a number of people. My sincerest gratitude is first and foremost extended to my husband and children for their understanding that it is in my soul to tell stories of the past and for their encouragement that I follow my dreams—especially to my daughter Amy, for her scholarly support and inspiring dialogue.

My appreciation once again goes out to the Amador County Archives for allowing me to use many of the images housed in their facility. Unless otherwise noted, the images used in this book are from the archives collection. Likewise, my gratitude is extended to Jim Fredrickson and Grant Vogel, for sharing rare photographs of the Amador Central from their collections to be used herein. Additionally, I am very grateful to Larry Bowler, Grant Vogel, and other members of the Recreational Railroad Coalition Historical Society for helping me along with my "railroad education" and for taking me on the marvelous speeder rides along the railroad. My thanks also go to my editor, John Poultney, for his patience and understanding through the many fits and starts I experienced along the way to completing this project.

I would also like to give acknowledgement to the work of those who have influenced and contributed to the compilation of this book, including to previous Amador Central historians, to Shelly Davis-King and Judith Marvin, who helped to save the railroad from destruction, and to Leslie McLaughlin, a dear friend and railroad fan who is no longer with us.

Introduction

It was once said that the history of the industrial development of the American nation is largely the history of American railroads. The ability to move products across great distances transformed the country, providing new opportunities to small, self-sufficient communities. As the rails spread out across the land, the increase in commerce developed alongside a growing romantic fascination with the new mode of travel and the faraway places that beckoned the traveler. For the residents of Amador County, the construction of the Amador Central Railroad brought both of these dreams to life. The story of this railroad is one of economic ups and downs and the ongoing dedication of the residents of a rural California county to keep a small but vital railroad in operation.

Construction of the Amador Central Railroad started in 1904 under the name of the Ione & Eastern Railroad; however, the story of this line begins several decades earlier and is inextricably linked to the Central Pacific Railroad (CPRR) and the larger story of the mining industry in Amador County. As early as 1870, talk of building a railroad in Amador had begun. An early idea proposed accessing Amador by rail from Stockton via the town of Copperopolis in Calaveras County, while another considered construction of an extension of the Sacramento Valley Railroad from Latrobe to Sutter Creek. These early imaginings died out, one by one, until the want of coal to power Central Pacific steam engines and gravel to ballast rail beds became the motivating factors for accessing Amador by rail. This was accomplished in 1875 when the "Big Four" of Central Pacific fame—C.P. Huntington, Charles Crocker, Mark Hopkins, and Leland Standford—built the Amador Branch Railroad. The line ran across the Sacramento Valley, from Galt to Ione, over a distance of 27.2 miles. Although this line provided an access to Amador County, it was known that, for Amador County to take full advantage of rail transportation, an extension of the rails into the heart of the county was needed. This prompted the formation of the Amador Traction Company (ATC) in early 1904. The line was to carry electric cars from Ione to Jackson, with power supplied by the American River Electric Company. However, by April, the ATC had folded and was taken over by the electric company, which eventually found opportunities to invest its money elsewhere and backed away from the project.

Within two weeks, Jackson Dennis, who was a partner in the ATC, took over the reins and formed the Ione & Eastern Railway Company with other local businessmen. The electric railway had now changed to a standard gauge line that would run steam engines. Survey of the line began in May 1904 and grading was started by July. The Ione & Eastern did not wait for completion of the line to begin operations. In January 1905, contractors began to lay track out of Ione, and within three weeks had reached the small settlement at Ranlett, the location of a Newton Copper Mine. The rails were completed to Martell by June 1905, and construction began on the depot buildings and the turntable. With the rail line finally completed, the dream of connecting freight and passenger service from Amador to the rest of the nation had finally been realized.

Over the next three years, the Ione & Eastern expanded its interests. In 1905, it purchased the stage line of Fred Rabb to facilitate more efficient timing of stagecoach service in line with passenger trains. It also purchased the freight business of David McCall, which included freight teams, a traction engine, and all of McCall's freight contracts. A passenger coach was purchased in November 1905, and in addition to local service, it offered excursions to the Oakland Pier every Sunday and on holidays. However, its success was short-lived. In 1908, the company failed when it was unable to pay on bonds that had been issued to Charles Erickson for his construction of the railroad. With this failure, the first chapter in the history of the railroad came to an end, but it was not the end of the line. On September 24, 1908, Erickson incorporated the Amador Central Railroad Company and took over the line the following year.

The Amador Central Railroad Company got off to a rocky start, with costs outweighing profits the first five years. This turned around when Erickson put into action advice from a California Railroad Commission audit and purchased a new engine to reduce operating costs. When Erickson died in 1910, his wife, Meta J. Erickson, took over as president of a thriving railroad. Although the line prospered over the next two decades, like many other businesses, it suffered when the Great Depression hit Amador County. In December 1932, the Amador Central suspended mixed train service and resorted to hauling only freight. Then, the railroad lost its biggest customers when mines in Amador County closed. Abandonment of the line was applied for and granted in November 1938. Once again, it seemed that Amador County was not meant to have a railroad; however, local residents came to the rescue. A group of Amador businessmen, including the owners of the Ione Fire Brick Company and the lumber company at Martell, organized the new Amador Central Railroad Company, and the abandonment was suspended.

Under management of the new owners, the railroad was back in operation by the autumn of 1938. Improvements were the first order of business, and a regular maintenance program was initiated. Despite several fires and equipment problems, the turn into the next decade brought the upswing in prosperity that they were hoping for. In 1940, the Amador Lumber Company built a new mill at Martell, which proved to be a boon to the railroad that lasted until World War II broke out and once again the mines were shut down, this time by presidential order. The railroad managed to hang on, but by the end of the war, all again seemed lost. In January 1945, the Winton Lumber Company, successor to the Amador Lumber Company, purchased all outstanding stocks and bonds of the railroad, and in December, they purchased the railroad properties. Once again, the Amador Central was saved from destruction.

The Winton Lumber Company set about making improvements to both equipment and operations. The changes were recognized by the Interstate Commerce Commission, which noted the fine condition of the engines and equipment, stating it was much superior to other Class 3 railroads. Winton operated the line until 1964, when American Forest Products took over the lumber and railroading operations. In 1988, the holdings were sold to Georgia Pacific, which held them until 1997 when it sold out to Sierra Pacific Industries. In 2004, Sierra Pacific petitioned for abandonment and dismantling of the line. Local historians and preservationists, including the author, feared the railroad would be lost forever; however, after six years of negotiations, the Amador Central was saved once again when Sierra Pacific sold it to the Amador County Historical Society and the Recreational Railroad Coalition for a dollar. The two non-profit organizations now manage the line under a joint-venture agreement.

One

How About a Railroad?

The story of the Amador Central Railroad actually began outside Amador County and was prompted by the commercial endeavors of men who had no direct interest in the local economy. Without the connection of Amador County to greater California by rail there would have not been a need to build the Amador Central. Numerous companies sought to complete this task but it was not until the Central Pacific Railroad became involved that a rail link between Amador and the outside world came to fruition.

As early as 1870, talk of building a railroad into Amador County was circulating. In 1873, the first attempt was made by the Stockton and Ione Railroad Company. Their plan was to build a railway from Stockton to Copperopolis, in Calaveras County, and from there into Ione. Within two weeks of incorporation, the new firm was consolidated with the Stockton & Copperopolis Railroad Company, and plans for the line were put into motion. Although a portion of the railway was built, it never reached Ione. After several fits and starts over the next two years, the two companies went broke. Private investments could not keep the project afloat, and with the suspension of the Bank of California, all funding for the enterprise dried up, leaving the company bankrupt.

At the same time the Stockton Company was attempting to build into Amador, other parties were looking to connect Amador to the Sacramento Valley. In February of 1873, a rumor was in circulation that the Central Pacific Railroad Company was considering the construction of an extension of the Sacramento Valley Railroad from Latrobe to Sutter Creek. More talk about town told that the company had also talked with mine owners in Amador County about laying rails from Galt to the coal mines near Ione. The motivation behind this proposal was Central Pacific's need for coal to fuel its locomotives. The line to Sutter Creek was never built but by November of 1876 the Amador Branch Railroad into Ione was completed and the door was opened to build a railroad inside Amador County.

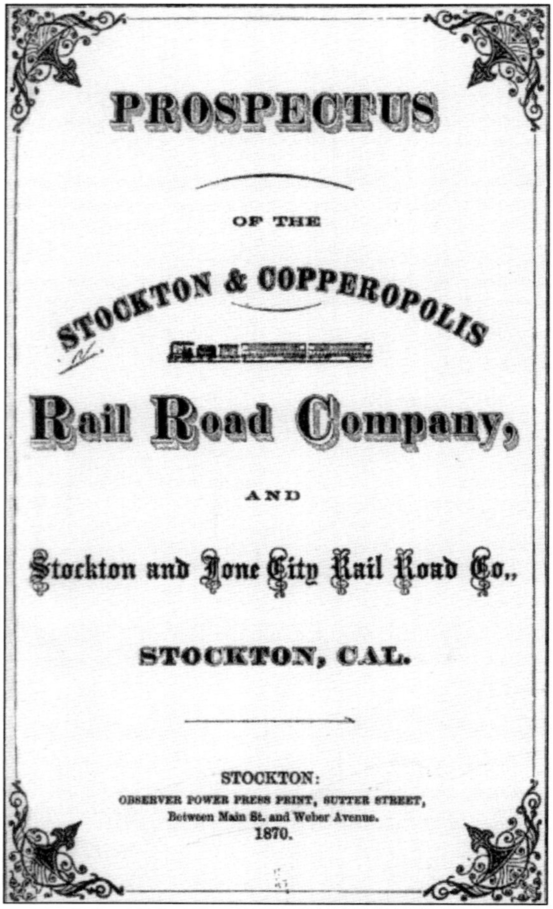

PROSPECTUS

OF THE

STOCKTON & COPPEROPOLIS

Rail Road Company,

AND

Stockton and Ione City Rail Road Co.,

STOCKTON, CAL.

STOCKTON:
OBSERVER POWER PRESS PRINT, SUTTER STREET,
Between Main St. and Weber Avenue.
1870.

The Stockton & Ione Railroad Company was one of the firms that proposed to bring rails into Amador County. Designed as a three-foot-wide, narrow gauge branch off the Stockton & Copperopolis Railroad, it was to stretch from Holden to Ione, providing rail service to transport coal out of Amador County. Only a few miles of track were laid before the endeavor failed. (Author's collection.)

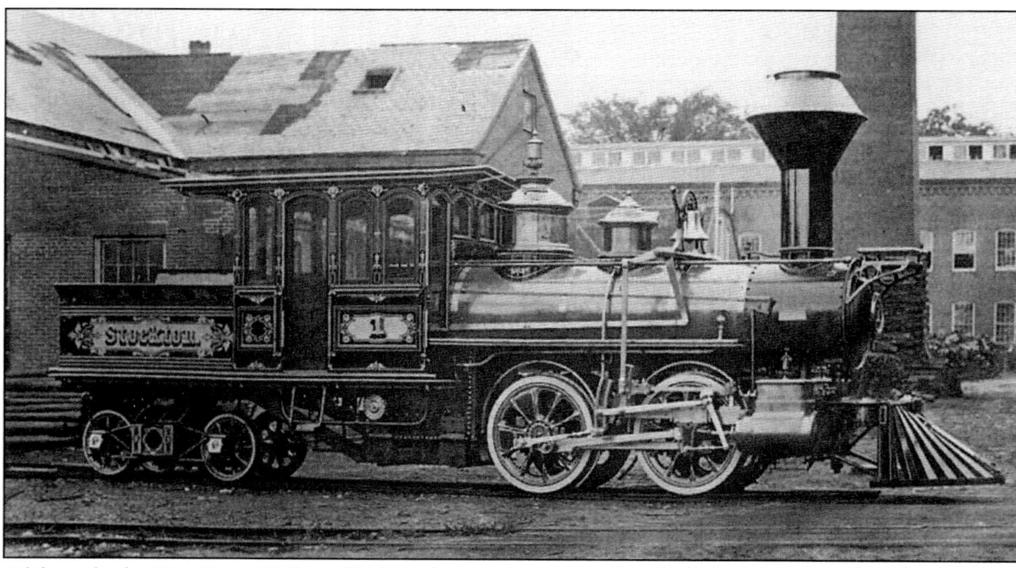

Although the Stockton & Ione Railroad was never completed, the company ordered engines to run on the line before it failed. Pictured here is a Mason Bogie 0-4-4-T model, one of two of this type ordered by the company.

This 1871 map shows the proposed route of the Stockton & Ione Railroad between Holden and Ione, cutting through the Jackson Valley. Despite repeated efforts to build the line, the company failed in 1876, when the Bank of California put a stop to funding the enterprise. (Author's collection.)

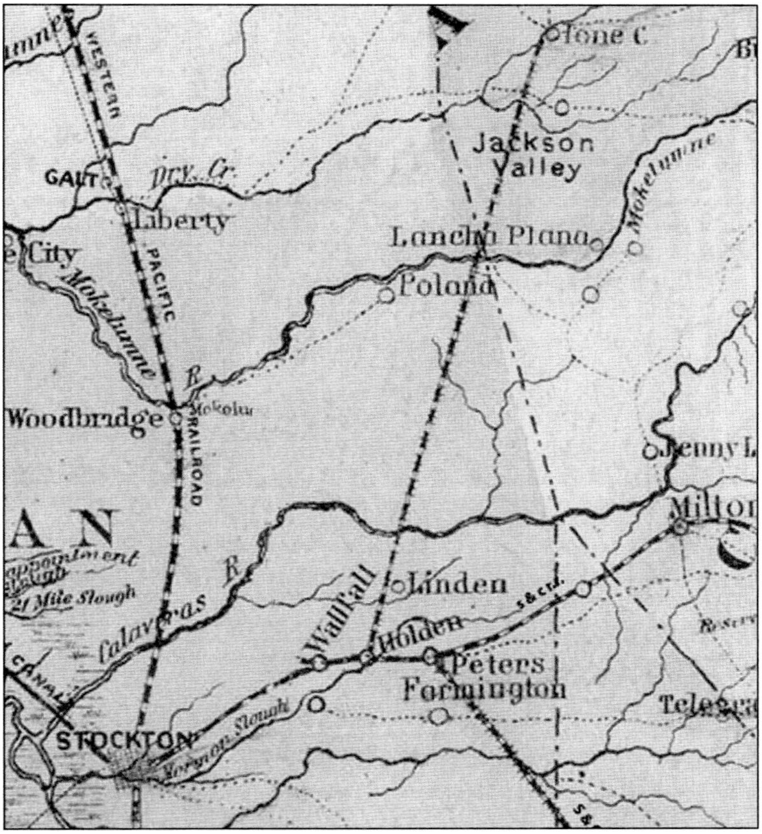

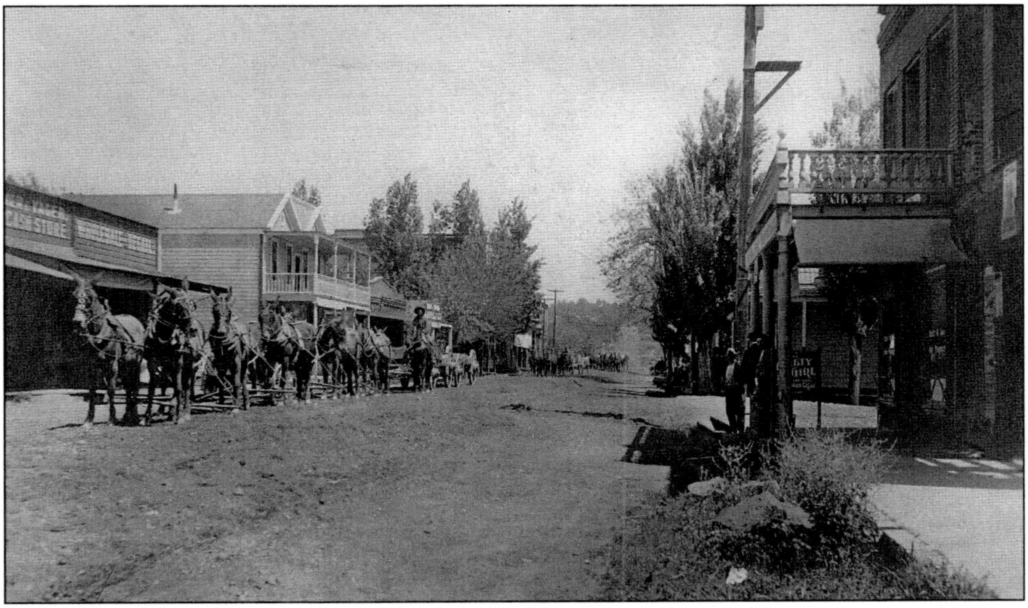

Ione City was to be the terminus of the Stockton & Ione City Railroad. This photograph, taken in the late 19th century, provides a view of Main Street and shows how freight was hauled into town via mule teams. Not only would the railroad improve the transportation of goods, it would also provide residents with a more efficient mode of travel.

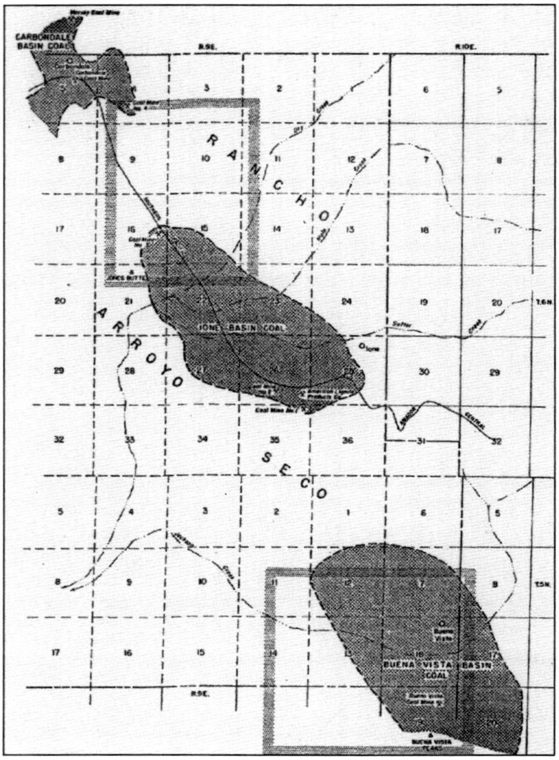

The main motivation for building a railroad to Ione was to provide rail access to the coal mines surrounding the town. This resource was needed to power the increasing number of locomotives moving up and down California. This map, compiled in the 1950s, shows the location of coal found in the area. (Courtesy California Division of Mines.)

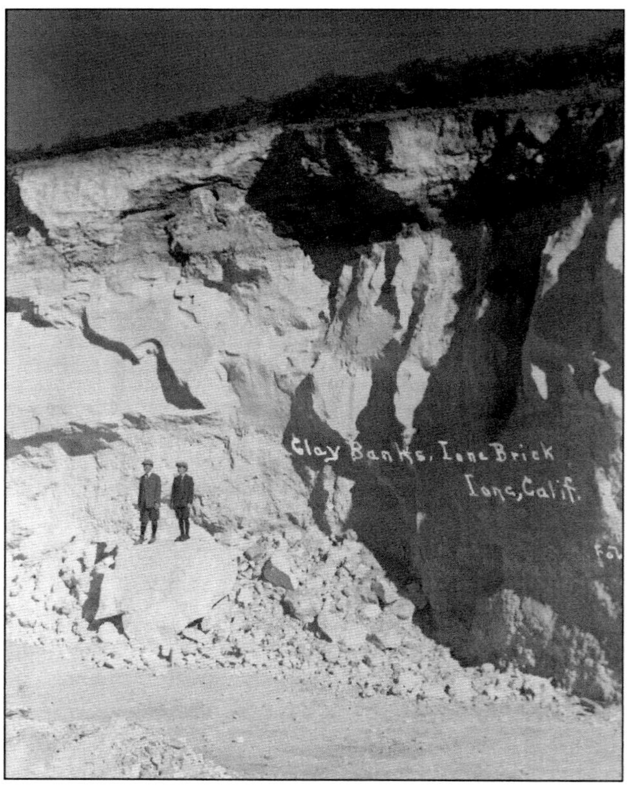

Coal was a valuable commodity to railroad companies in the late 19th century, as it was used to power their locomotives. The coal found in the Ione area is known as brown lignite. In this photograph of the Ione Brick Works clay pit, a deposit of lignite can be seen as the thick, dark line several feet below the natural ground surface.

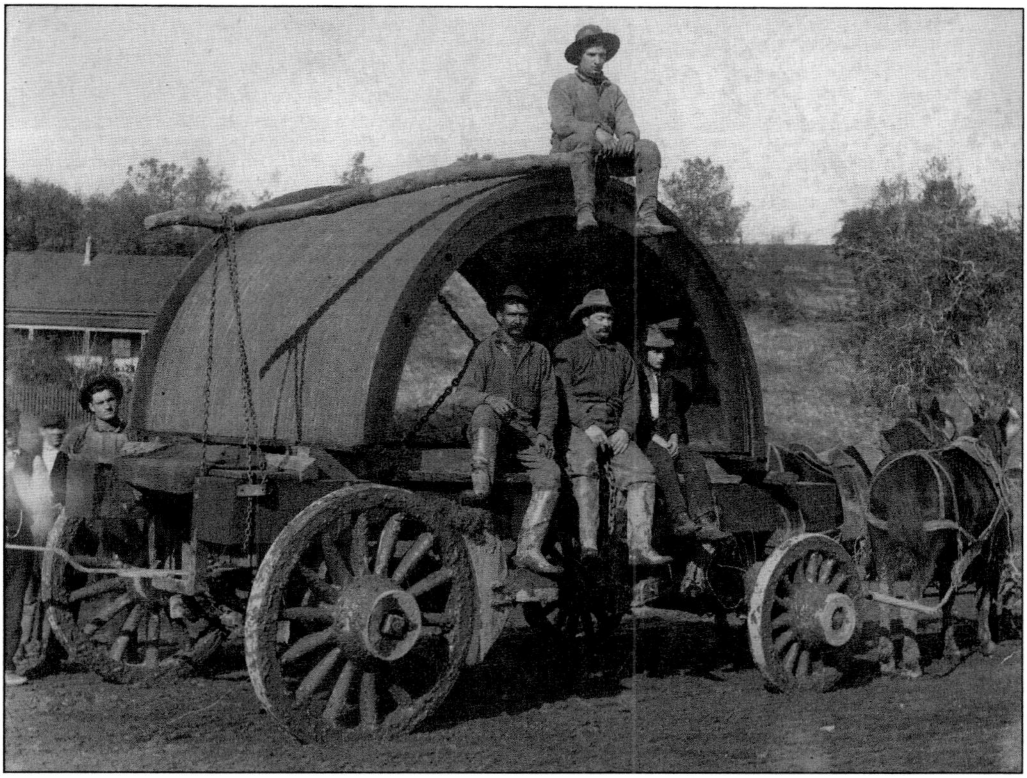

Amadorians for some time realized the benefits of having a railroad come to the county. Transportation of mining equipment and other goods by wagon was slow and tedious compared to train transport. In this photograph, men stop to pose while hauling a mine drum over a muddy dirt road with a mule team.

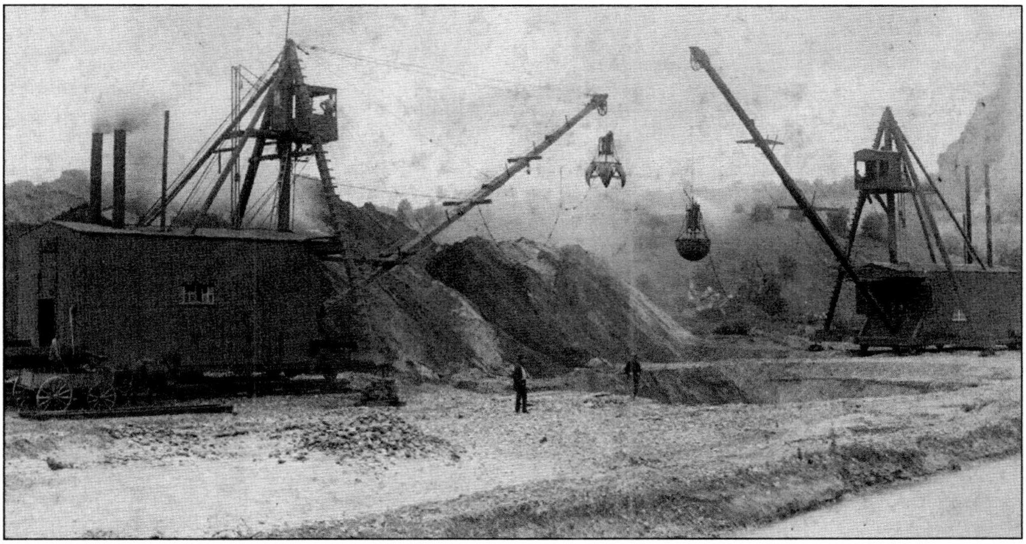

Another motivation for railroad builders included Amador County's gravel resources. Gravel was needed to ballast railways. One of the larger producers of this commodity was the Arroyo Seco gravel mine at Irish Hill, just west of Ione. This mine, among others, produced megatons of gravel and a fair amount of gold.

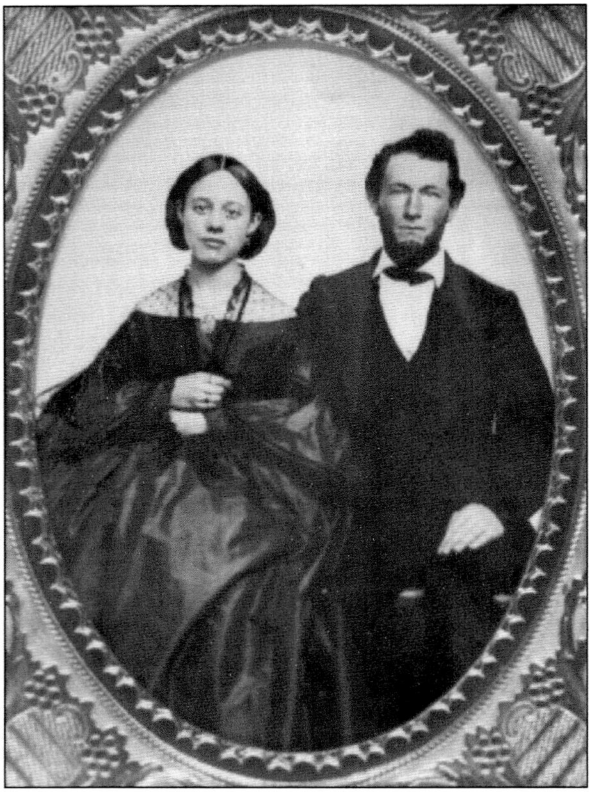

Although the main players in the proposal to build the Stockton & Ione City Railroad were based in Stockton, Amador businessmen rallied local support for the line. John Keyes, pictured with his wife, Clara, was a Sutter Creek businessman who helped gain financial support for the company by selling subscriptions of stock to residents of the county.

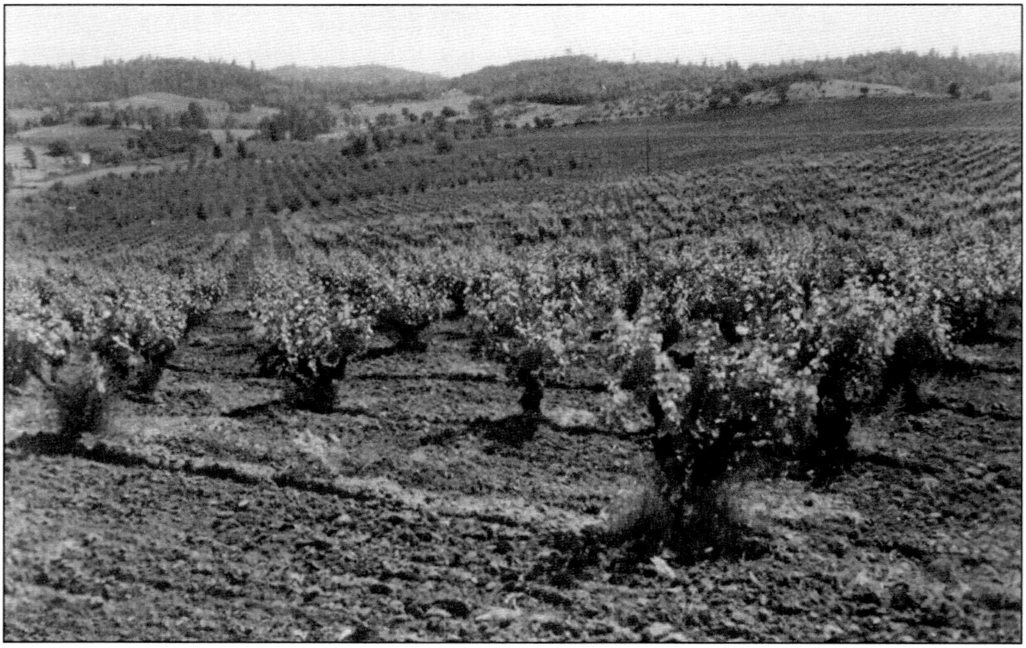

Amador newspapers of the day touted the benefits of a railroad coming into the county, with nearly a full column dedicated to the campaign in every issue. One article provided an extensive list of the economic benefits to the area, including the idea that "hundreds of thousands of tons of grapes" from Amador vineyards, such as the one pictured here, would be made available to the world.

Despite the failed attempt to build the Stockton & Ione City Railroad, even into the 1880s there was hope that San Joaquin County interests would succeed at reaching Amador by rail. Pictured here is an unused land release for another proposed venture, the Stockton & Amador Narrow Gauge.

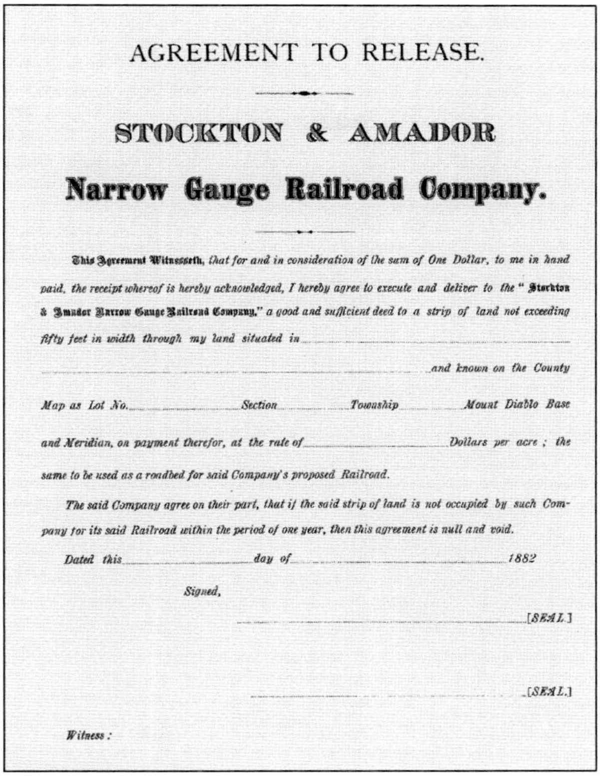

AGREEMENT TO RELEASE.

STOCKTON & AMADOR

Narrow Gauge Railroad Company.

This Agreement Witnesseth, *that for and in consideration of the sum of One Dollar, to me in hand paid, the receipt whereof is hereby acknowledged, I hereby agree to execute and deliver to the* "**Stockton & Amador Narrow Gauge Railroad Company,**" *a good and sufficient deed to a strip of land not exceeding fifty feet in width through my land situated in* __________ *and known on the County Map as Lot No.* _____ *Section* _____ *Township* _____ *Mount Diablo Base and Meridian, on payment therefor, at the rate of* _____ *Dollars per acre ; the same to be used as a roadbed for said Company's proposed Railroad.*

The said Company agree on their part, that if the said strip of land is not occupied by such Company for its said Railroad within the period of one year, then this agreement is null and void.

Dated this _____ *day of* _____ *1882*

Signed,

__________ *[SEAL.]*

__________ *[SEAL.]*

Witness :

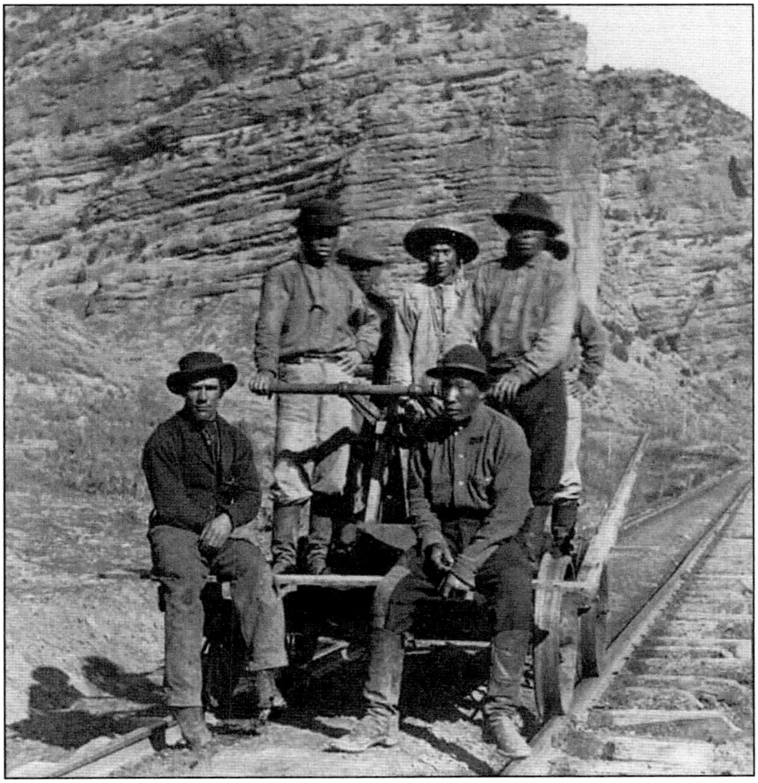

Chinese workers were employed to build the Transcontinental and other early railroads; likewise, they were hired to work on the Stockton & Ione City line. Because of prejudices, they were often blamed for failures. During one work stoppage, rather than tell investors the bank put a halt to the work, owners said the Celestial workers found the ground to hard to work and refused to continue until rains softened the earth.

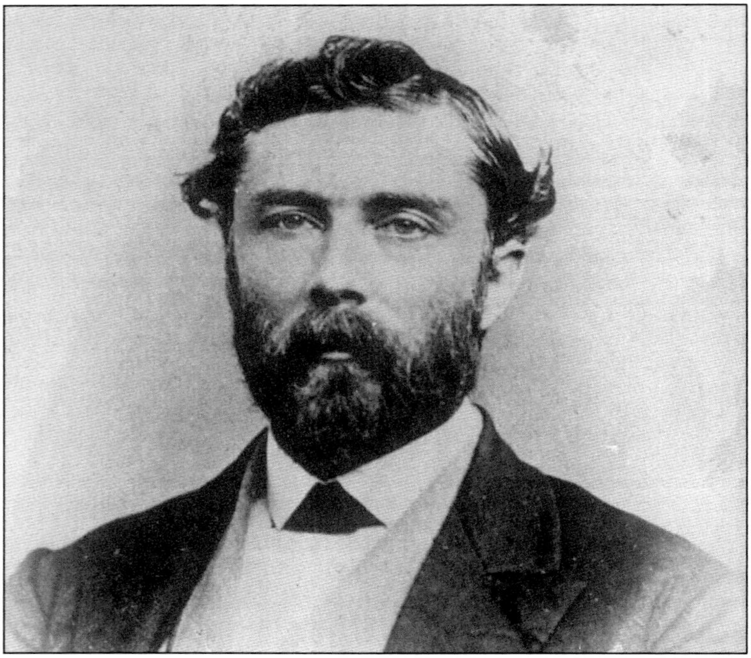

Long before the Stockton & Ione Railroad Company started work on its line, Theodore Judah, engineer of the Sacramento Valley Railroad, had visions of building a branch of that line from Latrobe into Ione, a plan that never came to fruition. Judah went on to lobby for construction of the transcontinental railroad, which led to approval of the Pacific Railroad Act in 1862.

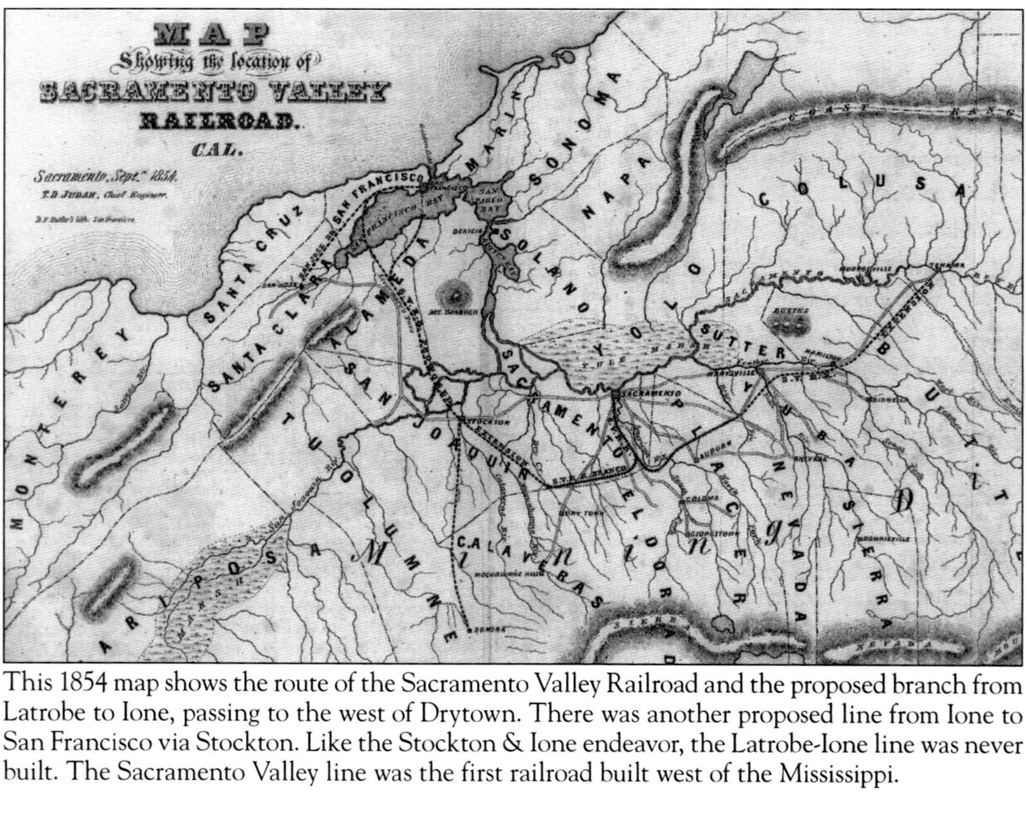

This 1854 map shows the route of the Sacramento Valley Railroad and the proposed branch from Latrobe to Ione, passing to the west of Drytown. There was another proposed line from Ione to San Francisco via Stockton. Like the Stockton & Ione endeavor, the Latrobe-Ione line was never built. The Sacramento Valley line was the first railroad built west of the Mississippi.

It took high rollers like Mark Hopkins, pictured here, to bring the rails to Ione. He, along with his three partners, Charles Crocker, Collin Huntington, and Leland Standford (the Big Four of Central Pacific fame), built the Amador Branch Railroad between Galt and Ione. Hopkins and Crocker had a vested interest beyond railroads—they partnered with local men in operating the Ione Coal and Iron Company.

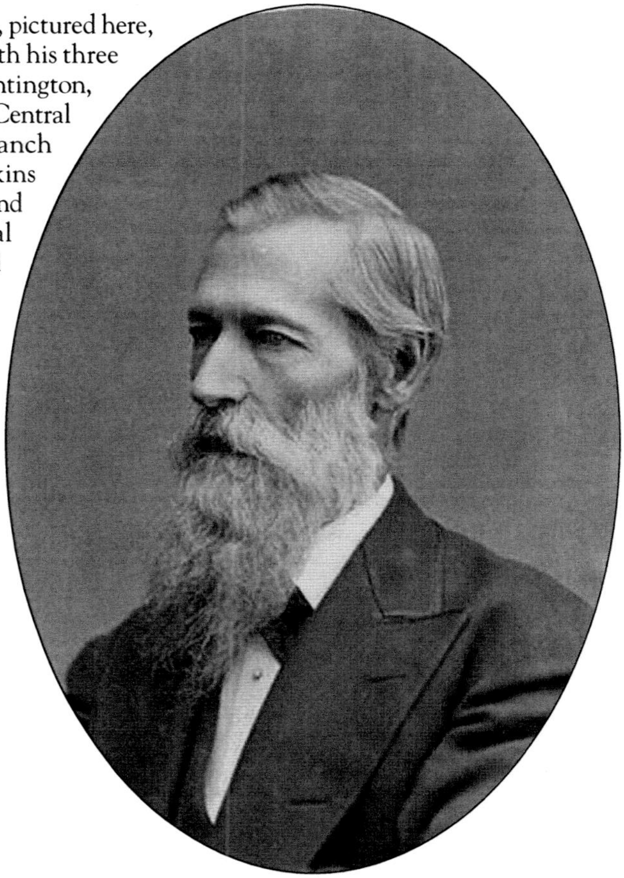

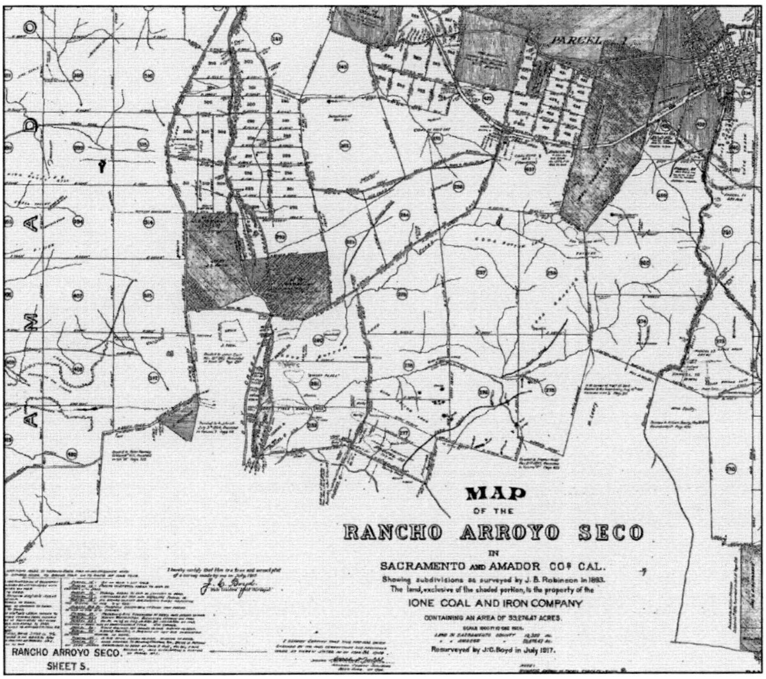

This 1917 copy of an 1893 map shows the property of the Ione Coal and Iron Company in the immediate vicinity of Ione. Not shown are its extensive holdings well beyond the Ione city limits. Coal was first discovered in the area in the 1850s. With the need for coal to power Central Pacific locomotives, it is no surprise that the Big Four found value in building the Ione line.

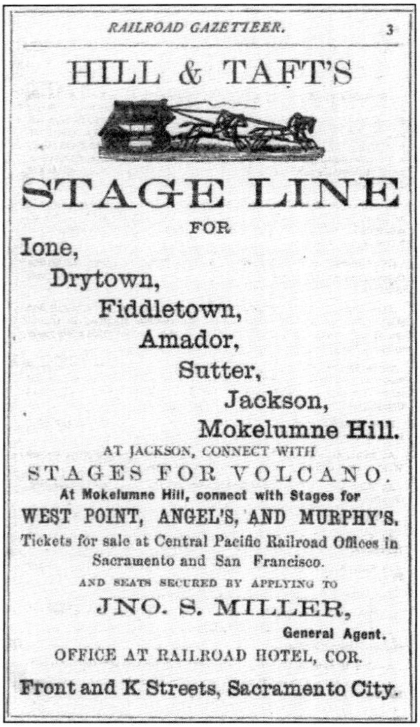

The Central Pacific Railroad Company (CPRR) recognized early the need for rail connections to Amador County, as evidenced by this 1870 stage line advertisement placed by H.S. Crocker and Company in the *Pacific Railroad Gazetteer.*

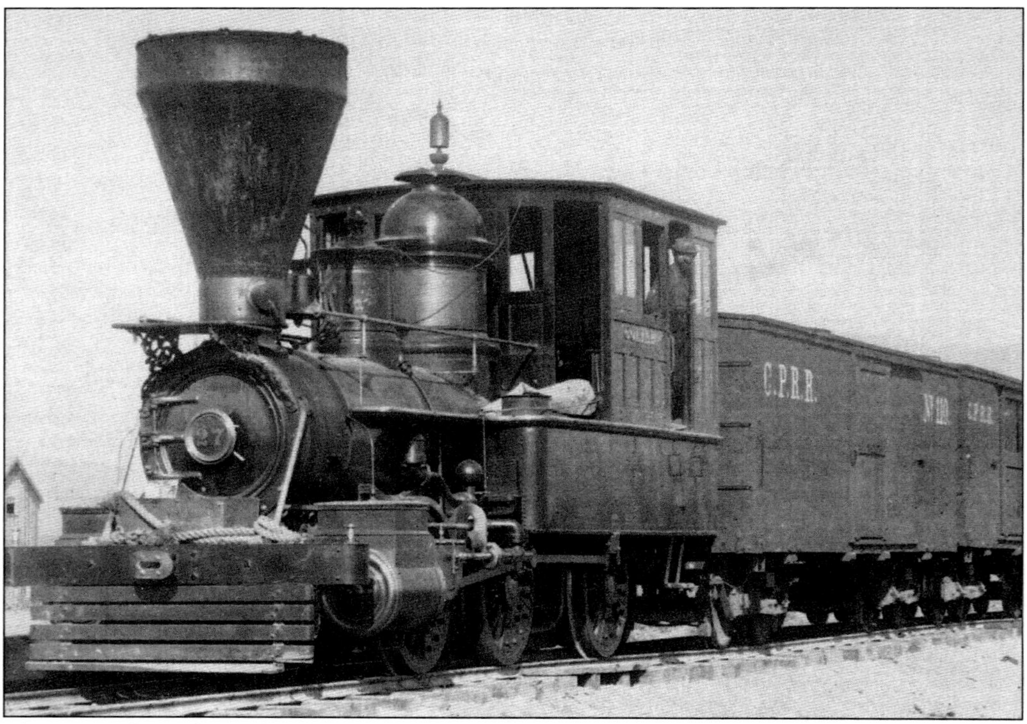

The Central Pacific Railroad was in need of large amounts of coal, hence their desire to build a line to the mines near Ione. By the time the Amador Branch was under construction, the CPRR was operating a large number of steam engines, such as this one, No. 27 on its roster, also known as "Goliath." (Author's collection.)

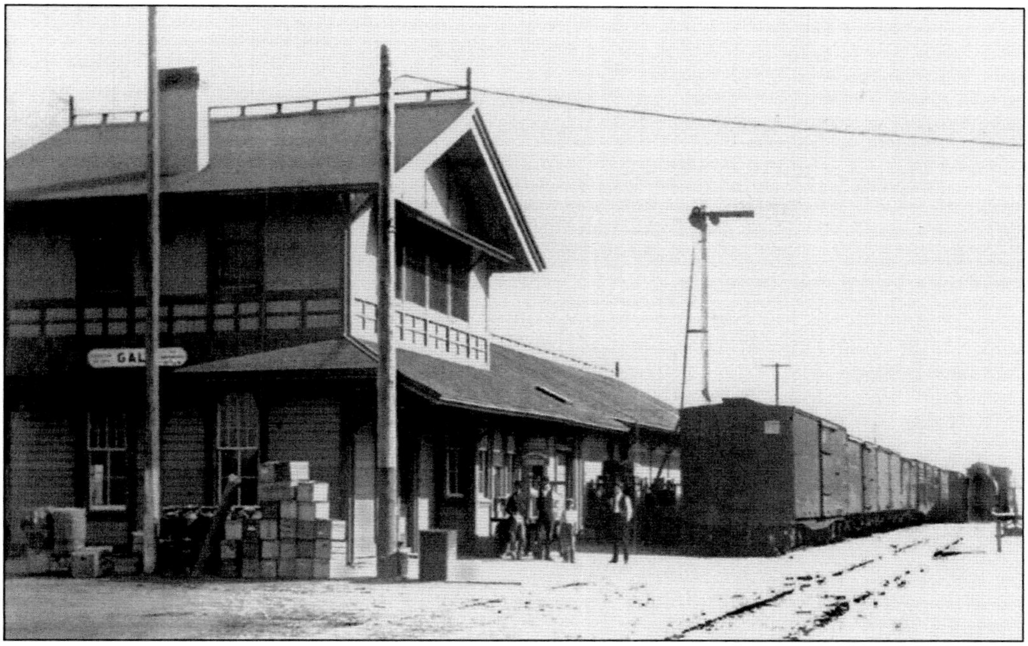

Pictured is the depot in Galt, California, which was built in 1869 by the Western Pacific Railroad Company. Situated on the main north-south rail route up and down the state, it was the jumping-off point for the Amador Branch Railroad.

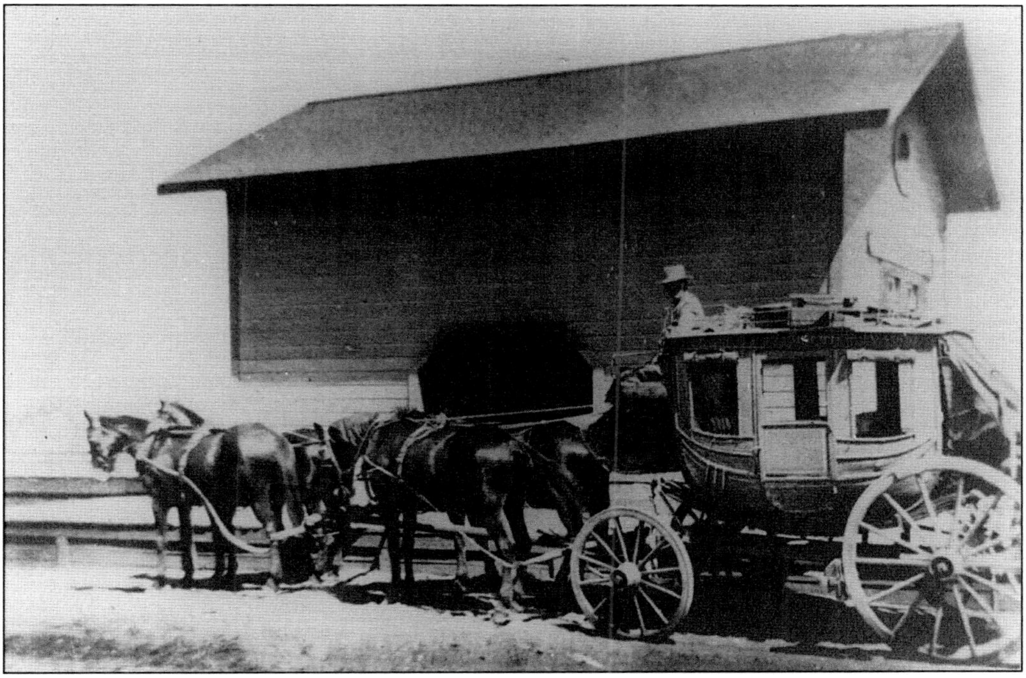

This rare photograph shows a stage in front of the railway station at Carbondale. Earlier known as Buckeye, it was one of the station stops on the Amador Branch Railroad. It was here that the Central Pacific threatened to end the rails unless Ionians raised $8,000 to extend the line to their town. Carbondale is now just a memory, with a namesake road that passes where this station once stood.

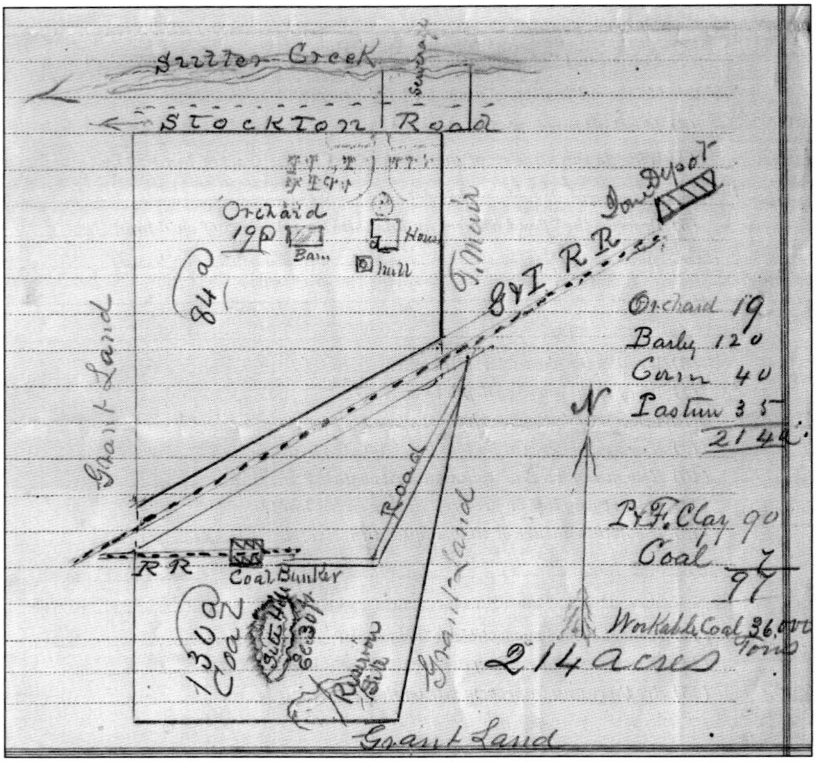

Ionians were well aware of the value of their coal. Prepared for a proposal to sell property to the state of California for the construction of Preston School, this 1889 map details the availability of coal on the land and its convenient proximity to the railroad.

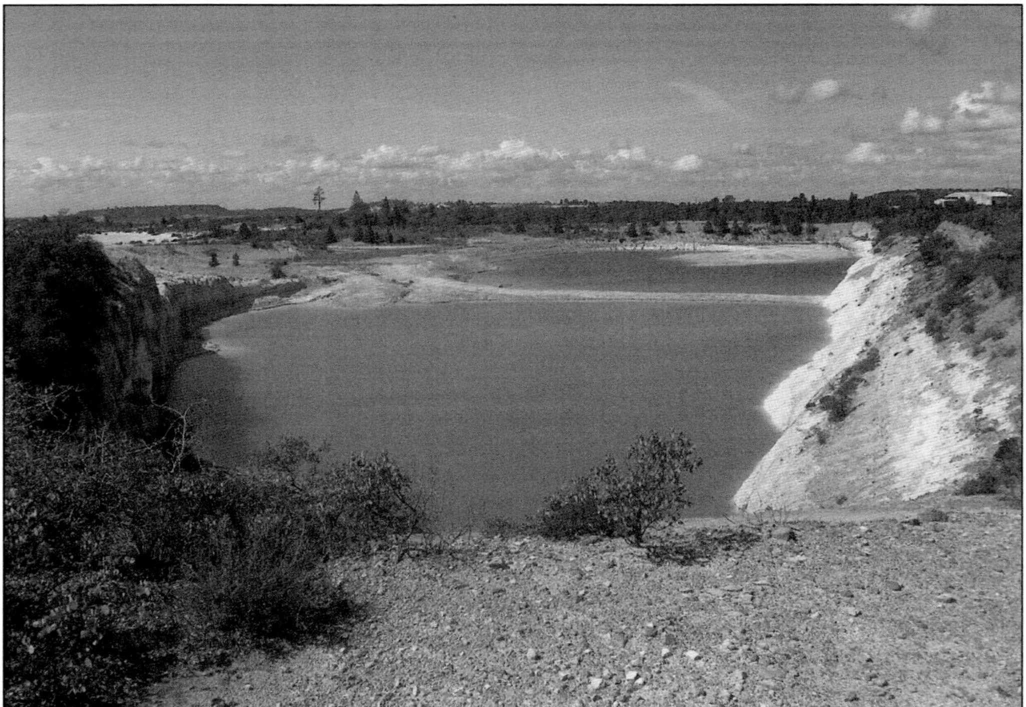

After completion of the main line of the Amador Branch Railroad, several spur lines were built to nearby clay mines where coal deposits were located, including the Yaru Clay Pit, pictured here.

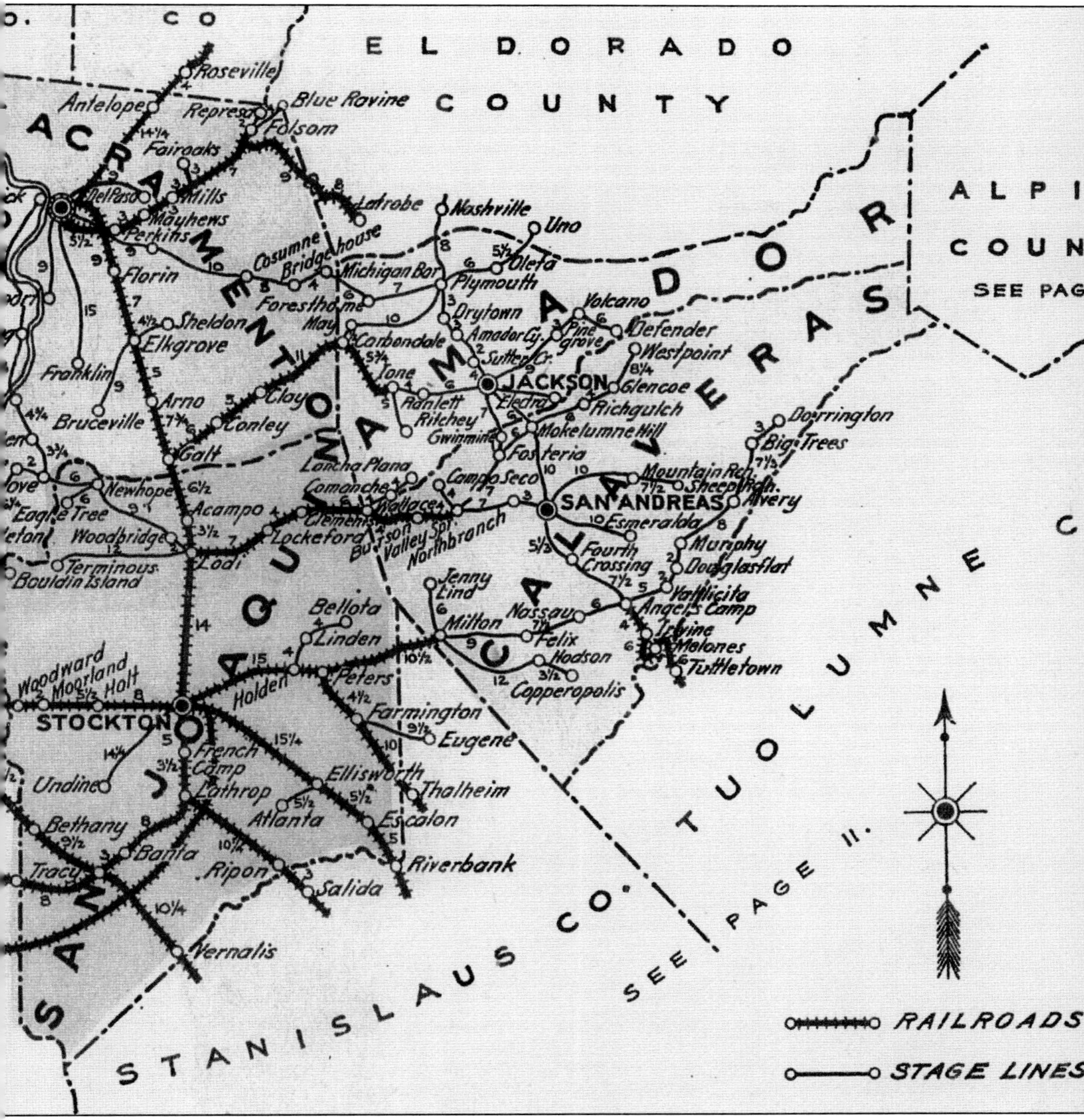

This 1904 map shows the route of the Amador Branch Railroad from Galt to Ione. This railway was completed in November 1876. Once this line was completed it opened the long sought after rail connection between the Sacramento Valley and Amador County, setting the stage to build the Ione & Eastern Railroad, the original name for the Amador Central.

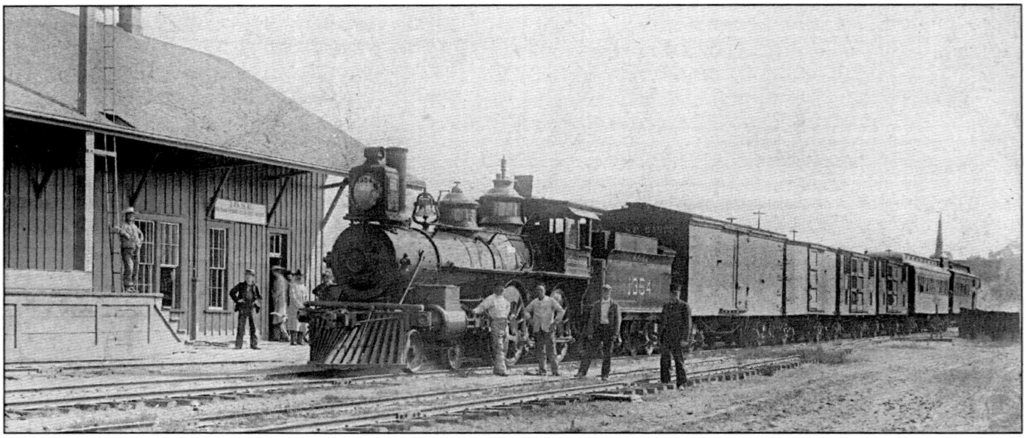

Within a week of track completion, freight traffic began on the line. It was not until a sidetrack to the Mule Creek gravel pit was completed and the gravel used to ballast the rail bed that general traffic began. In December 1876, passenger service commenced, and a freight car was used as a ticket office. Construction of the depot building, pictured here, was completed the following January.

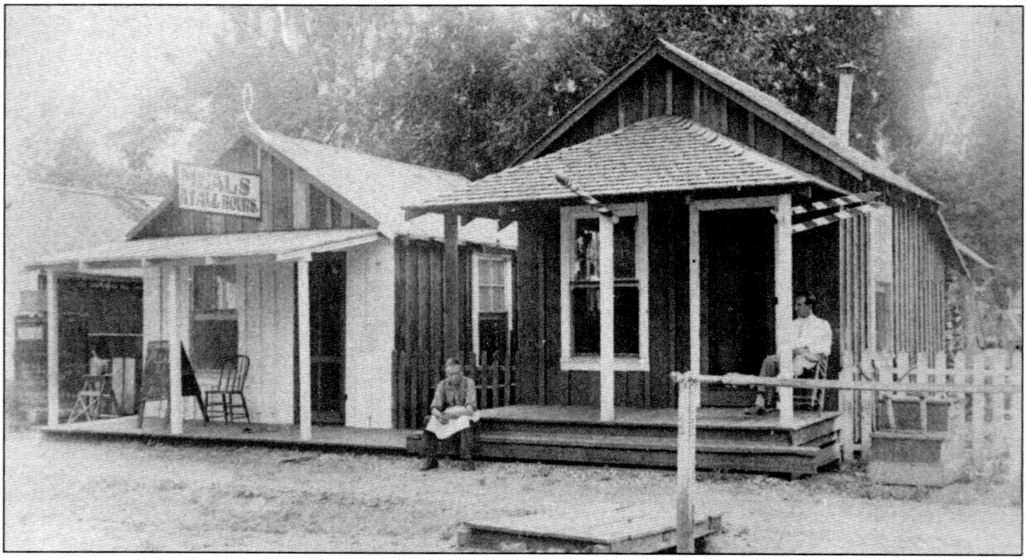

Prior to the arrival of the railroad, many small businesses hauled goods in by wagon, a lengthy and tedious journey from the Sacramento Valley. The two businesses pictured were owned and operated by Jake and Callie Haller, and Jake's brother Jim. Once the railroad came to town, Jake supplemented his income by running a dray wagon, hauling freight from the depot to stores in Ione.

Completion of the railroad into Ione brought added business and work for the residents. John Dabney Perkins, known to his friends as "J.D.," was a local businessman who dabbled in many different professions, including mining, teaming, and brick making. He came to Ione in 1876, served as the postmaster, and in 1877 was hired to be in charge of freight on the Amador Branch railroad.

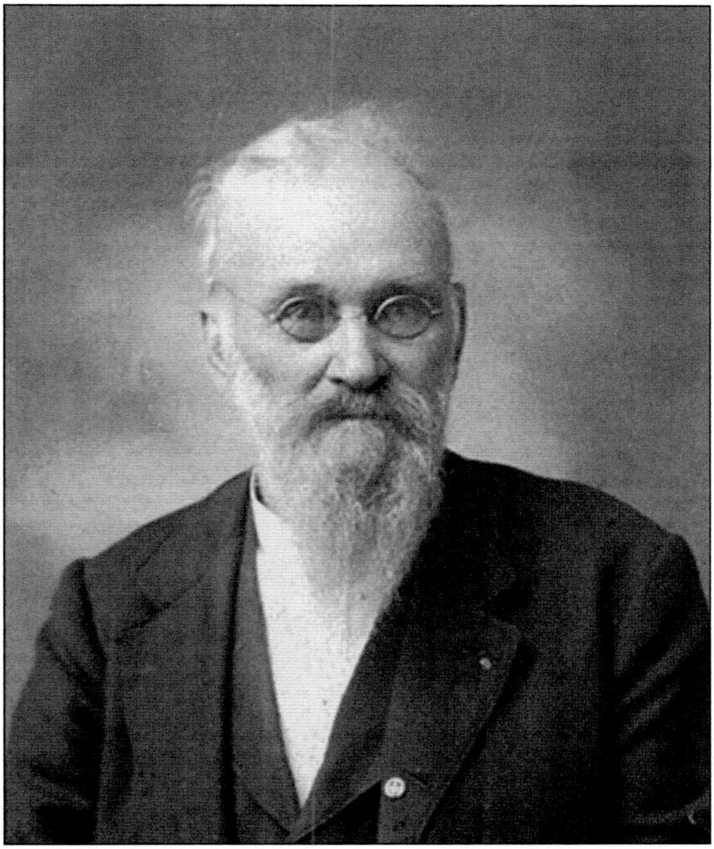

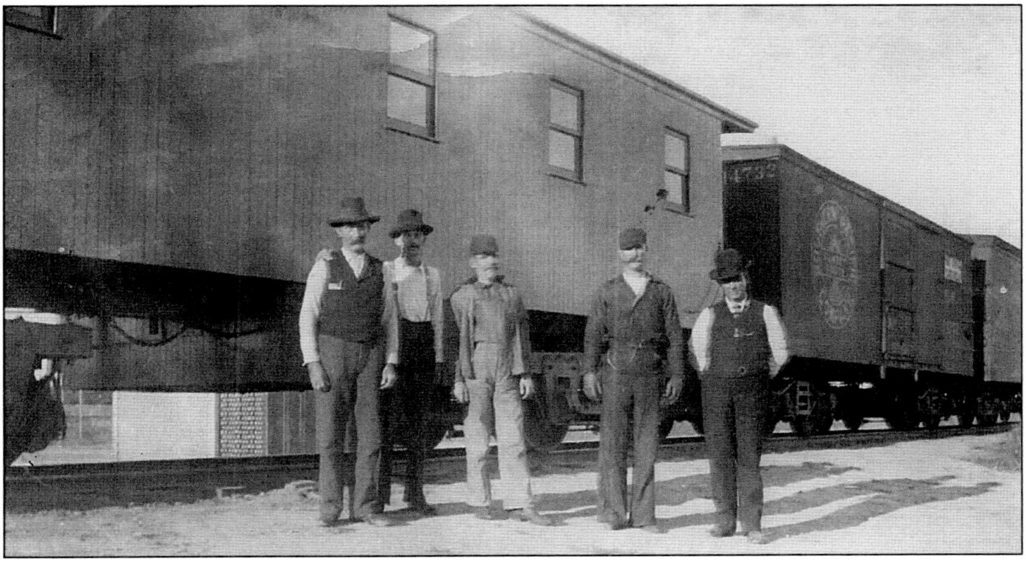

Many local men got steady work with the railroad and although the Amador Branch changed hands several times, many retained their jobs. The Central Pacific Company ran the line until 1885, when it was taken over by Southern Pacific. In 1888, it was consolidated into the Northern Railway and eventually became part of the Union Pacific system. This photograph was taken at the Ione rail yard.

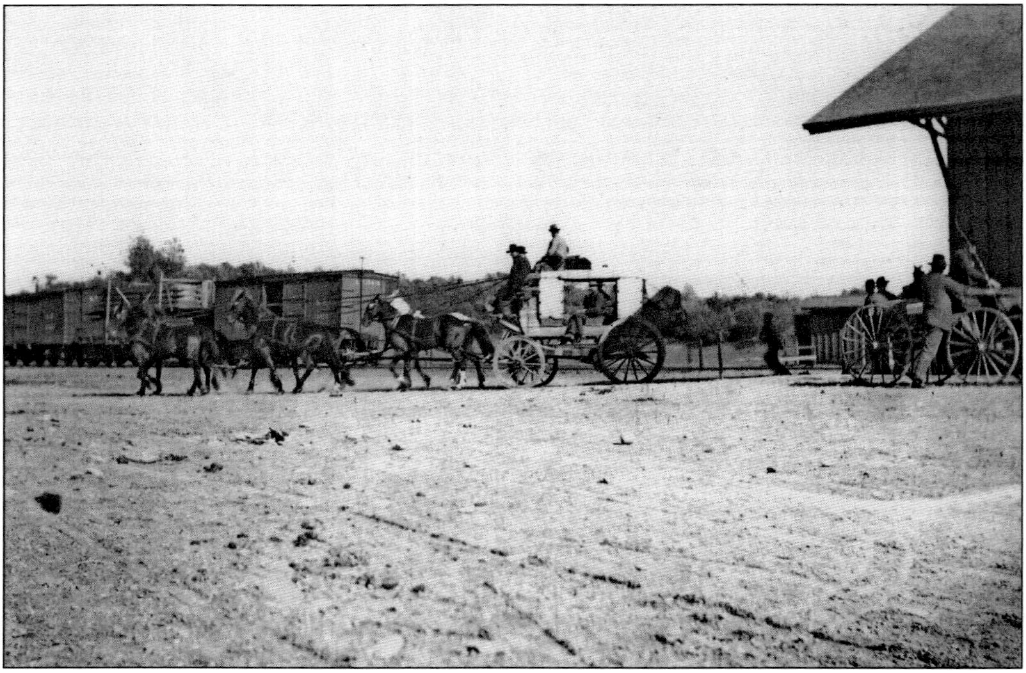

Amador residents quickly recognized the benefit of having the railroad come to Ione. Within a week of completion, freight was being shipped in and out of the county at a steady pace. Soon thereafter, passenger service was offered. In this early photograph of the Ione depot, a stagecoach and buckboard are available for travelers at the station.

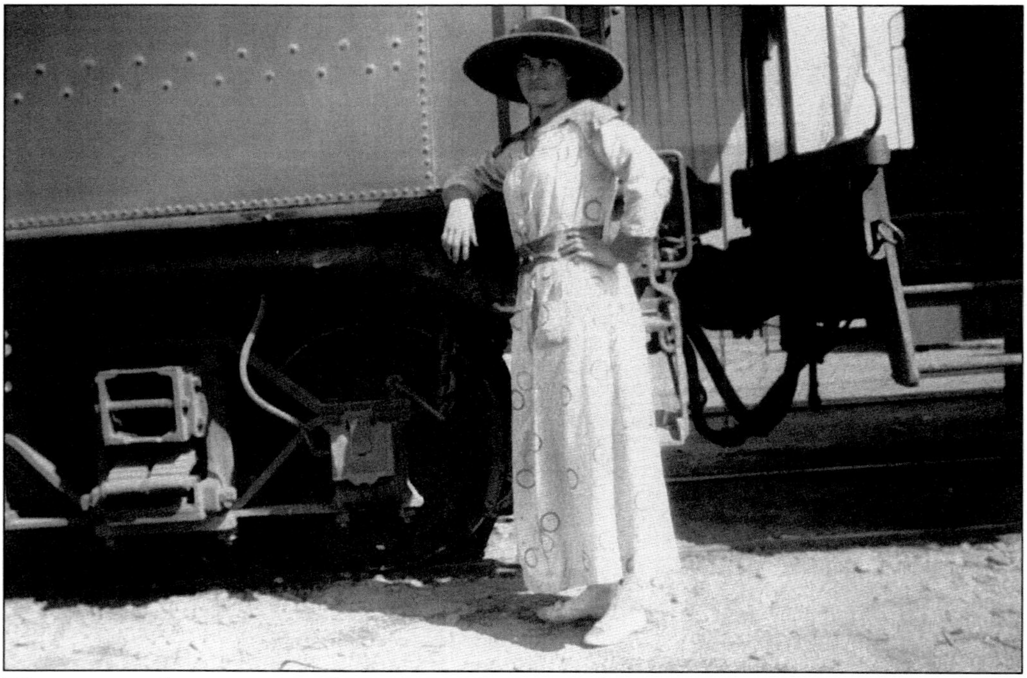

There is something romantic about a train. Having a rail station in Ione remained a novelty well into the early 20th century. In this photograph, Reyes Padgett poses in her traveling clothes, next to a car stopped at the Ione rail yard.

Two

Birth of the Ione & Eastern

The construction of the Amador Branch Railroad into Ione brought increased business and trade into Amador County. Coal and gravel were shipped in immense quantities around California to fuel locomotives and ballast rail beds. Likewise, other goods produced in Amador found their way to outside markets much more quickly and at less expense for the suppliers. The increase in trade for local businessmen continued; however, shipments of coal soon dwindled, as it was discovered that the low grade of lignite supplied by the Amador mines proved to be less efficient than higher grades found elsewhere in California.

Although the Amador Branch provided improved business associations outside the county, residents thought that an extension of the line into the heart of Amador was needed. This prompted the formation of the Amador Traction Company. The company envisioned building an electric rail line from Ione to Jackson. Like several other Amador railroad efforts, this company failed, and the project was taken over by the American River Electric Light Company, which had proposed selling electricity to the Amador Traction Company. Despite the organization and failure of no less than four "paper railroads," including the Amador Railroad Company, the Amador, Plymouth & Jackson Railroad Company, and the Amador Electric Railway & Light Company, the residents of Amador continued to press on with their efforts.

On April 12, 1904, the Ione & Eastern Railway Company was incorporated by local businessmen and financiers out of San Francisco, including Jackson Dennis, who had promoted the failed Amador Traction Company. They intended to build 14 miles of electric railway from Ione to Jackson and Sutter Creek. Power would be supplied by the American River Light Company. After much wrangling and reorganization, the line was changed from an electric line to a standard gauge that would run steam locomotives. Finally, with the organization of the Ione & Eastern, the dream of having a railroad inside Amador County was about to become a reality.

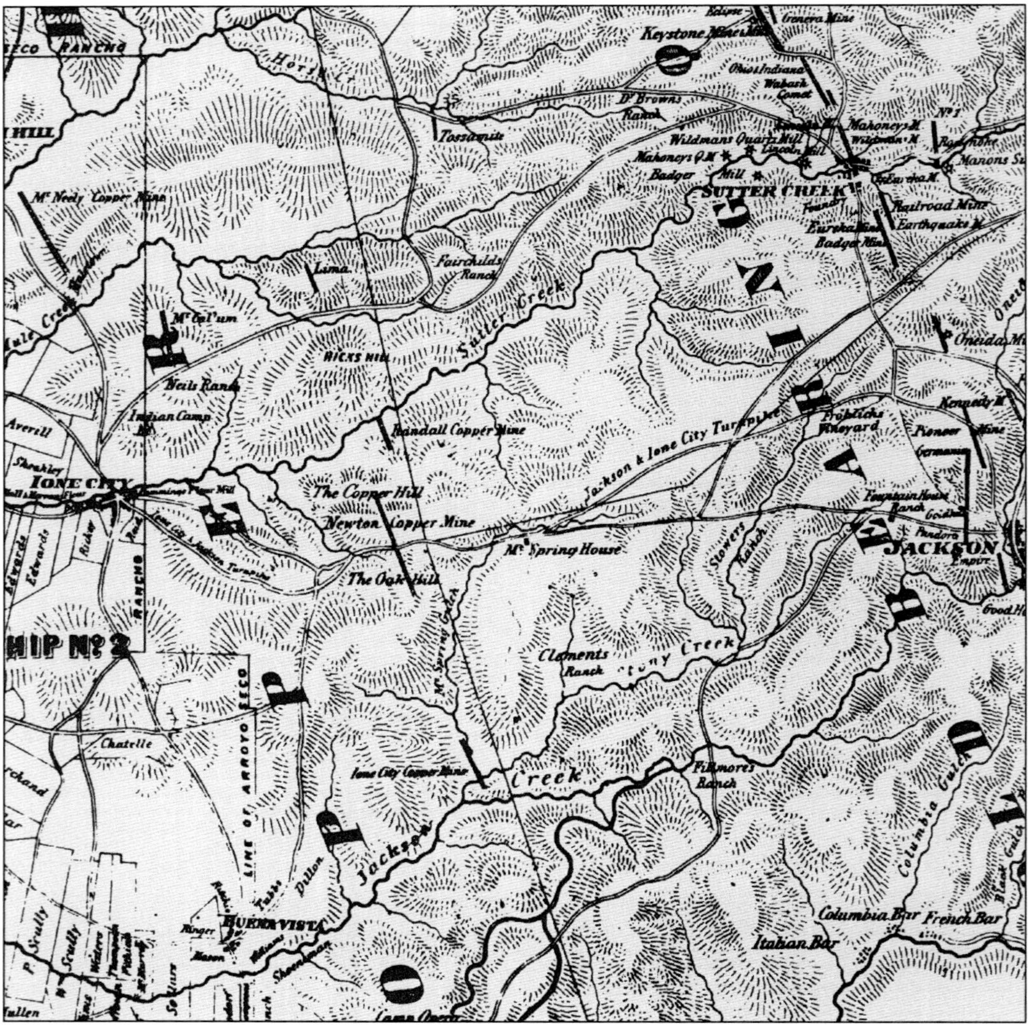

This section of the 1866 Amador County map shows the roads between Ione, Jackson, and Sutter Creek. Travel over the Jackson and Ione City Turnpike and the Sutter Creek–Ione Road was both difficult and time consuming. The change in elevation and hilly terrain presented many challenges, especially to freight companies that hauled goods via wagon over muddy and rutted roads. A new railroad between the towns would eliminate these difficulties; however, the visionaries who sought to complete such a railroad knew they had their work cut out for them. This demanding project would attract the interest and investment of some of the most astute and successful businessmen in California and draw on the skills of one of the best engineers in the United States.

NARROW GAUGE TO JACKSON.

Senator Brown, who introduced the bill for the construction of a railroad from Ione to a point near Jackson, informs us that it is intended to push the matter through as expeditiously as possible. The construction of a V flume from the reservoir above Sutter Creek to Ione, has been talked of for some time. It would appear that the building of a narrow guage railroad could be accomplished for about twice the amount that a flume would cost, while the advantages of a railroad over the flume would be immense. This has inclined the Amador Lumber Company to favor a narrow guage in preference to the flume. The scheme is to make Jackson the terminus, so as to command a large portion of the Calaveras trade, which now goes direct to Lodi or Stockton, The total cost of the road, twelve miles in length, is estimated at $80,000. The promoters think that stock to this amount can be placed without much difficulty, between Amador, Calaveras, and the Central Pacific Railroad Company,

Serious work to build a railroad from Ione into Amador County got underway when Sen. Frank Mason Brown took the helm. Prior to the construction of a railway, approval of the state government was required. As noted in this article (right), in March 1878, Brown introduced a bill into the California state legislature to provide for the construction of such a line. The bill passed but Brown did not live to see the railroad built. He drowned in 1889 while on a survey through the Grand Canyon, scouting a route for another proposed railroad. A memorial to him was scratched in a rock at the site by one of his companions (below).

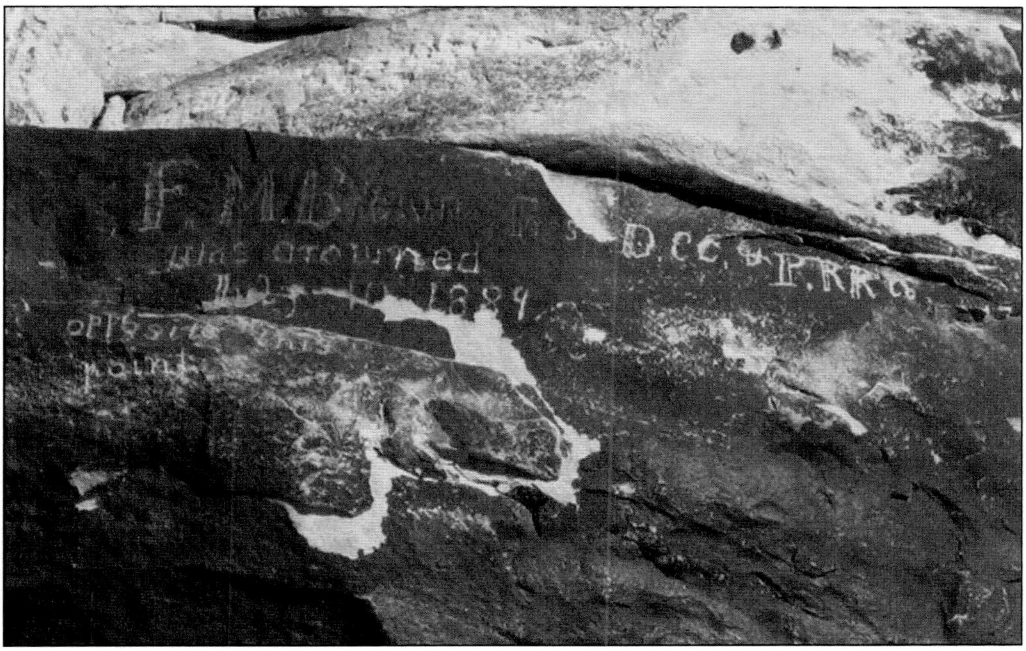

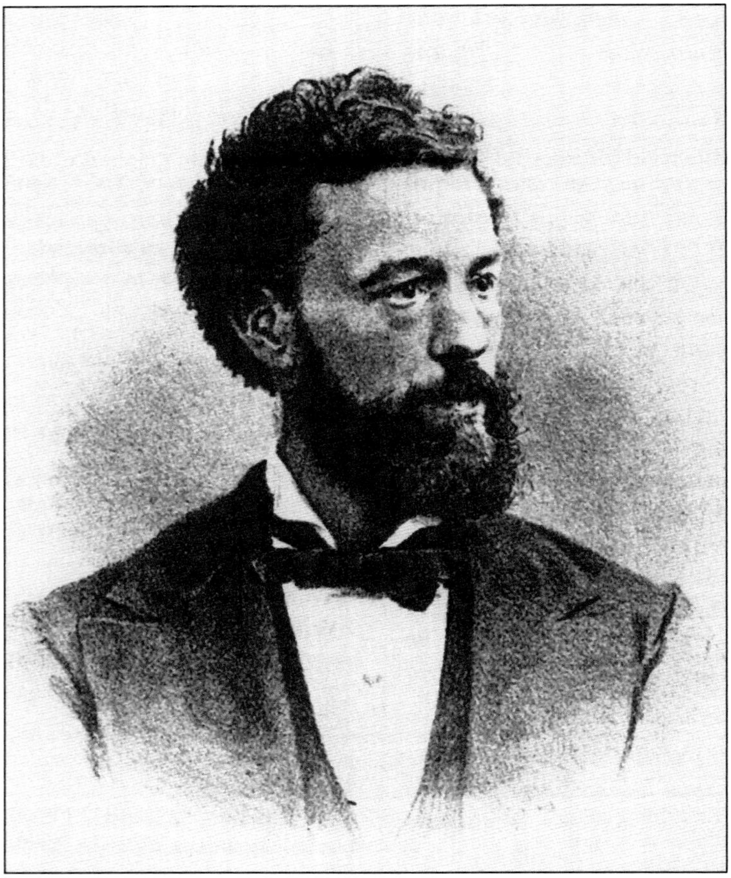

Richard Webb, pictured in this lithograph from the 1881 *History of Amador County*, was one of the organizers of the Amador Electric Railway & Light Company. Webb was a prominent businessman, well known throughout the county as editor of the *Amador Republican* and later, the *Amador Ledger*. He was also one of the incorporators of the Jackson Gaslight Company and invested in Amador mining interests.

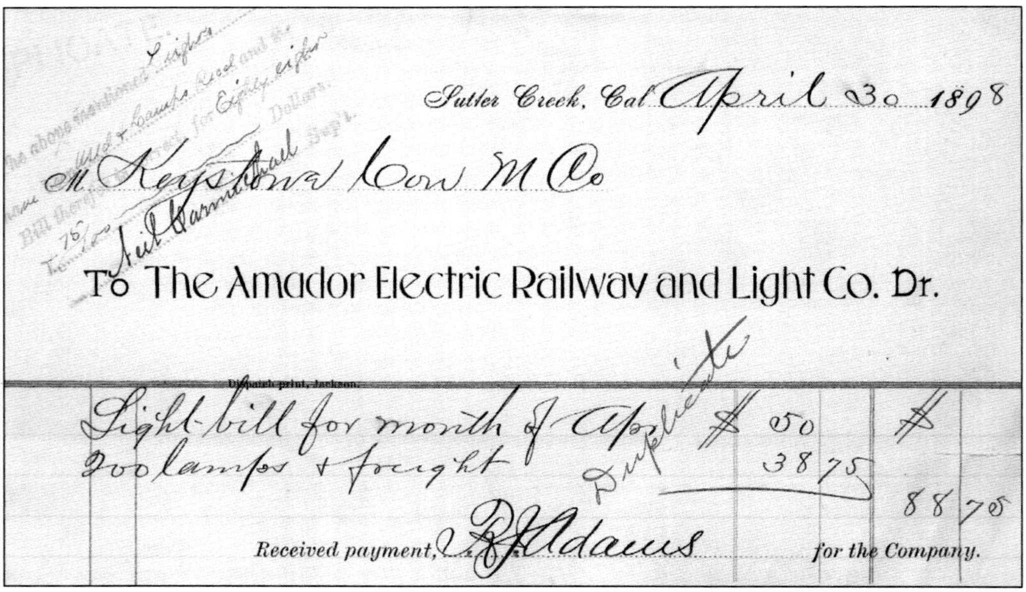

Sutter Creek, Cal. April 30 1898

M Keystone Con M Co

To The Amador Electric Railway and Light Co. Dr.

Dispatch print, Jackson.

Light bill for month of April	$ 50	$
200 lamps + freight	38 75	
		88 75

Duplicate

Received payment, R J Adams for the Company.

The Amador Electric Railway & Light Company was one of the firms organized to build a railroad in Amador County. Although its plans failed, it later constructed an electric grid that supplied power first to Sutter Creek and then other neighboring towns.

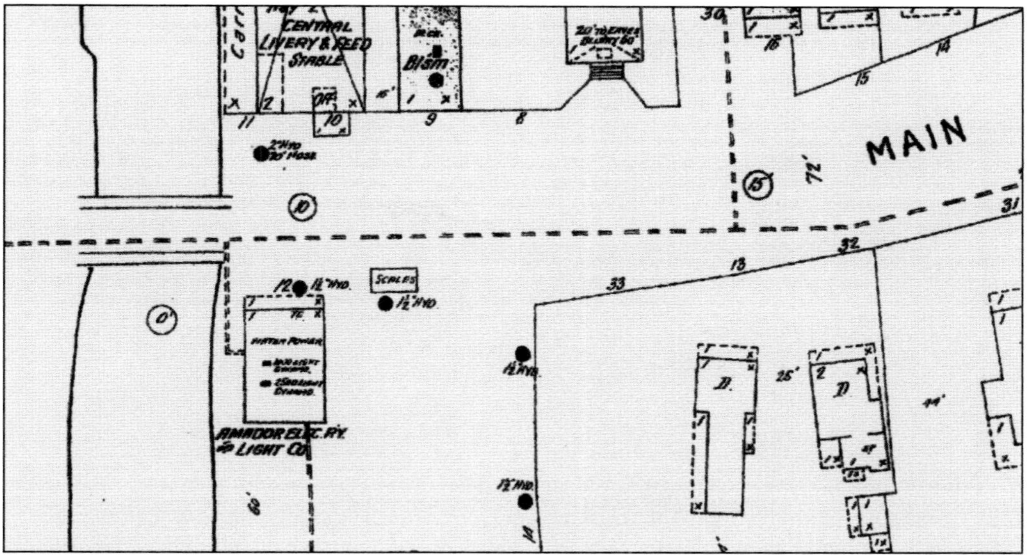

This portion of the 1898 Sanborn Fire Insurance Map of Sutter Creek shows the location of the building constructed by the Amador Electric Railway & Light Company to house its water-powered electric dynamos. The motors were never employed to power a railroad, but did provide electricity to Amador residents and mines as far away as Jackson.

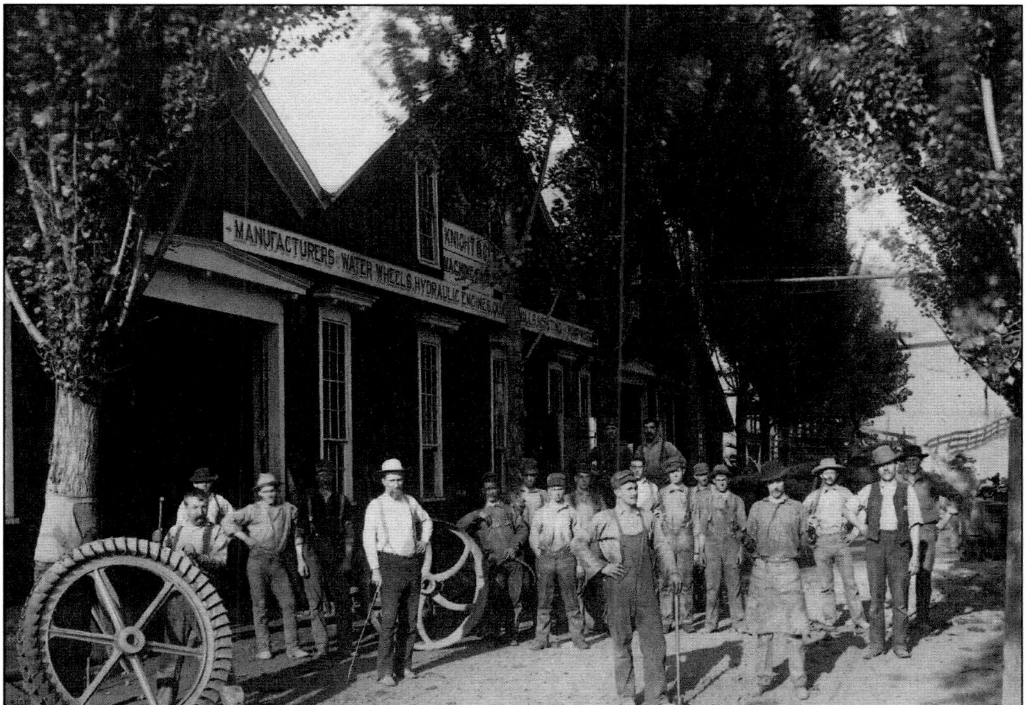

Samuel Knight (left of center with cane), well known for his Knight Waterwheel, was another investor in the Amador Electric Railway & Light Company. When this company first supplied electricity to residents of Amador, the power was generated by a dynamo shipped in from the East Coast. By 1896, Knight replaced the motor with his prototype alternating current dynamo, powered with water supplied by the Blue Lakes Water Company.

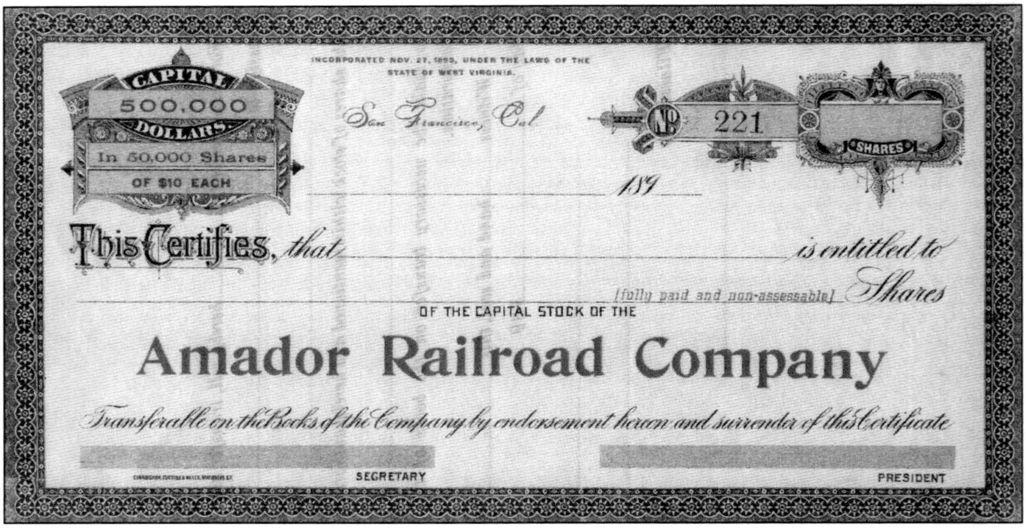

INCORPORATED NOV. 27, 1893, UNDER THE LAWS OF THE STATE OF WEST VIRGINIA.

CAPITAL 500,000 DOLLARS In 50,000 Shares OF $10 EACH

San Francisco, Cal ____________ 189__

No 221 ____ SHARES

This Certifies, that ______________________ is entitled to ______ (fully paid and non-assessable) Shares

OF THE CAPITAL STOCK OF THE

Amador Railroad Company

Transferable on the Books of the Company by endorsement hereon and surrender of this Certificate

SECRETARY PRESIDENT

Investors from around the state soon wanted to climb onto the bandwagon and build a railroad inside Amador County. In 1893, a charter was issued for the Amador Railroad Company, which eventually failed. The incorporators hailed from San Francisco and included Stephen H. Emmens, the famed charlatan scientist who supposedly transmuted silver into gold and sold it to the US Mint.

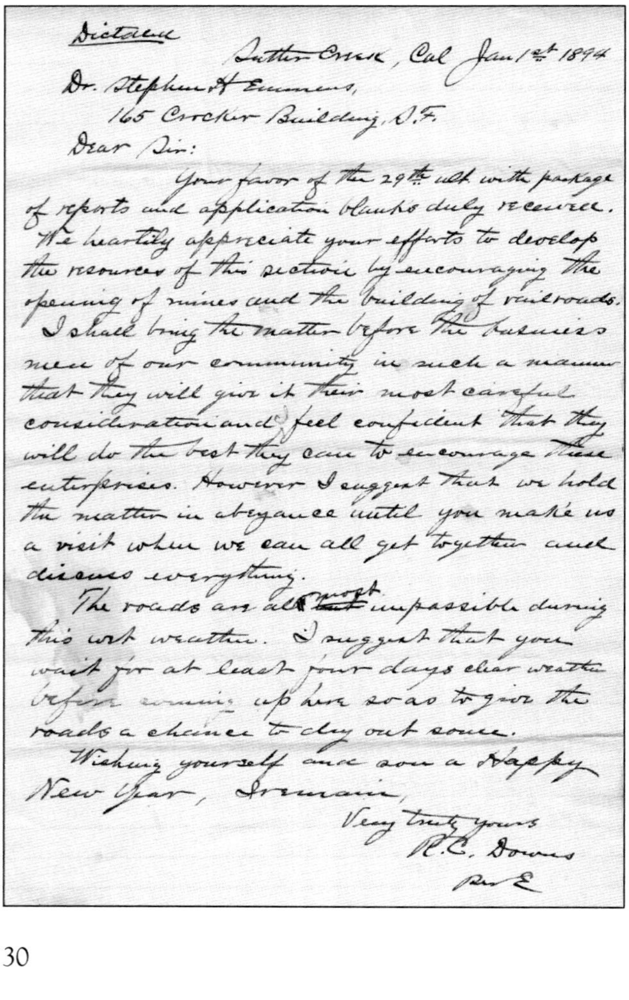

Dictated

Sutter Creek, Cal Jan 1st 1894

Dr. Stephen H Emmens,
165 Crocker Building, S.F.

Dear Sir:

Your favor of the 29th ult with package of reports and application blanks duly received. We heartily appreciate your efforts to develop the resources of this section by encouraging the opening of mines and the building of railroads. I shall bring the matter before the business men of our community in such a manner that they will give it their most careful consideration and feel confident that they will do the best they can to encourage these enterprises. However I suggest that we hold the matter in abeyance until you make us a visit when we can all get together and discuss everything.

The roads are almost impassible during this wet weather. I suggest that you wait for at least four days clear weather before coming up here so as to give the roads a chance to dry out some.

Wishing yourself and son a Happy New Year, I remain,

Very truly yours
R.C. Downs
Per E

Emmens was well connected to Amador County, and although Amador residents did not provide any of the organizational capital for the Amador Railroad venture, he did have local support. In this 1894 letter to Emmens, local mining mogul and businessman R.C. Downs expresses his thanks to Emmens for his efforts, and offers his services to promote the building of the railroad.

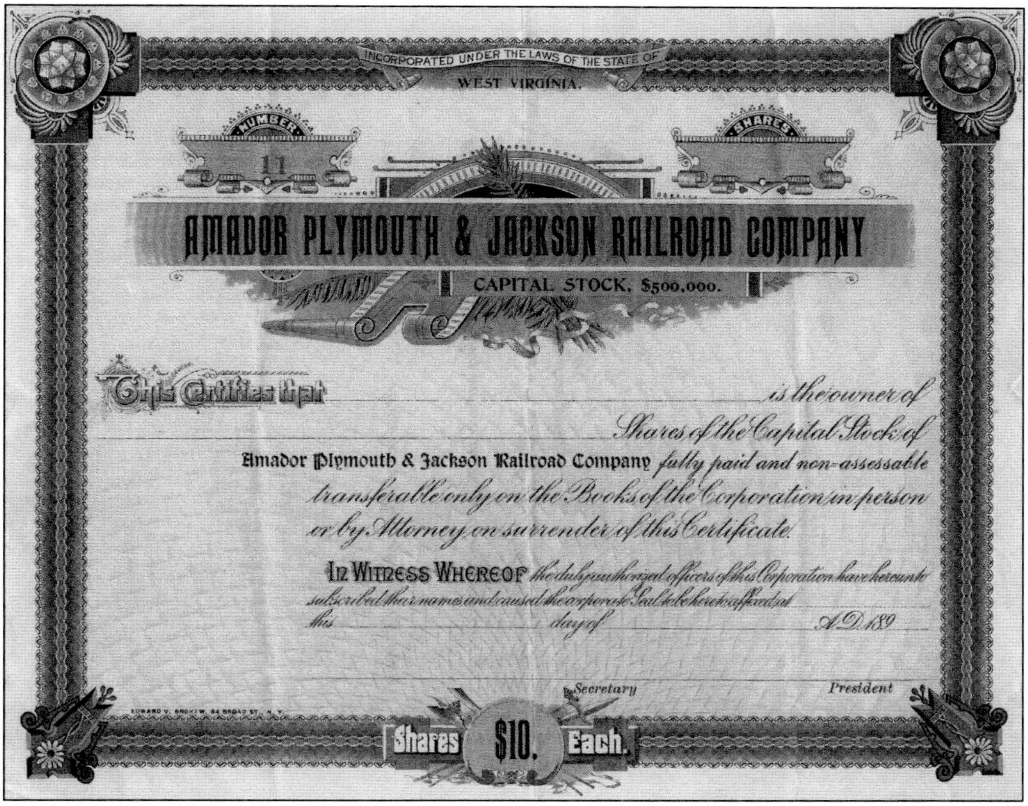

In 1895, a charter was issued out of West Virginia for the Amador, Plymouth and Jackson Railroad Company, a revived effort of Stephen Emmens and his son Newton. However, this time, Emmens garnered local support from Amador City businessmen H.C. McCoy, L.G. Hastings, and O.E. Martin. All three were businessmen with longtime connections to other entrepreneurs in Amador County. Capital for the company was authorized at $500,000, but like other railroad organizations, the startup investment was small. Like its predecessor, this company also failed.

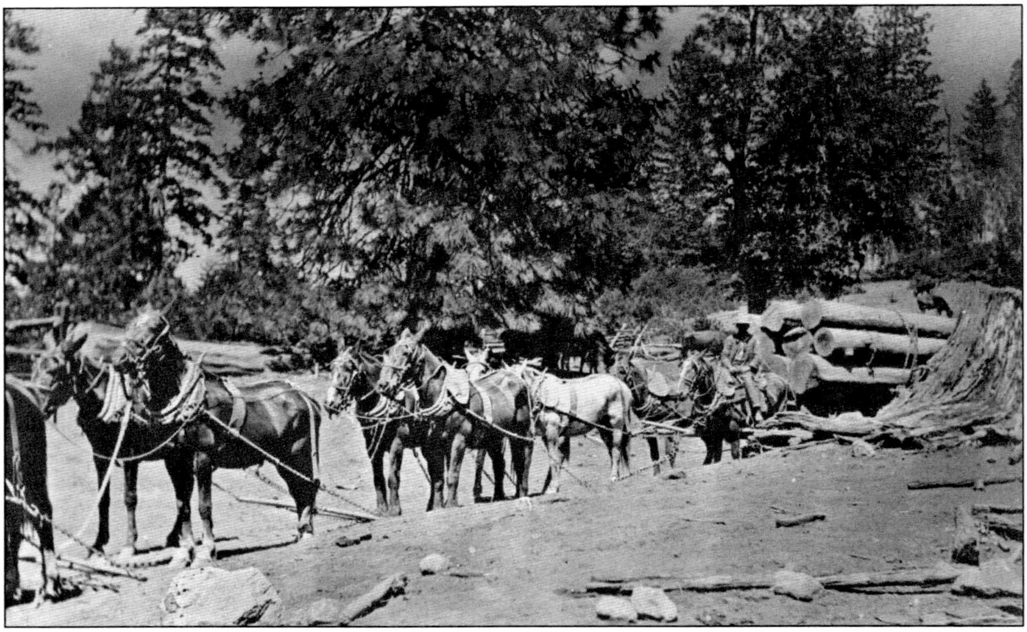

It seems that the primary goal of the Amador, Plymouth & Jackson Railroad Company investors was to transport lumber. There was money to be made from the timber stands in the Sierra Nevada. Their proposal, like others, was to extend the rails into the mountains and increase the speed by which their goods reached the lowlands—a step up from hauling logs down the mountain by mule or oxen.

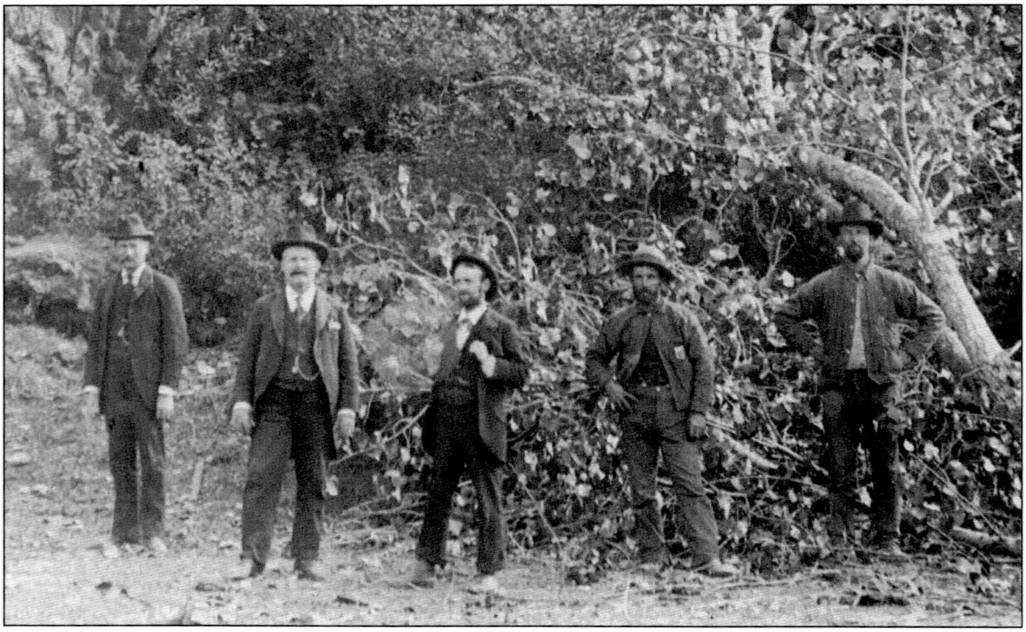

David Gutman, pictured second from left, was an Amador businessman who helped organize the Jackson, Sutter & Amador Railway Company. This firm planned to build a line from Ione to Martell with extensions to Jackson, to Middle Bar on the Mokelumne River, and to Plymouth via Sutter Creek, Amador City, and Drytown. The line from Ione to Martell was surveyed, and maps were prepared, but the company eventually disbanded.

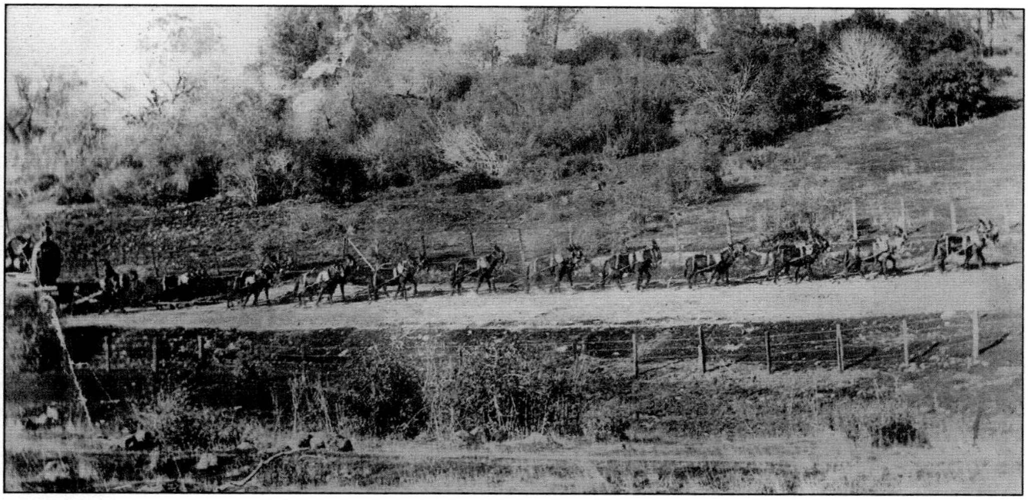

Many of the promoters of the numerous Amador railroad ventures were engaged in the freighting business and also ran stage lines. They recognized the benefit of moving their goods in and out of Ione via rails rather than the steep and rough Ione-Jackson Road, the main east-west route between the towns. In this photograph, a 20-mule team pulls mining equipment up one of the grades along that road.

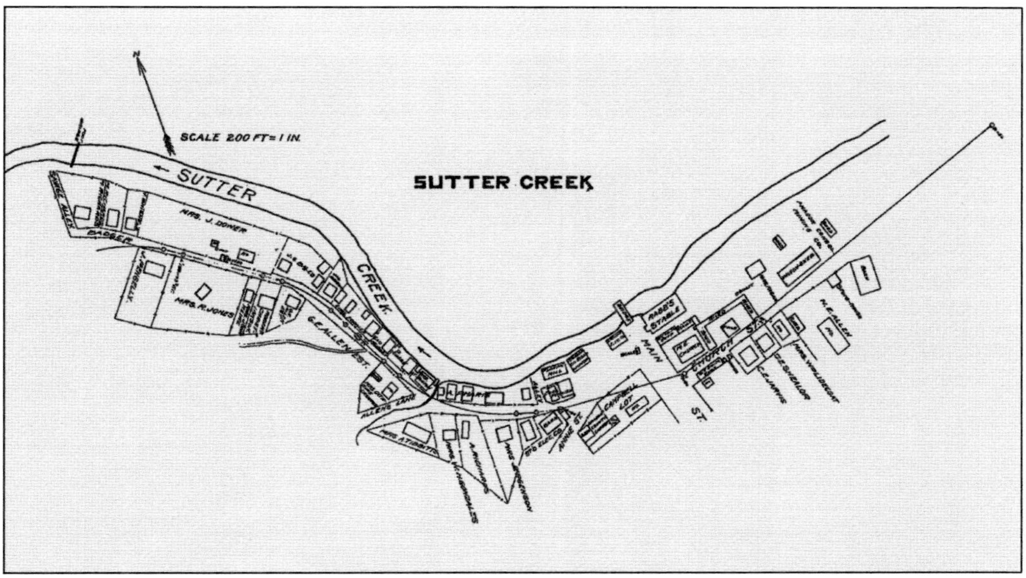

When Gutman and others incorporated the Jackson, Sutter Creek & Amador Railway, they employed well-known engineer Henry E.C. Feusier to survey and prepare maps. Pictured is Feusier's map of the route through Sutter Creek. Feusier worked as surveyor and engineer on several proposed Amador lines and prepared the final maps for what was to become the Ione & Eastern Railroad.

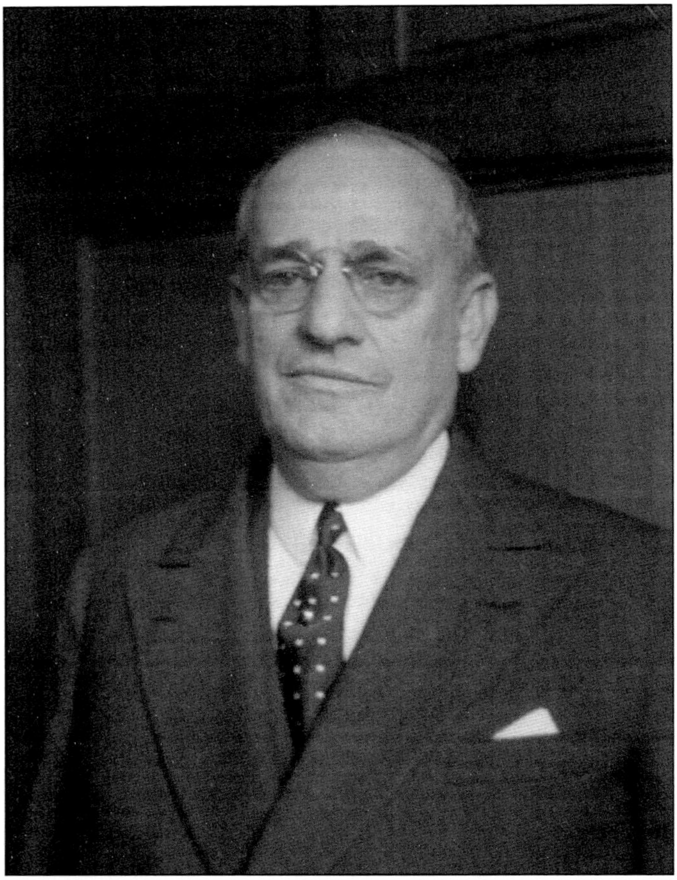

In 1904 when the Amador Traction Company incorporated, the Fleishhacker brothers, owners of the American River Light Company, agreed to supply power to the proposed electric line. By March, the fledgling railroad company had already signed contracts with freight receivers and hired Feusier, who had already surveyed lines from Ione to Martell, Sutter Creek, and Jackson. Like others before, it collapsed by April 1904. Herbert Fleishhacker (left) and his brother Mortimer (bottom) took over the railroad company. One week after the failure of Amador Traction Company, the Ione & Eastern Railroad was organized, and the Fleishhackers once again agreed to supply power.

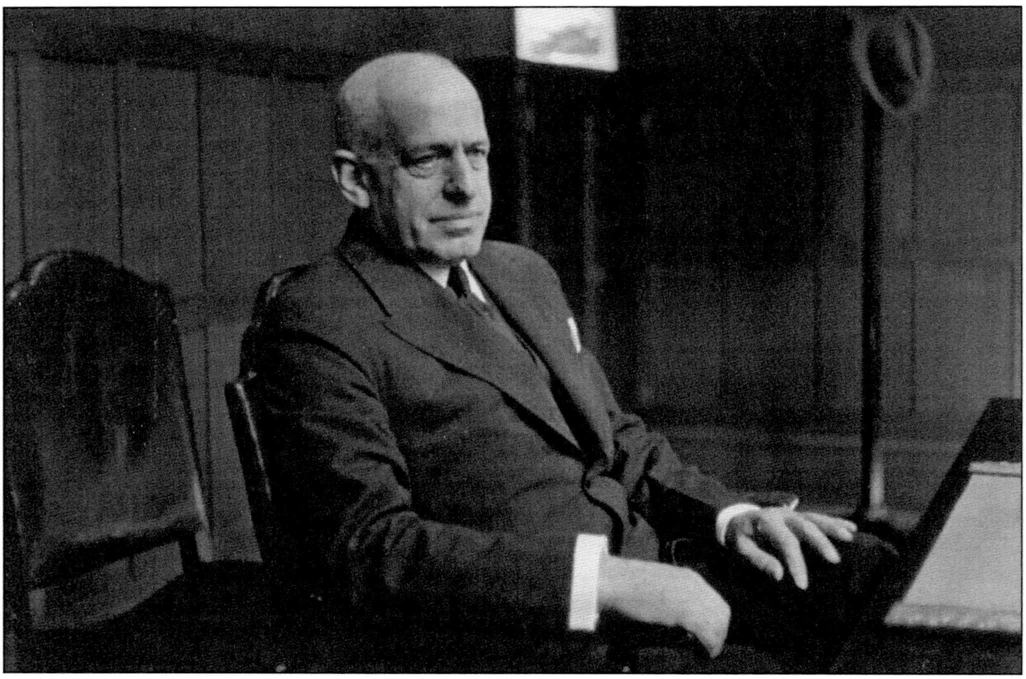

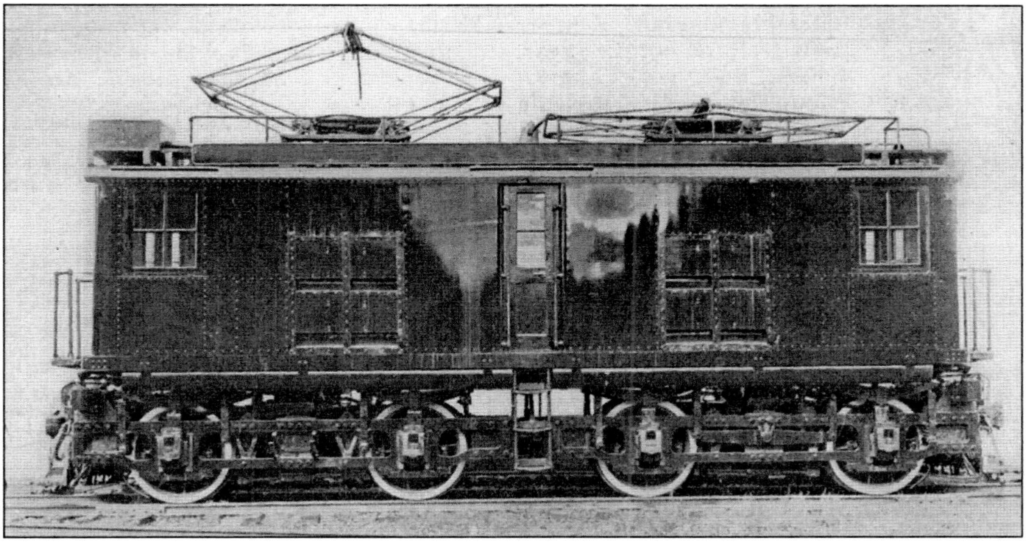

When the Amador Traction Company proposed building an electric railway from Ione to Martell, Sutter Creek, and Jackson, it planned to employ electric locomotives like the one pictured here. The choice to make this an electric line stemmed from the concern that the elevation climb from Ione into the aforementioned towns was too steep and curvy in too short a distance for heavy steam locomotives to make the grade without extreme difficulty.

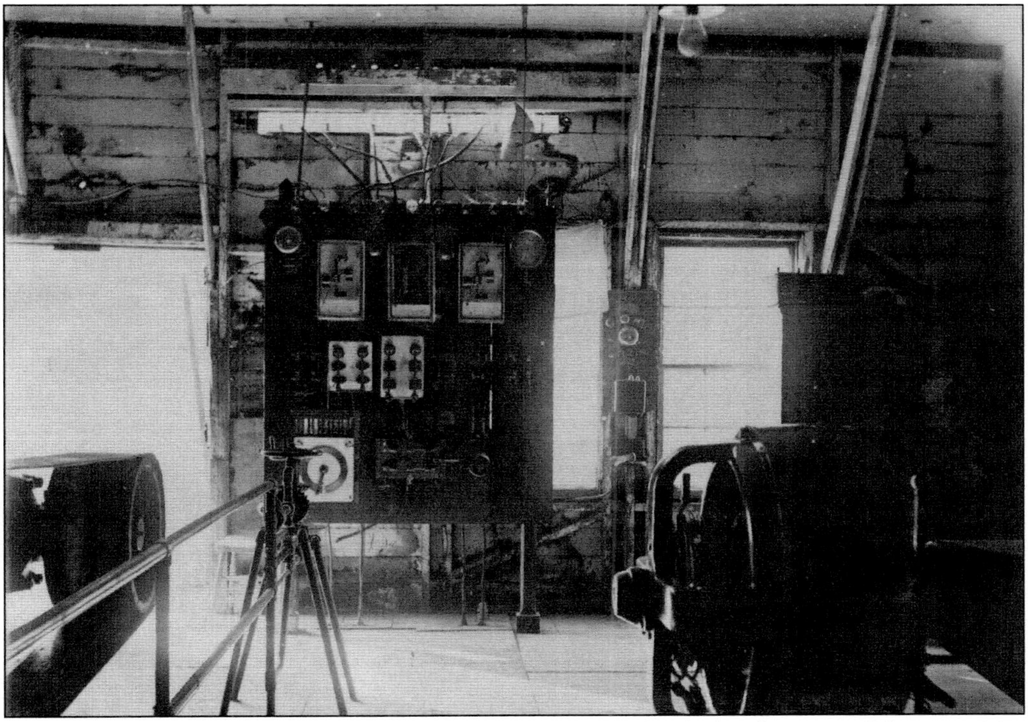

Pictured is the main electrical control room at Preston School of Industry. In February 1904, Edward Records, representing the American River Electric Company, paid a visit to L.M. Holbrook, the electrician at the school, to view the school's power system. Records, with the assistance of Holbrook, proposed placing another steam-powered dynamo at the school to supply power to the town and the Amador Traction line until a larger facility could be built.

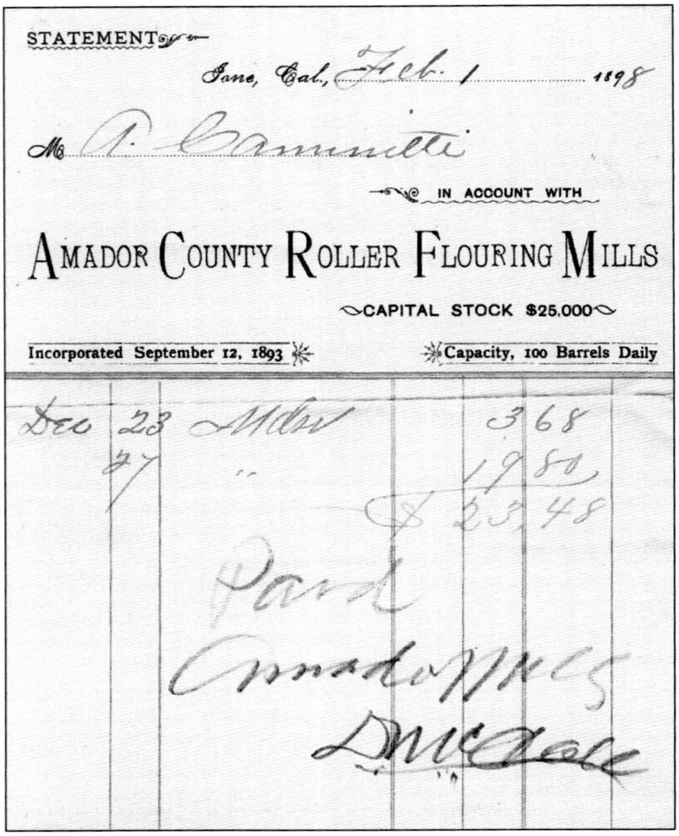

STATEMENT

Ione, Cal., Feb. 1 1898

M

IN ACCOUNT WITH

AMADOR COUNTY ROLLER FLOURING MILLS

CAPITAL STOCK $25,000

Incorporated September 12, 1893 — Capacity, 100 Barrels Daily

Dec	23		3	68
	27	"	19	80
			$ 23	48

David McCall, owner of the Amador Roller Flour Mill in Ione, was the principal organizer of the Amador Traction Company. McCall held many business interests in Amador County. In addition to the mill, he also operated a teaming business hauling goods between towns in Amador County. The freight business was later sold to the Ione & Eastern Railroad.

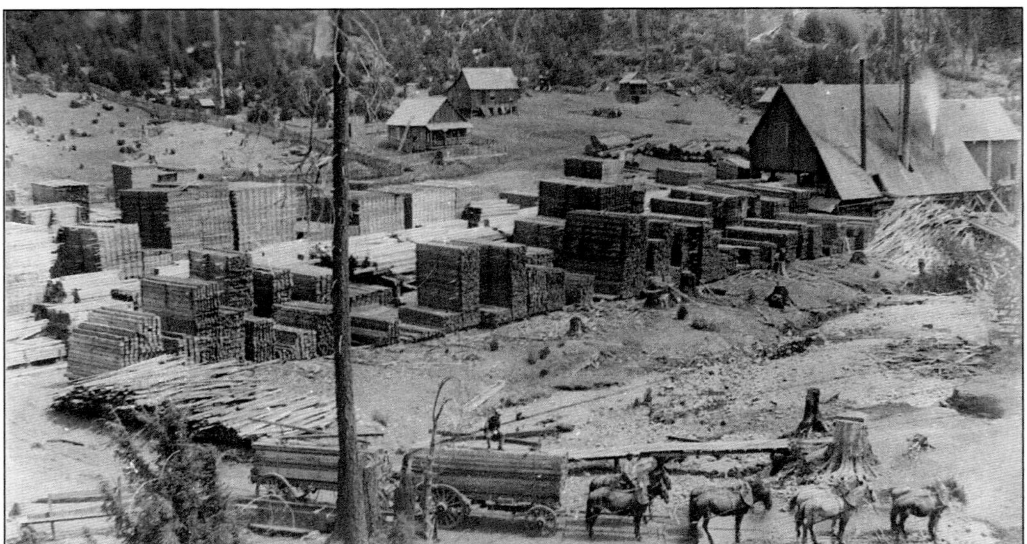

Thomas Chichizola partnered with David McCall in organizing the Amador Traction Company. Chichizola was one of the owners of the Amador Lumber Company and also operated a general store in Jackson Gate. Pictured here is the Chichizola sawmill. Thomas hoped that a rail line, extending from Martell into the timber country, would increase shipments of lumber from the mill to customers outside Amador County.

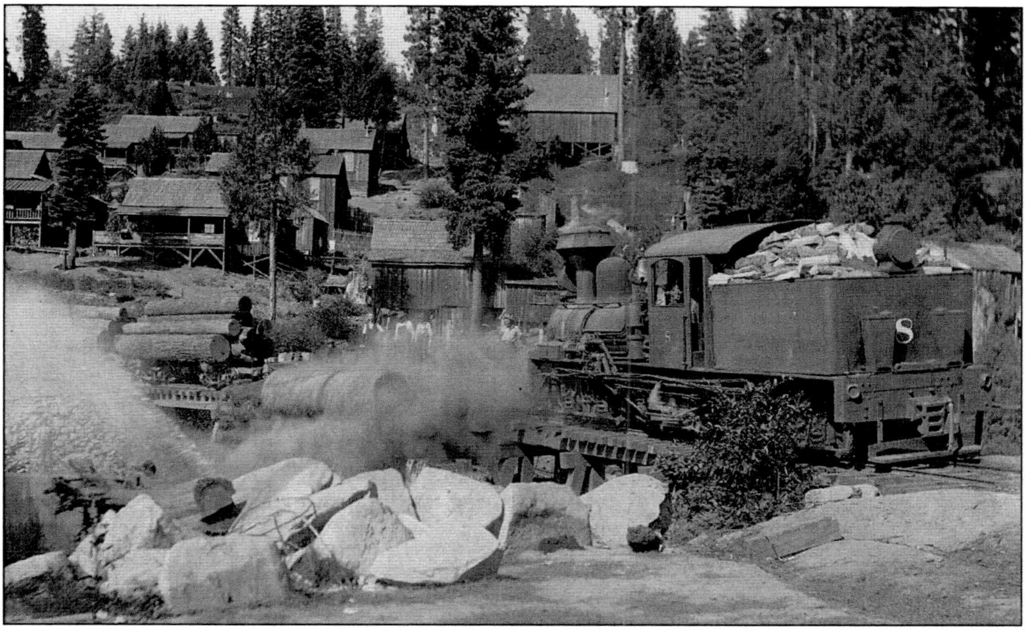

Promoters of the Amador Traction Company looked to the future of industry in Amador County. For them, the immense stands of timber in the Sierra Nevada Mountains were just waiting to be harvested. Logging companies had, for some time, put to use narrow gauge railroads throughout the forests of California to move timber to mills. A rail line into the forests of Amador County seemed only logical.

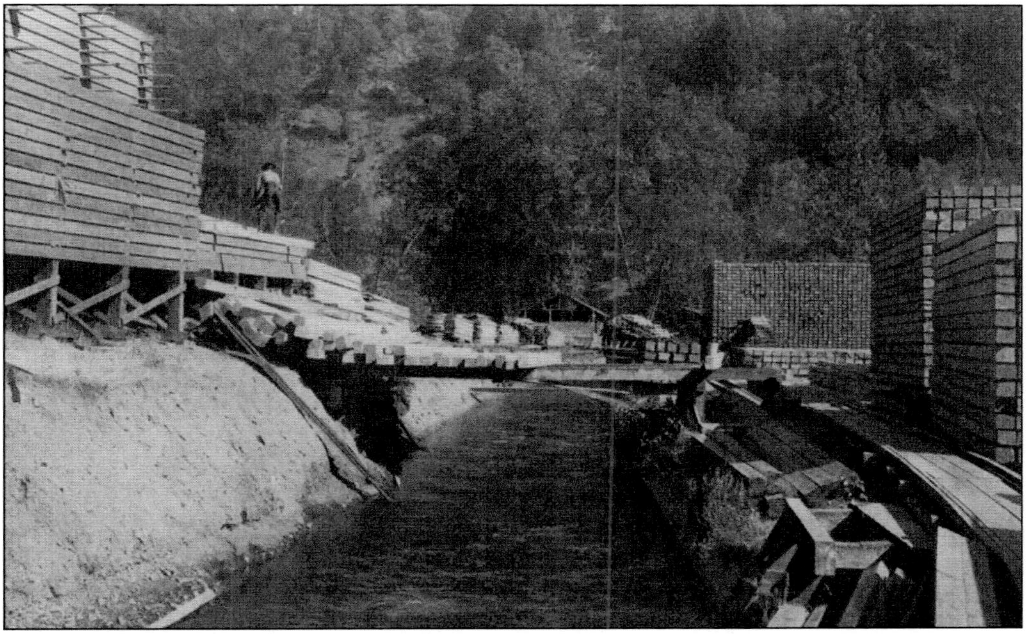

Canals and flumes served as important features to mining and logging operations throughout the Mother Lode region in California. Their primary function was to deliver water to power machinery for these industries; however, they were also employed to transport logs to lower elevations, where they were then loaded on wagons for transport. Building a railroad into the forests would provide a much more efficient way for the Amador Lumber Company to move the wood to a mill site near Martell.

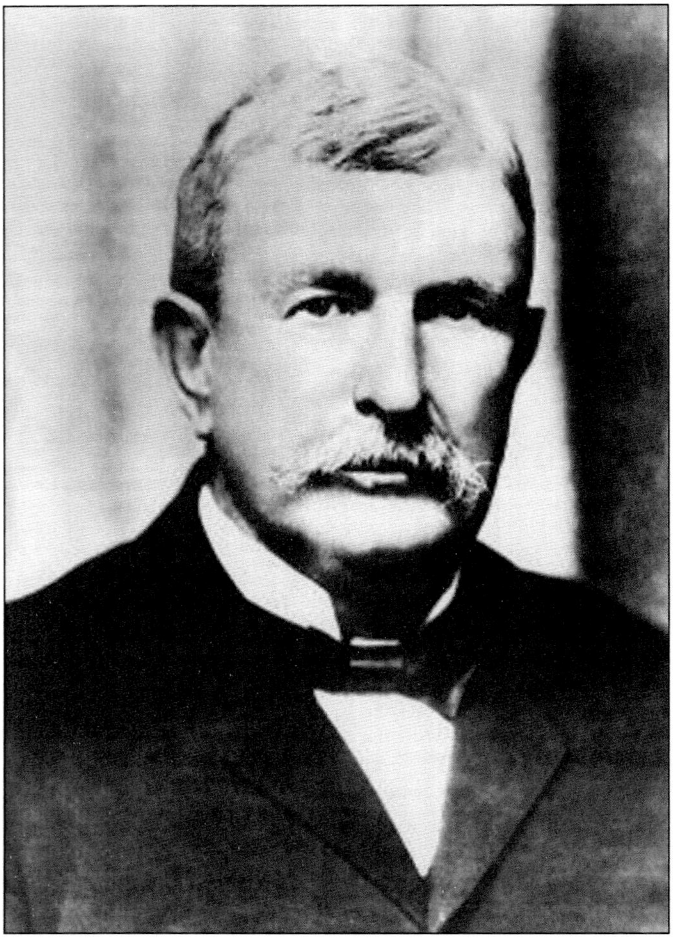

Ben Holt was another partner in the Amador Traction Company. Like his partners, Holt was a businessman and had an interest in lumber. As a young man, he worked in his father's sawmill in New Hampshire, where he managed the shipment of lumber to a family manufacturing company operated by his brothers in San Francisco. After his parents died, Ben followed his brothers to California, and they soon founded the Stockton Wheel Company, where they continued to manufacture wagon parts. Holt went on to design and patent the first practical steam traction engine that could burn wood, coal, or oil as a fuel. Although designed for farm use, it was soon adapted for use by foresters to haul logs out of the mountains. This type of engine, like the one pictured below, proved to be a boon to the logging business.

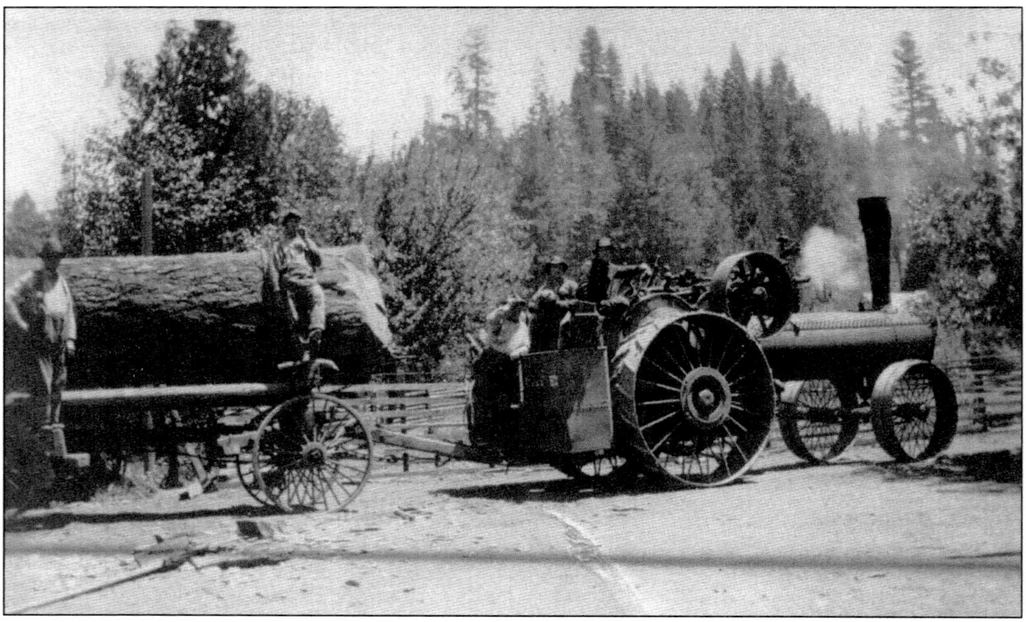

With the failure of the Amador Traction Company, all of the short-lived railroad ventures that were attempting to build a line east from Ione came to an end. The April 21, 1904, issue of the *Amador Record* announced the incorporation of the Ione & Eastern Railway Company. The father-and-son team of local businessmen Jackson and Wilford Dennis, along with investors from San Francisco, were determined to see their line completed.

RAILROAD NEWS,

A New Company Formed and a Road to be Built.

Tuesday of last week the Ione and Eastern Railroad Co., was incorporated in San Francisco, with the following directors and stockholders: Jackson Dennis and Wilford Dennis of this county, J. J. Fagan, William Pardy, R. E. Wallace, H. H. Ferns and S. C. Scheeline of San Francisco. The capital stock is $1,000,000. Jackson Dennis has subscribed $3,500, Wilford Dennis, R. E. Wallace and H. H. Ferns, $2,500 each, and the others $1,000 each. The treasurer is J. J. Fagan. It is estimated that the road will be fourteen miles in length, from Ione to this section. Electricity will be the motive power to be furnished by the American River Power Co.

It is presumed that the gentlemen who took preliminary steps toward forming the Amador Traction Co. found an investment for their money in some other channel, hence let the project go by the board, but Jackson Dennis would not let it down and immediately set about organizing another company, which he soon succeeded in accomplishing, as the first paragraph in this article shows.

At a meeting of the directors Jackson Dennis of Sutter Creek was chosen general manager. Shortly afterward he selected a corps of engineers who are now in the field making the preliminary survey. When this is completed a route will be selected and the final survey made. Then will follow the securing of a charter and rights of way. It is expected that grading will be under way in two or three months.

Jackson Dennis has been working on the project of building a road into this section for a number of years past, in the face of strenuous hatchet wielding of knockers, but he did not swerve from his purpose, and when the railroad is an accomplished fact these same knockers will rise up and call him blessed. No one with brains enough to fill a thimble will dispute the fact that a railroad will be of great benefit to this county, hence it is hard to understand why there should be any opposition at all.

The route of the railroad has not been selected. No doubt it will be done to the satisfaction of investors who can be depended upon to look out for their interests. Jackson and Sutter Creek will each be tapped by the new road as these places are expected to furnish most of the traffic.

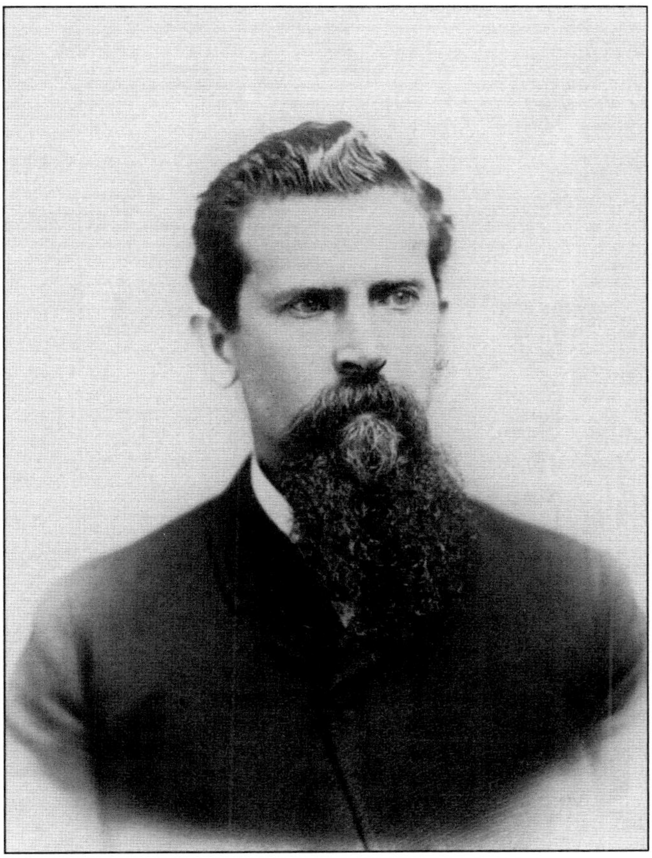

One of the first orders of business for the Ione & Eastern Railway Company was to obtain a right-of-way along the corridor previously surveyed by Henry Feusier. Many landowners were eager to have the railroad built as quickly as possible. Ione resident and businessman John Marchant (left) was the first of many to grant a right-of-way through his land.

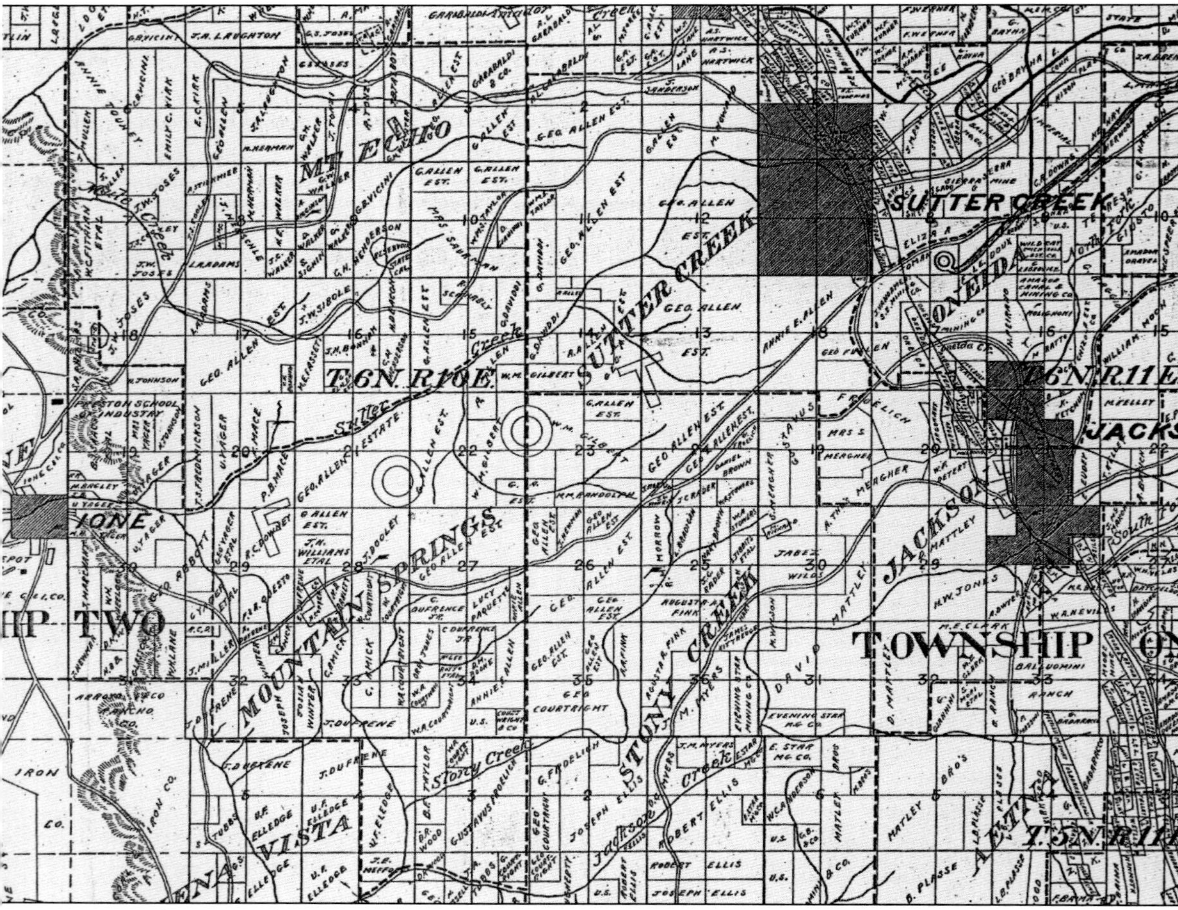

As shown on this 1904 map, numerous residents held parcels of land between Ione and Martell. Within several months, all gave their permission for the rails to cross their land. On August 4, 1904, the Atlas Contract and Supply Company employed 40 men to begin grading work on the Ione & Eastern Railroad, opening a door to new economic and social possibilities for Amador County residents and businesses.

Three

Into the Heart of Amador

Railroads are like ideas—when connected to the world at large, the possibilities for growth are limitless. The opportunity for Amador County to connect to the outside world by rail had become a reality with the construction of the Amador Branch Railroad. However, transport of goods and passengers to the Ione depot by wagon was still necessary. Support for the railroad often centered on the fact that travel became very difficult during winter and spring, when rains virtually ruined the roads. When the Ione & Eastern Railway Company was organized with sound financial support, the newspapers were abuzz and continually reported on the efforts to build what was to become "an avenue to success and prosperity" for Amador.

On Monday, August 4, 1904, the Ione & Eastern Company broke ground near the Southern Pacific depot in Ione. It immediately put to work a crew of 50 men. The following week, two carloads of horses arrived to be used in the grading operations. As the grading work progressed up the line, construction crews laid ties and tracks right behind them. When in full force, the size of work crews increased to eventually become well over 500 men and just about as many horses. The men lived in work camps set up along the route. When track was laid about halfway, boxcars came for the men to sleep in during heavy rains.

Their work was no easy task. They were to build a railroad just less than 12 miles in length, with nearly 100 curves, and face an elevation increase of over 1,244 feet. They would encounter soils ranging from hard clay that became slick and washed away in rains to solid rock that had to be blasted. They would also meet with several severe accidents along the way and would go on strike twice for higher wages. Despite these difficulties and months of inclement weather, the final track was laid at the Martell Station in May 1905, and a new era was opened up for Amador County.

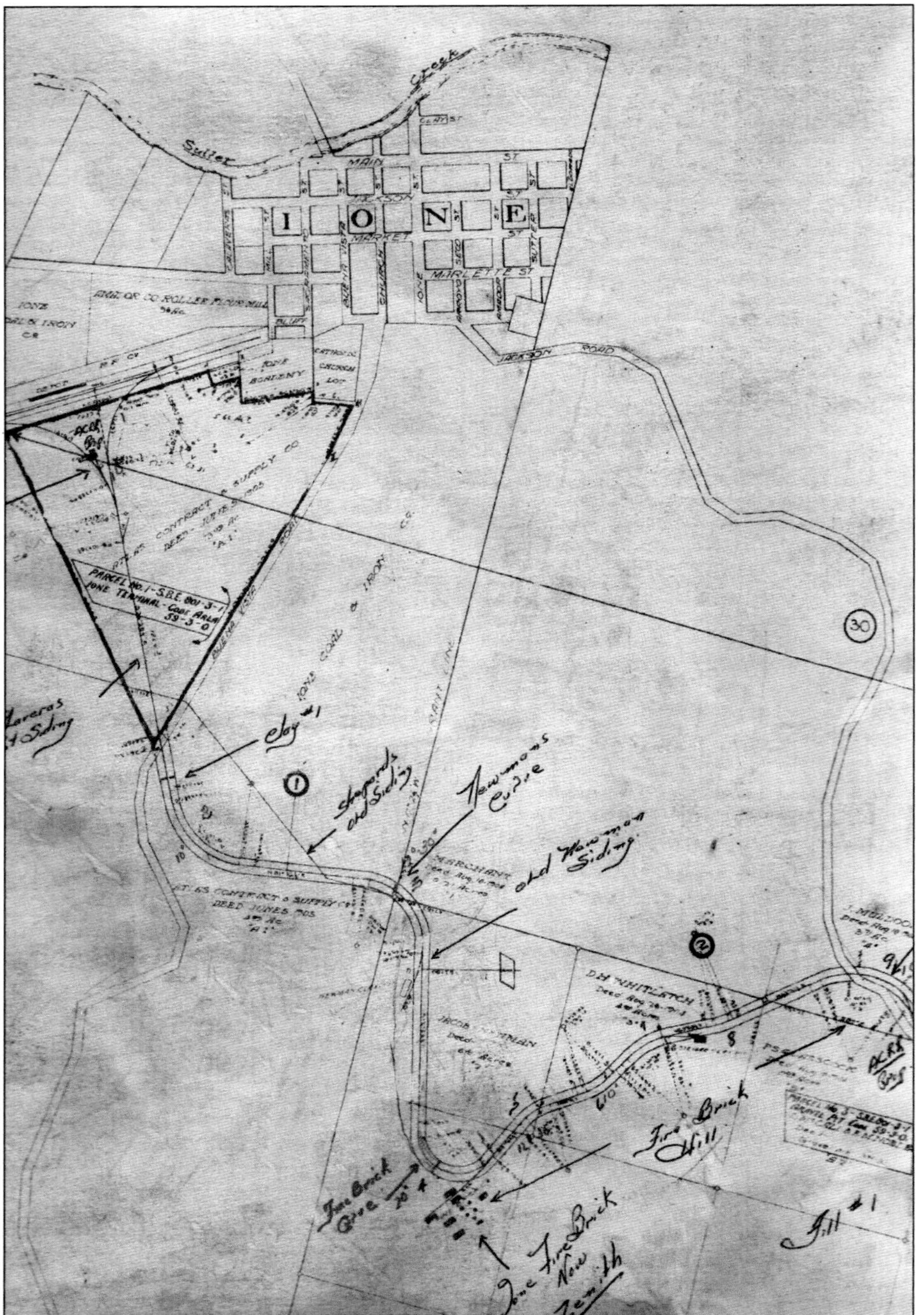

Pictured is the westernmost section of the original survey map laying out the route of the Ione & Eastern Railroad, from Ione to where it crosses the old Ione-Jackson Road, now State Route 104. The handwritten notes on the map mark important features along the line that became known under familiar names associated with either land owners or mines. When looking at names on the map, it is easy to understand why backers of the railroad invested so much personal interest in its construction. The Amador County Roller Mills, owned by David McCall, is located immediately adjacent to the Ione rail yard, and the Ione Coal and Iron Company owned a large parcel of land just outside of Ione. (Courtesy Grant Vogel.)

Also included on the survey map on page 42 were lists of the names of those who deeded to the railroad a right-of-way through their property, for a mere $10 each. There were so many of these allowances made that they were grouped into parcels. This list for parcel No. 2 contains the names of landowners that are also shown as handwritten locals on the survey map.

PARCEL No. 2 - SBE 801-3-1

RIGHT-OF-WAY - CODE AREA 59-3-0.

Grantor	From Sta.	To Sta.	Area		Deed
Atlas Cent & Sup Co	24+58	46+60	4.82	Ac	June 5 1905
J. Marchant	46+60	47+52	0.21	"	Aug. 10 - 1904
Jacob Newman	47+52	75+45	6.41	"	Not shown
D.H. Whitlatch	75+45	92+90	4.00	"	Aug. 26 - 1904
P.S. Glasscock	92+90	93+21	0.09	"	Aug. 10 1904
J. Muldoon	93+21	109+36	3.71	"	" " "
Wm H. Lane	109+36	125+23	3.64	"	" " "
J & F Miller	125+23	148+60			
	154+52	163+72	7.54	"	" " "
Jos Dufrene	148+60	154+52	1.39	"	" " "
Aug. Dufrene	163+72	169+33	1.29	"	Not shown
Josias Winter	169+33	201+84	7.23	"	
W.A. Amick	201+84	227+15	5.81	"	Oct 14, 1904
Aug Dufrene	227+15	231+00	0.88	"	Not shown
Newton Copper M.	231+00	249+62	4.27	"	" "
Nellie Courtright	249+62	266+00	3.28	"	Nov. 16, 1904
Jos Dooley	266+00	304+25[6]	8.78	"	Aug. 31, 1904
Allen Est Co	304+25[6]	311+40	1.64	"	Oct 25, 1904
Total Area Parcel 2 -			65.06	Ac.	

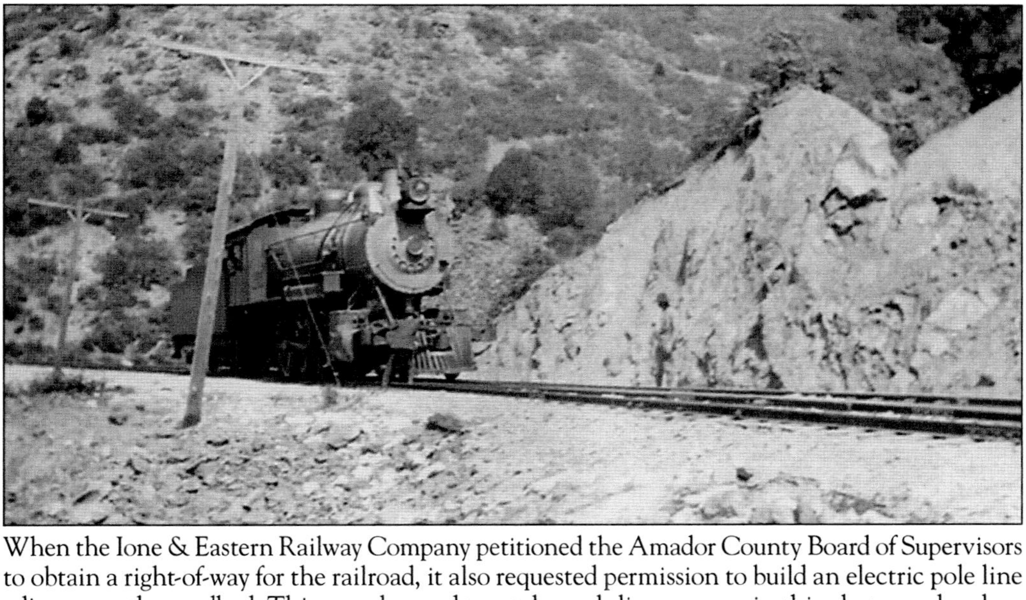

When the Ione & Eastern Railway Company petitioned the Amador County Board of Supervisors to obtain a right-of-way for the railroad, it also requested permission to build an electric pole line adjacent to the roadbed. This was changed to a telegraph line, as seen in this photograph, when it was decided to run steam locomotives instead of electric on the railroad.

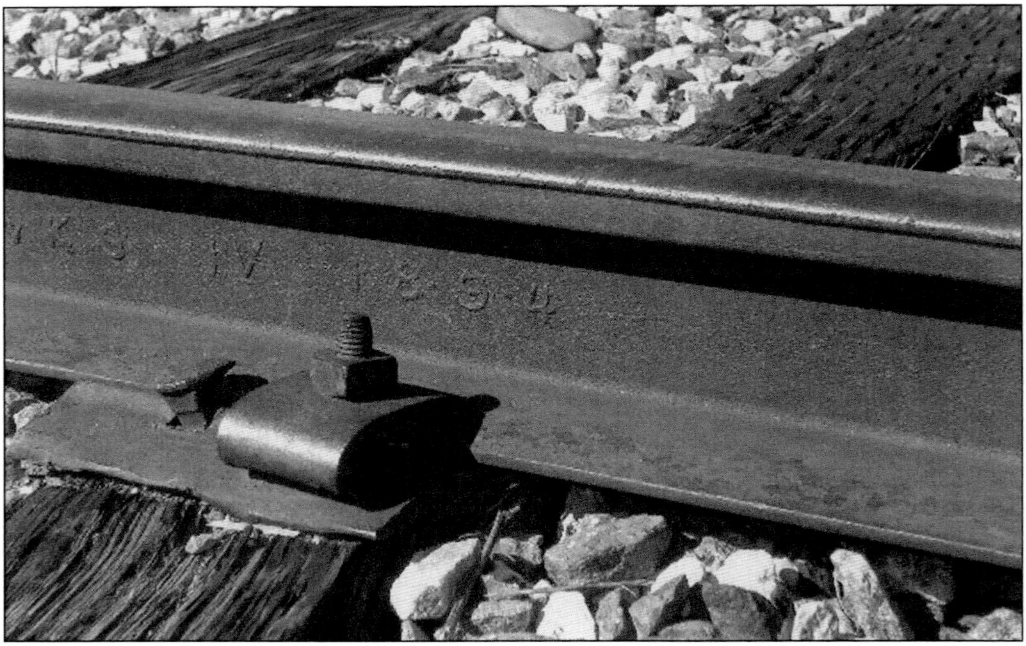

The contract between the Ione & Eastern Railroad and the Atlas Supply and Contract Company called for the construction of a subgrade for a standard gauge railroad to have a width of four feet, eight and a half inches between the rails, on a road bed 12 feet wide. The ties were to be made of fir, pine, or redwood, and the rails were to be no less than 45 pounds in per-yard weight. Many of the rails used were recycled from other railroad stock. Over time, much of the rail was replaced by 60-, 70-, 80-, and 90-pound rail to accommodate heavier loads. Today, the majority are of the 80-pound per-yard weight. The contract also included the placement of signals. The remains of a signal control box are shown in the photograph below. (Author's collection.)

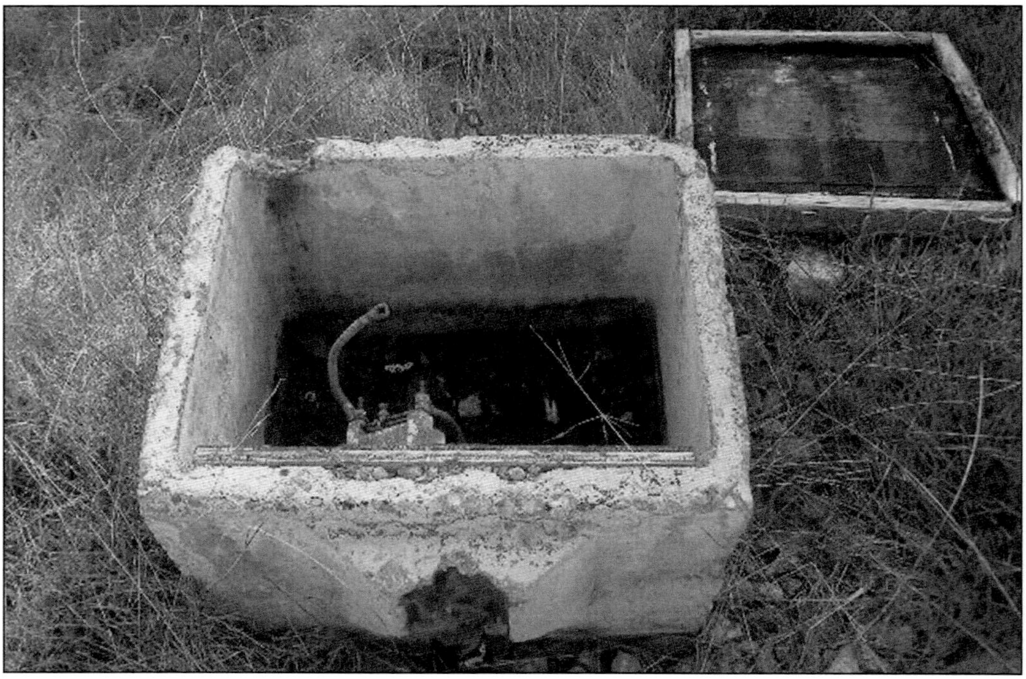

Jacob Newman (right), in partnership with his brothers, was involved in many business enterprises throughout Amador County, including the clay industry. The Newman Clay Company mine, located a mile east of downtown Ione, was adjacent to the Ione & Eastern tracks. Here, a siding was built into the center of the Newman operations to facilitate the transport of clay products. In the picture below, a boxcar sits on the siding, waiting to be loaded with product. The main tracks of the Ione & Eastern can be seen running across the center of the photograph.

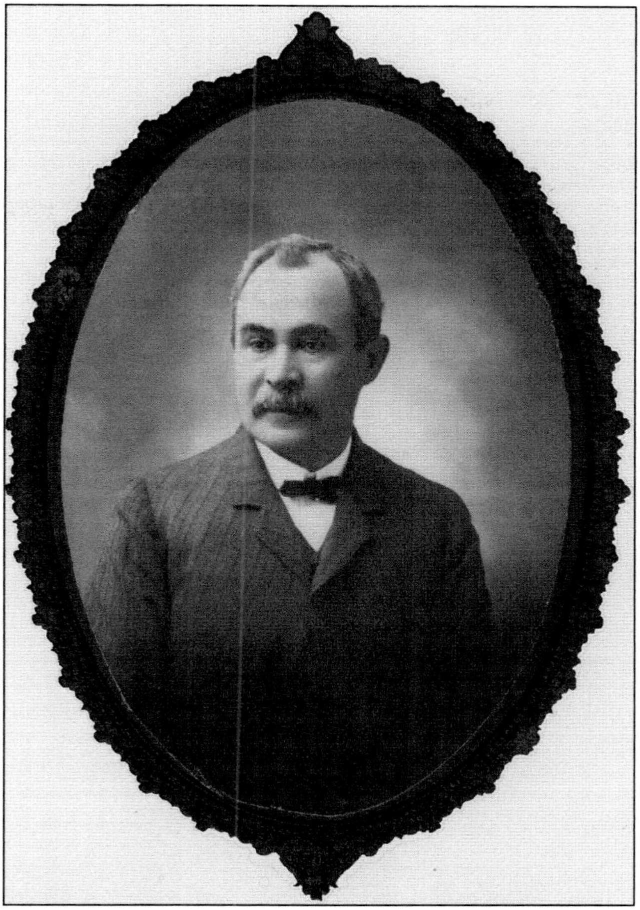

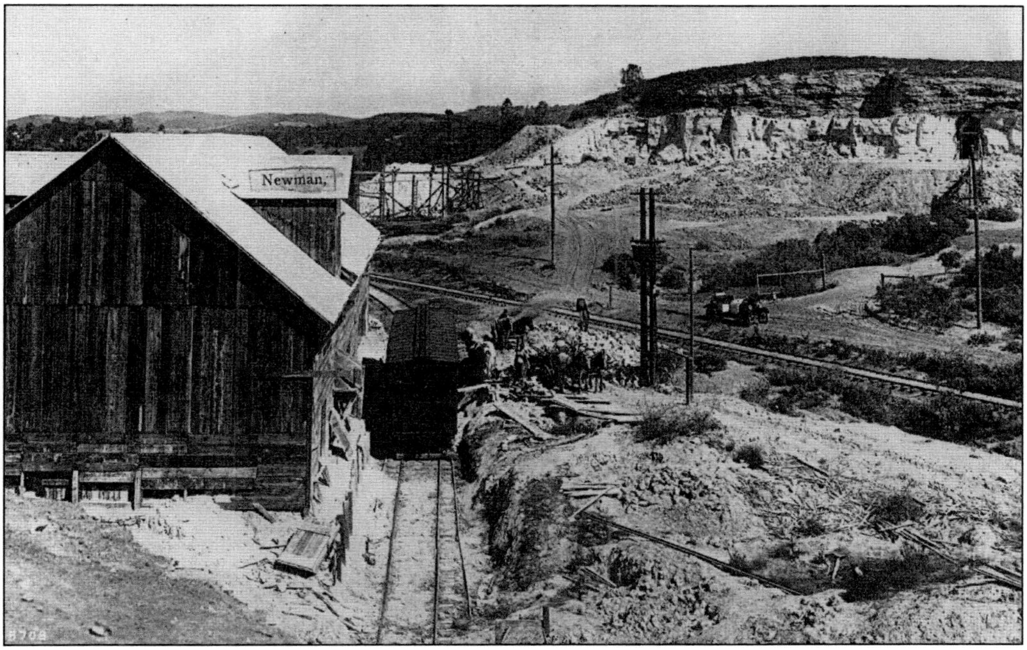

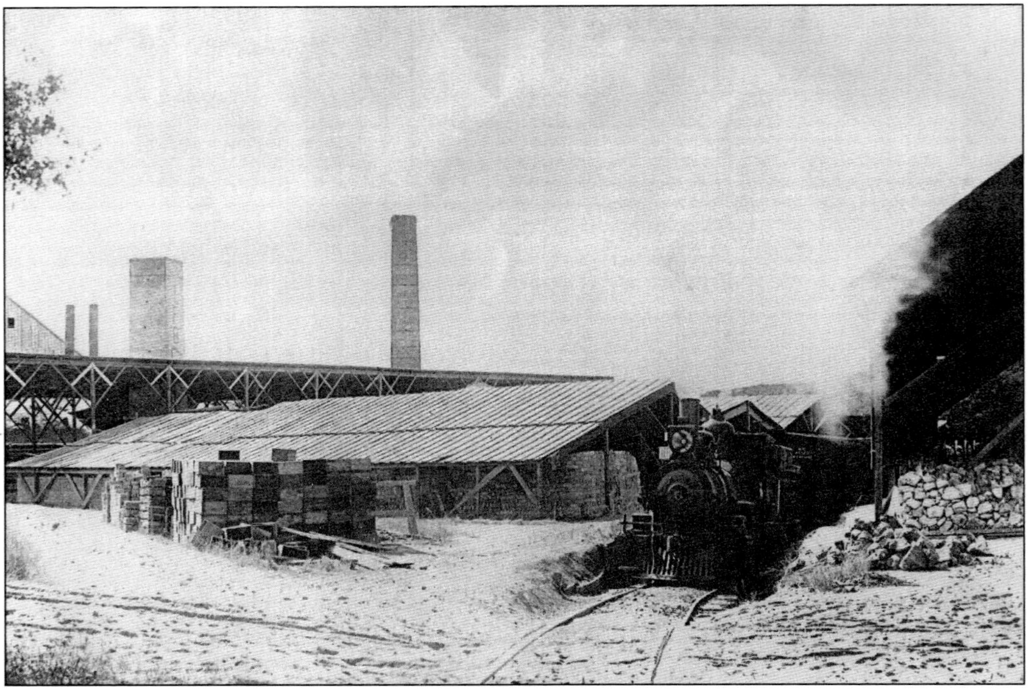

The Ione Fire Brick plant, situated a short distance to the south of the Newman clay pit, had been in business for a number of years before the Ione & Eastern was built. Like other mines in the area, all of its products were shipped out by wagon until the railroad became a reality, and a siding was built into the plant.

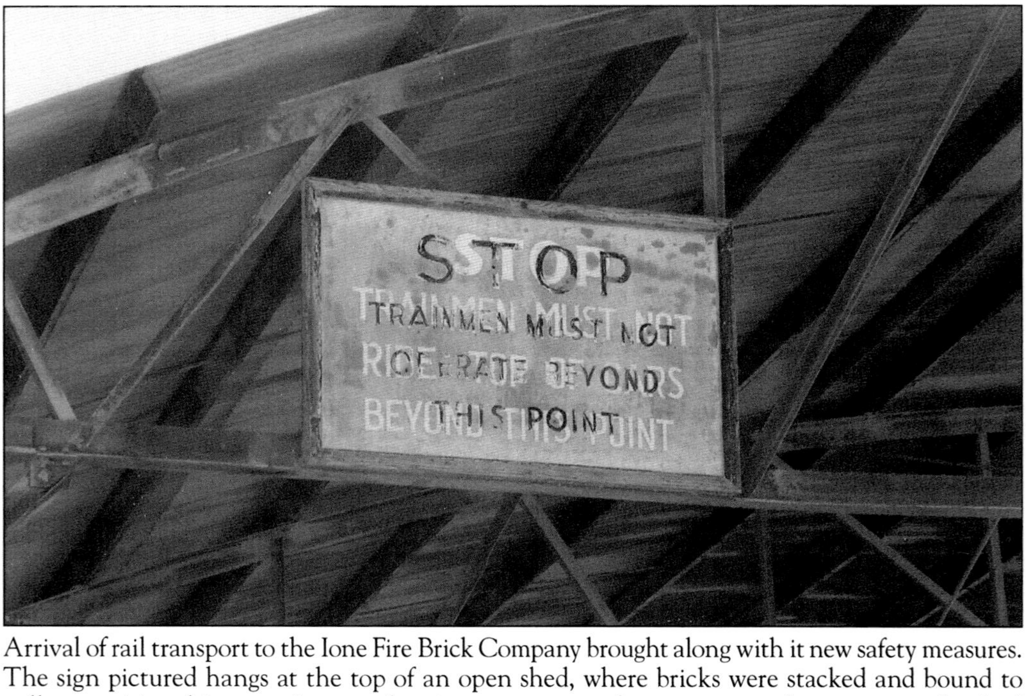

Arrival of rail transport to the Ione Fire Brick Company brought along with it new safety measures. The sign pictured hangs at the top of an open shed, where bricks were stacked and bound to pallets awaiting shipment. It warned trainmen against riding atop cars when entering the shed because of the low clearance of the trusses. (Author's collection.)

46

The siding built into the Ione Fire Brick Company split into two tracks; one went to one section of the yard near the factory, and the other went to the brick storage sheds. In this photograph, a car takes the tracks to the factory area.

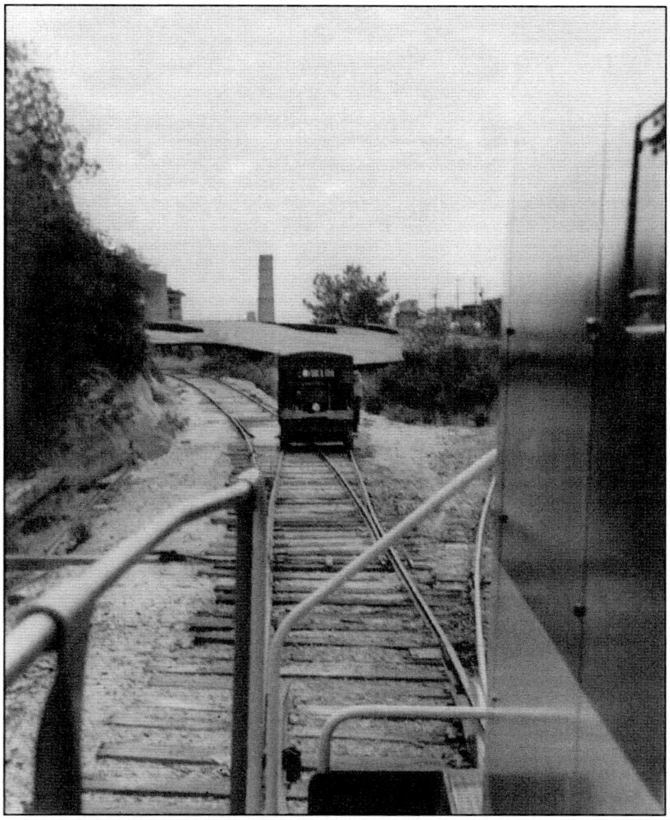

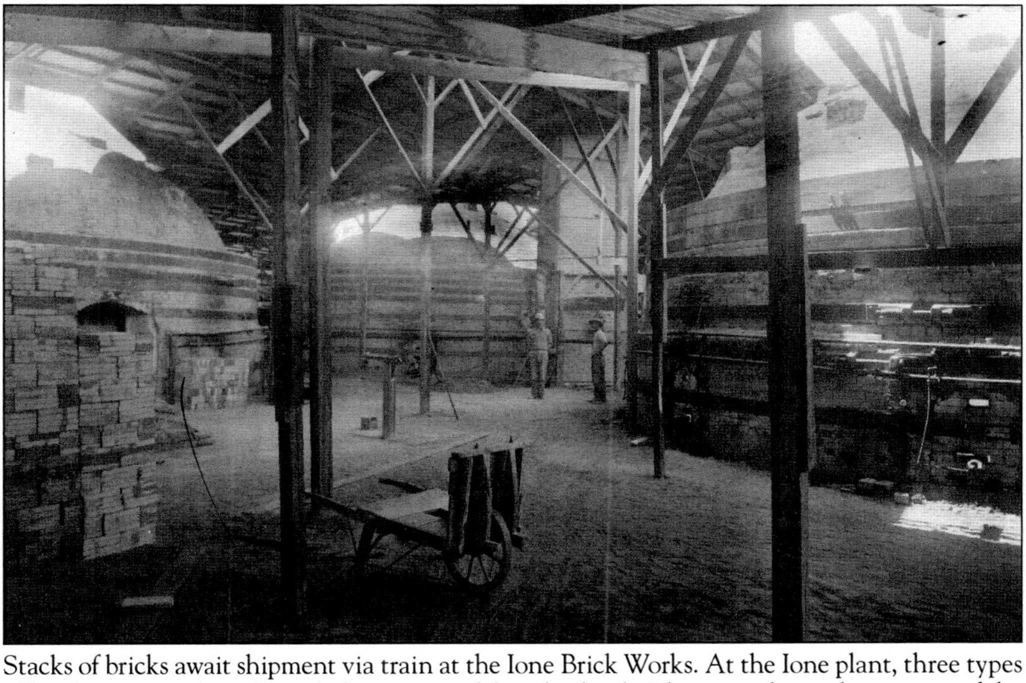

Stacks of bricks await shipment via train at the Ione Brick Works. At the Ione plant, three types of bricks were made: stiff-mud, dry-press, and fire-clay brick. This view shows the interior of the shed with the sign that warned trainmen of low clearance (shown on page 46).

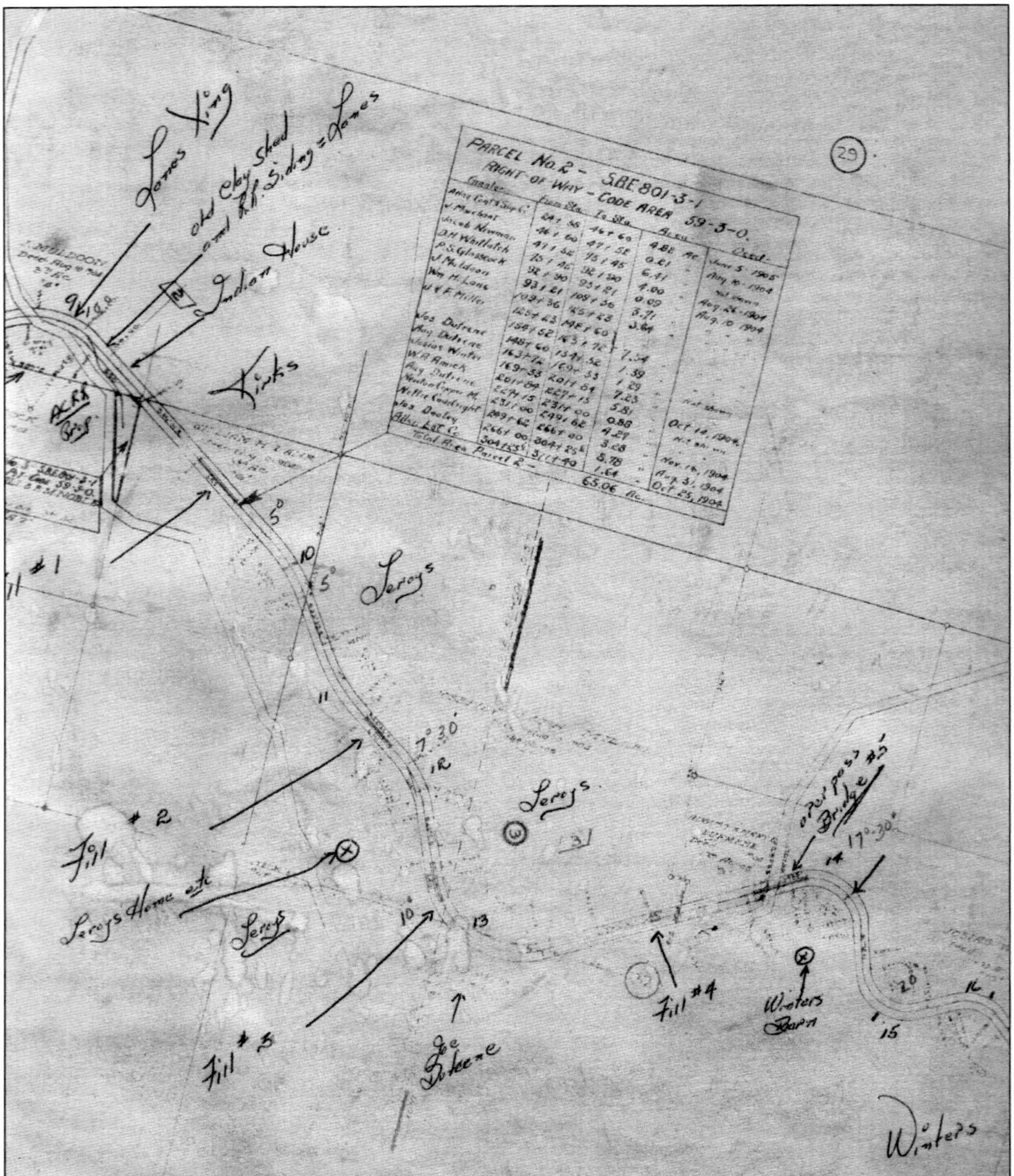

Pictured is another section of the original survey map laying out the route of the Ione & Eastern Railroad. This section shows the route of the railroad from the crossing of State Route 104 to just beyond the trestle that crosses State Route 88. The construction crews did not have much difficulty with grading, thanks to the flat ground near Ione, but by the time they reached just beyond Kinks, their work took on a slower pace. Here, the topography presented new challenges, requiring cutting and filling around hillsides and the construction of trestles across large gullies. In January 1905, the *Amador Ledger* reported that the embankment marked on this map as Fill No. 1, the highest on the railroad, was saturated with rain and kept sinking. Bridge No. 5, shown at the lower right, was the only trestle constructed to pass above a roadway. (Courtesy Grant Vogel.)

The hilly topography and an elevation increase of 1,244 feet in less than 12 miles presented special challenges when building the Ione & Eastern Railroad. Curves in the line, such as the one pictured, and the steep grade, which at one point reaches 3.8 percent, made it the curviest and slowest traveled railway in California. (Author's collection.)

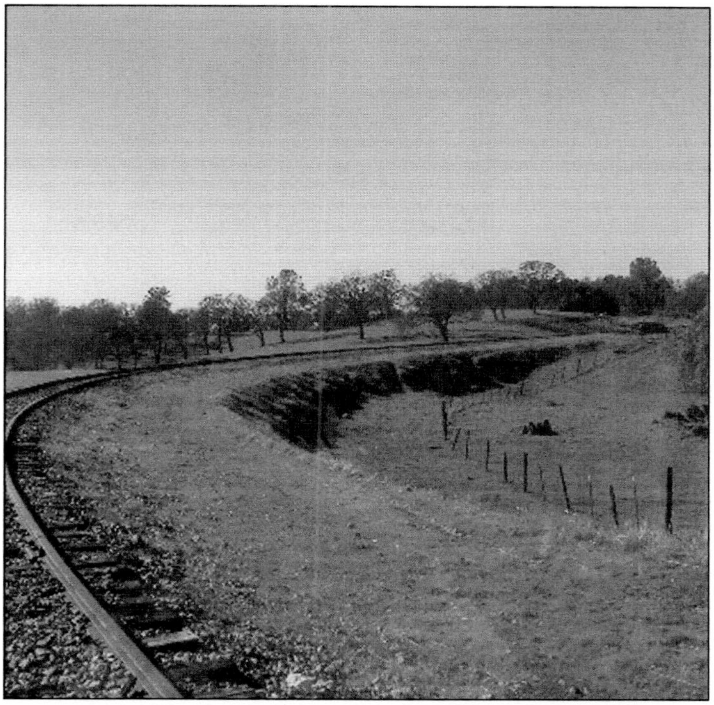

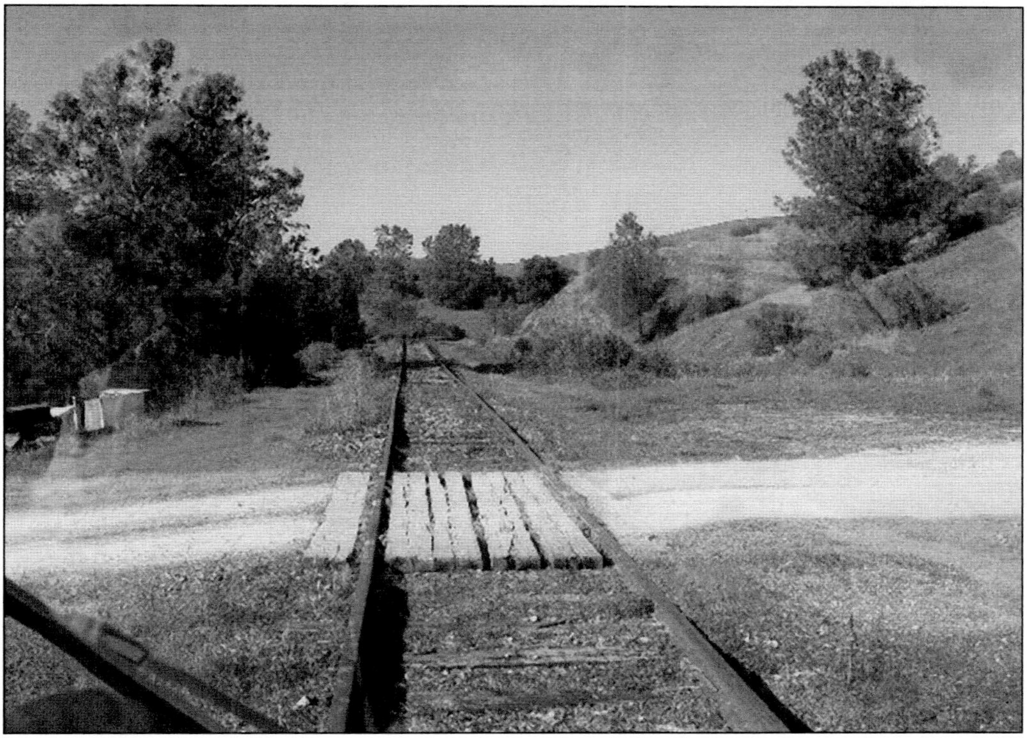

Along with the right of way granted to the Ione & Eastern by landowners, many people entered into separate agreements so that they could continue to access their property across the rails. Where the tracks crossed the farm road of William H. Lane, the company laid ties to allow him continued access by wagon. This location became known as Lane's Crossing. (Author's collection.)

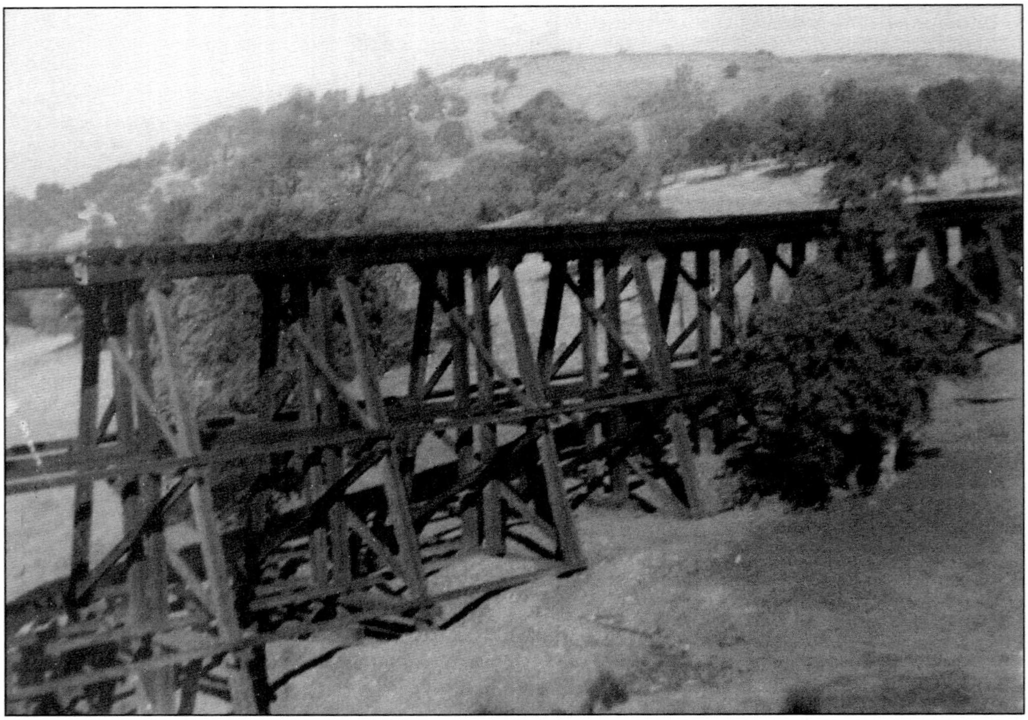

The Ione & Eastern tracks extended out of Ione over flat ground for about three miles, until they reached a point where the topography became hilly with deep ravines. The newspapers of the time reported that quick progress was being made at building the railroad up to this point. Here, the work slowed, and the work of constructing a total of 12 trestles between Ione and Martell began.

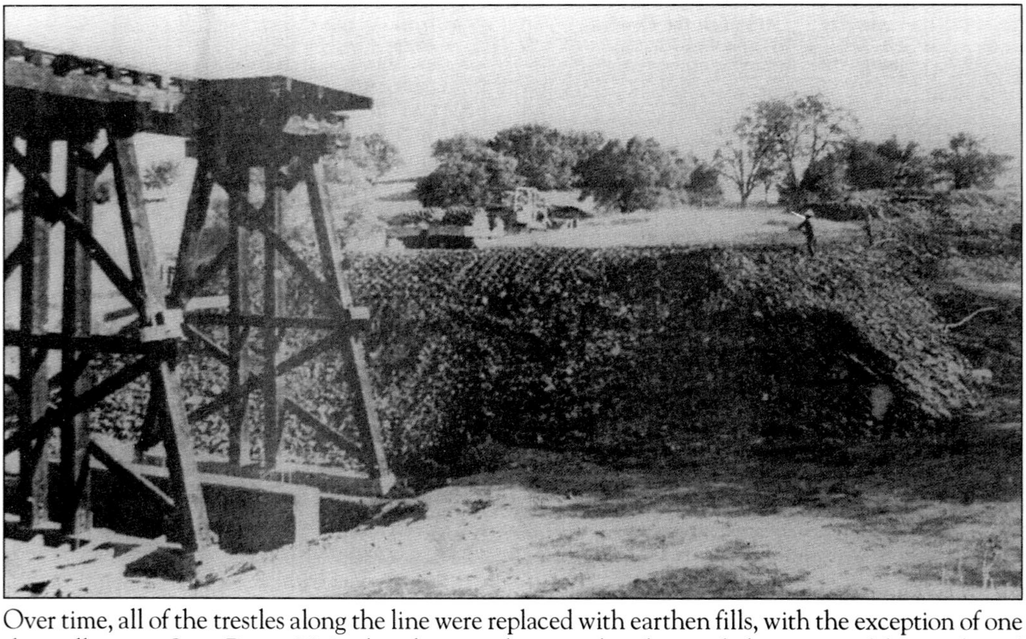

Over time, all of the trestles along the line were replaced with earthen fills, with the exception of one that still crosses State Route 88. In this photograph, a crew has dismantled a section of the trestle and has begun to fill and compact the area prior to replacing the tracks. (Courtesy Grant Vogel.)

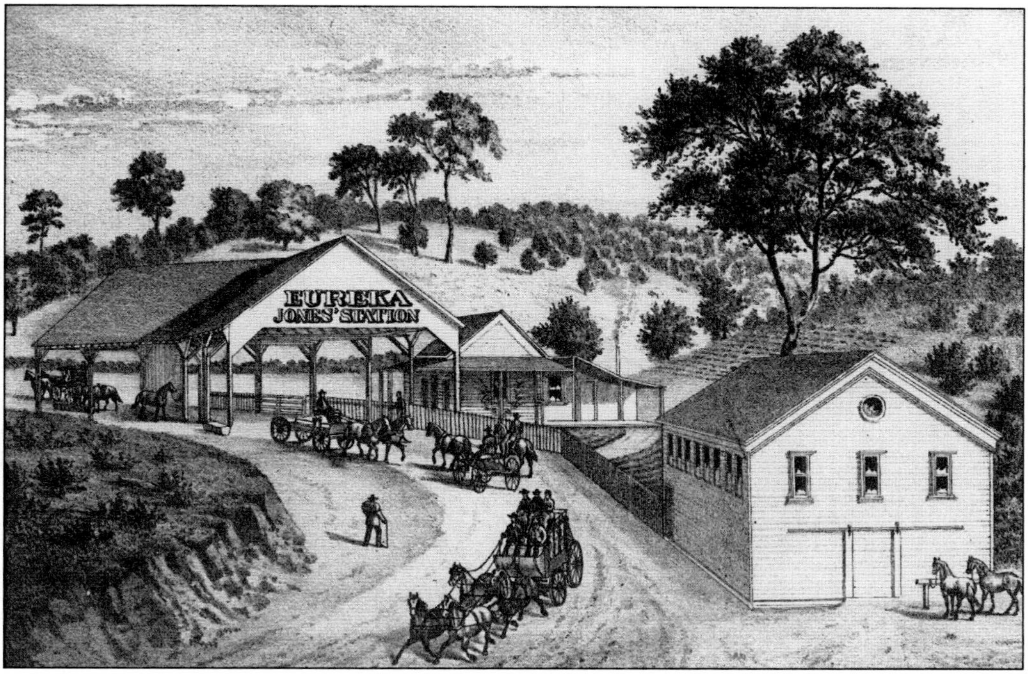

Within one month of breaking ground in Ione, the grading crew had reached Miller's Station, pictured in this lithograph with the name of an earlier owner. It was next to this stage station, on the road between Ione and Jackson, where the rails crossed above the road atop a large trestle.

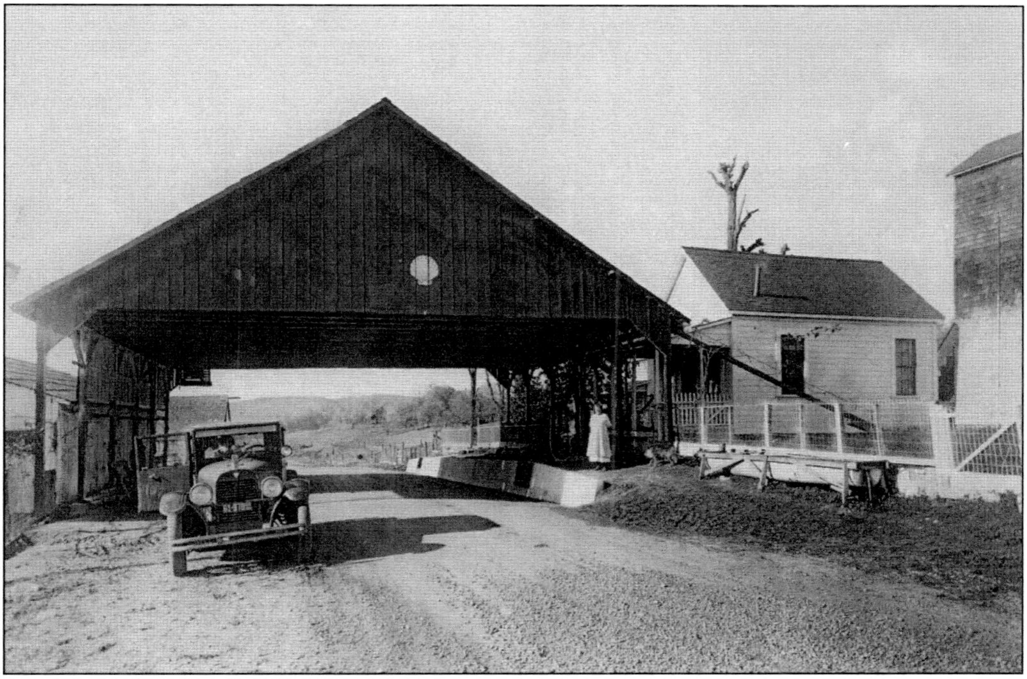
Pictured is Dufrene's Station, another landmark that once stood along the Ione-Jackson Road. A railroad workers camp with over 100 men and just about as many horses was set up near here in November 1904. Once the work was completed in this area, the camp was moved farther east. This photograph was taken well after the railroad was completed.

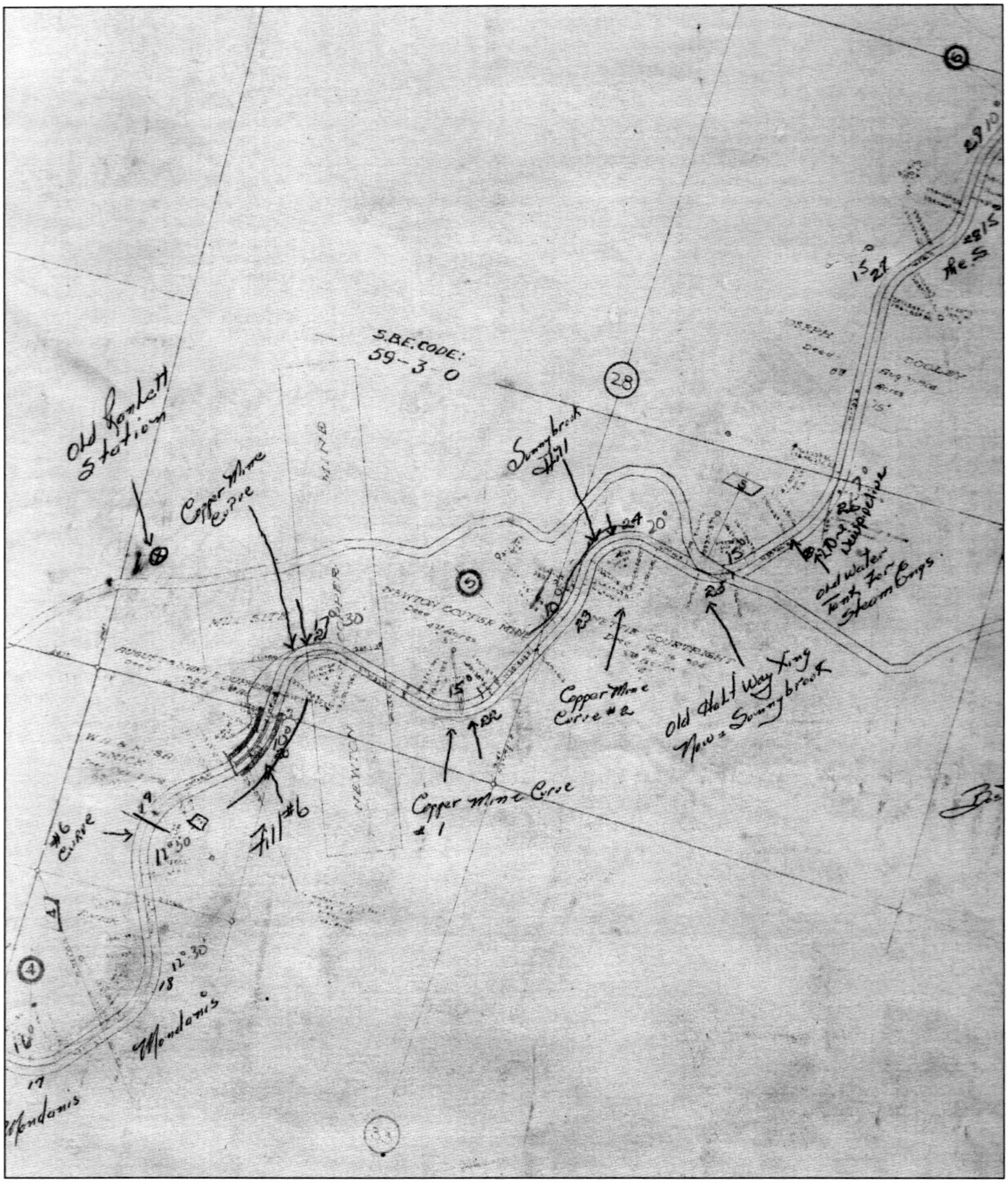

As the crews moved east, their work became much more difficult. The hillsides became steeper and the valleys and gullies deeper. Here, the route of the railroad takes on a much different character with numerous curves, many of which could only be graded after blasting through rock. Note that in this short section of the route, approximately three miles in length, there are a total of 10 curves. The area marked "Fill No. 6" was the location of a trestle, and the dark line running along Sunnybrook Hill is where the entire hillside had to be reinforced before track could be laid. (Courtesy Grant Vogel.)

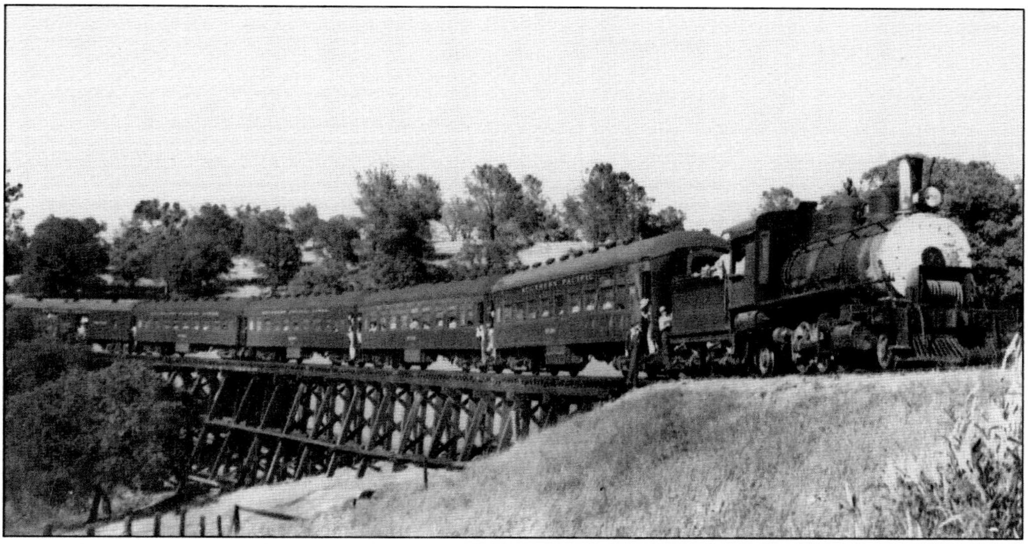

In mid-December 1904, the railroad contractors were met with several setbacks. The lower portion of an embankment that had been built up in the gully below Miller's Station collapsed because of wet and unstable ground. After viewing this photograph, it is easy to understand how the hilly terrain presented obstacles for construction crews. In this photograph, engine No. 7, affectionately known as "Iron Ivan," pulls several Southern Pacific passenger coaches over a trestle.

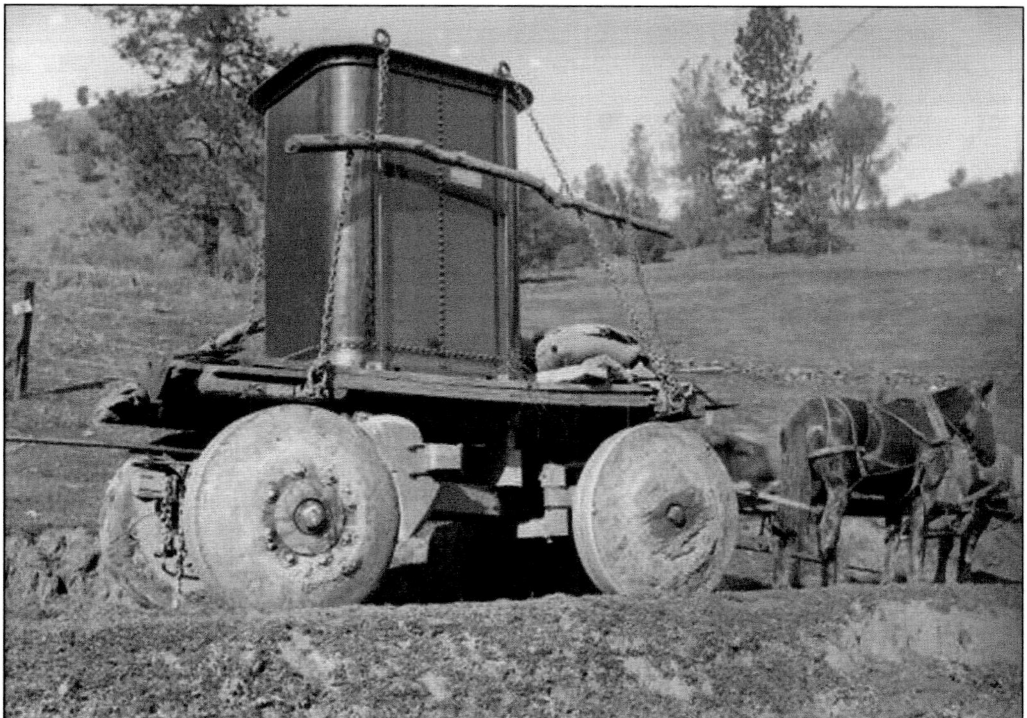

Laying the rails to Mountain Springs would reduce the difficulty of transporting heavy machinery to the Mokelumne River for construction of the Electra Powerhouse. When the bank collapsed below Miller's Station, a wagon loaded with a nine-and-a-half-ton transformer, like the one pictured here, went off the road and ended up in a gully when the bank gave way.

The condition of the road between Ione and Jackson—the main artery of traffic in Amador county—is deplorable beyond description. If anything were wanted to demonstrate the absolute necessity of railroad communication between these two points, it is supplied by the present condition of the wagon road. We call it a road; but it is far from deserving that distinction. It is a mud channel from beginning to end. Below the Mountain Springs it is plowed up so thoroughly by the heavy freight teams as to be almost impassable. Transportation over it in any shape is really dangerous. This side of Mountain Springs there is a hard bottom of rock, but this is covered nearly all the way with mud to the depth of three to six inches. After all the money that has been spent on this highway in the effort to make it fairly passable the year round, the conclusion is inevitable that the undertaking is a failure. The truth is forced home that the county is not equal to the task of keeping it in repair. We do not say this as a reflection upon the management of the road work. We are not discussing that proposition. It is enough to say that a portion of this road was macadamized under the supervision of the state board of highway commissioners. That particular piece of road went to the bad as quickly as the rest. The fact is the traffic has become too much for any such road, no matter how scientifically constructed. In an experience of nearly thirty years, we have never seen the road in a worse state than it is at present.

Amador residents were anxious to have the railroad completed. Suffering through one of the wettest winters in several years, they looked forward to having an alternative to traveling wet and muddy roads. This article appeared in the January 27, 1905, issue of a local newspaper. (Author's collection.)

The Ione & Eastern Railway Company lost no time in preparing for a brisk freight and stage business. Within two weeks of announcing that it would commence shipping freight, the company purchased David McCall's freight business and Fred Rabb's stage lines. Pictured here is an invoice from Rabb's livery business.

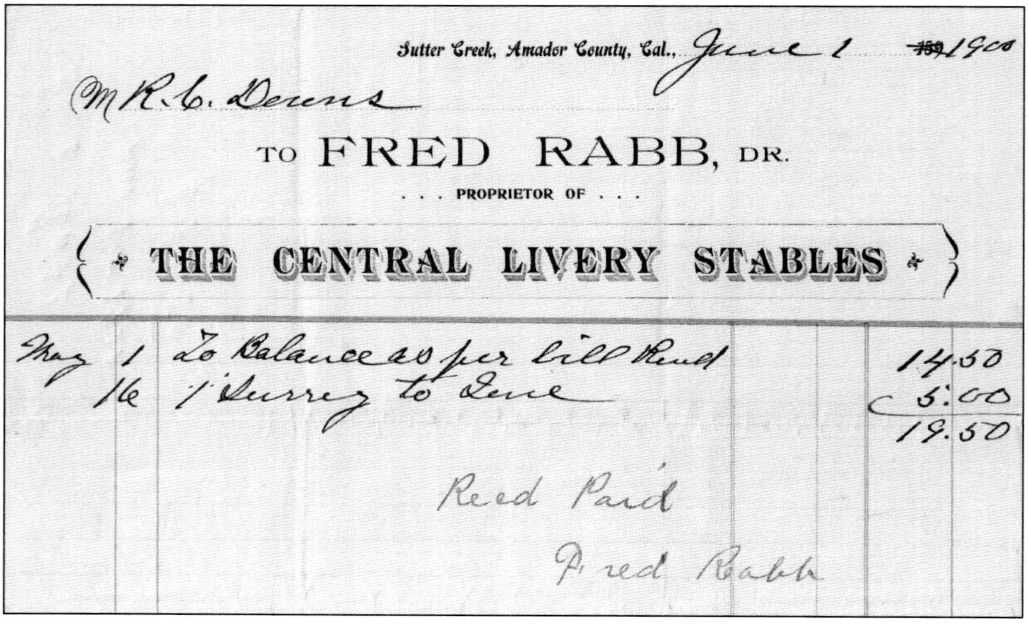
Sutter Creek, Amador County, Cal., June 1 1900

TO FRED RABB, DR.

. . . PROPRIETOR OF . . .

THE CENTRAL LIVERY STABLES

May	1	To Balance as per bill Rend	14.50
	16	1 Surrey to Ione	5.00
			19.50

Recd Paid

Fred Rabb

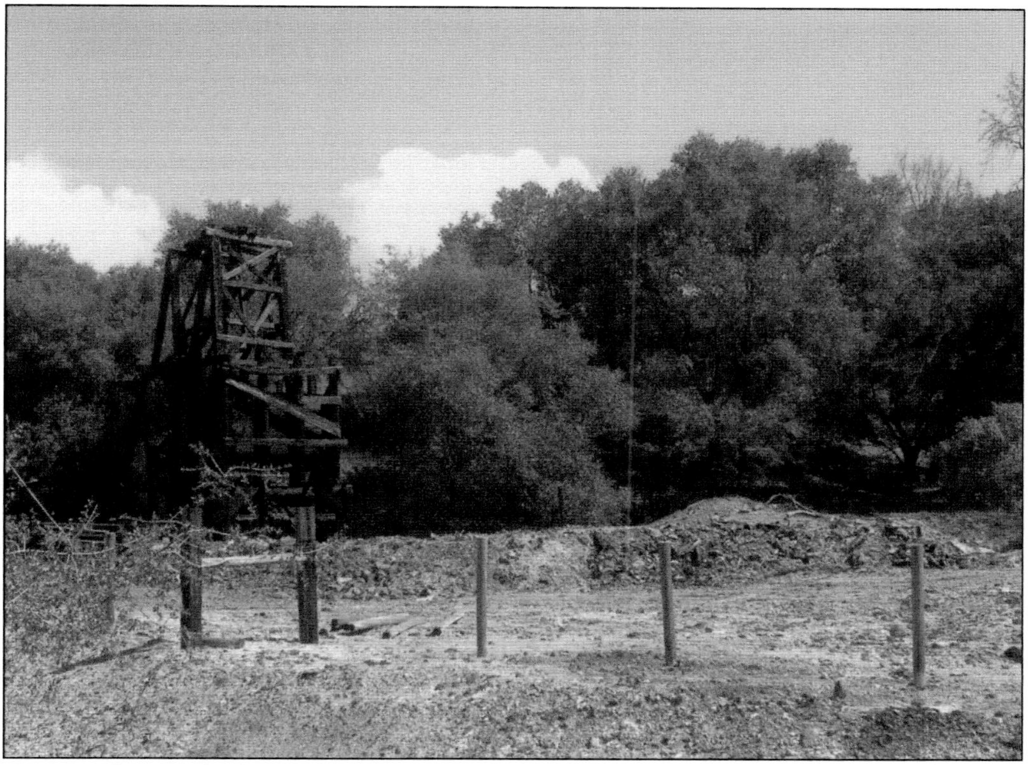

Once tracks were laid to Ranlett, a depot was constructed, and it became the first freighting center on the railroad. Freight was hauled to this point via rail and off-loaded to wagons. Today, all that remains of the settlement are the headframe and tailings of the Newton Copper Mine, as seen here. (Author's collection.)

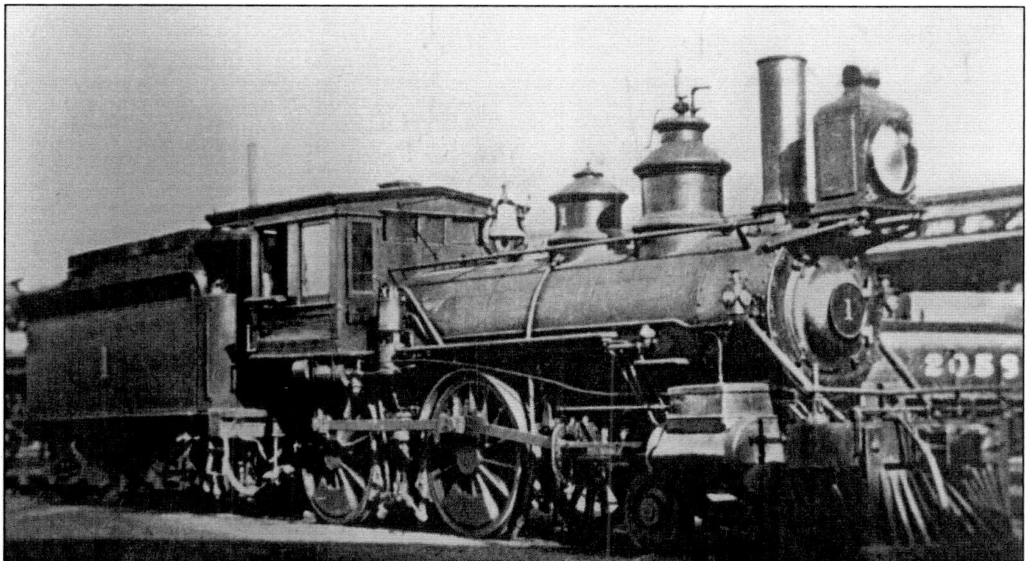

This Shay locomotive served as engine No. 1 on the Ione & Eastern. It was used as the construction engine and was the first to pull freight into Ranlett. It took the place of another when that engine was involved in a wreck between Lodi and Ione. (Courtesy Jim Fredrickson.)

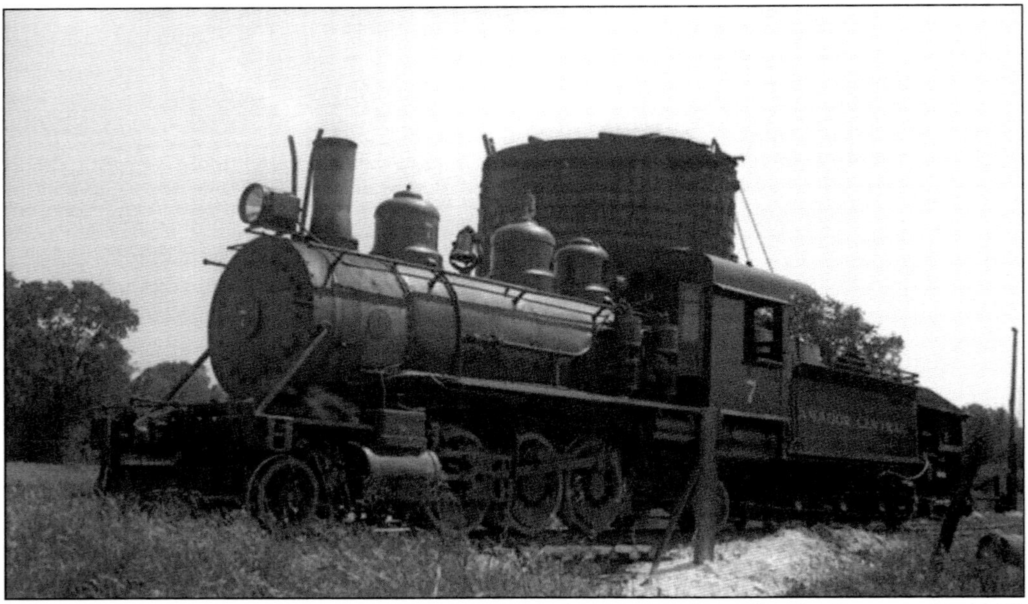

With the help of the construction locomotive, work progressed rapidly. On January 20, 1905, the *Amador Dispatch* reported that tracks had been laid as far as David Kerr's place on the Ione-Jackson Road, also known as the Halfway Station. Here, a water tank was erected to supply the steam locomotives. In this picture, taken years later, engine No. 7 stops to take on water.

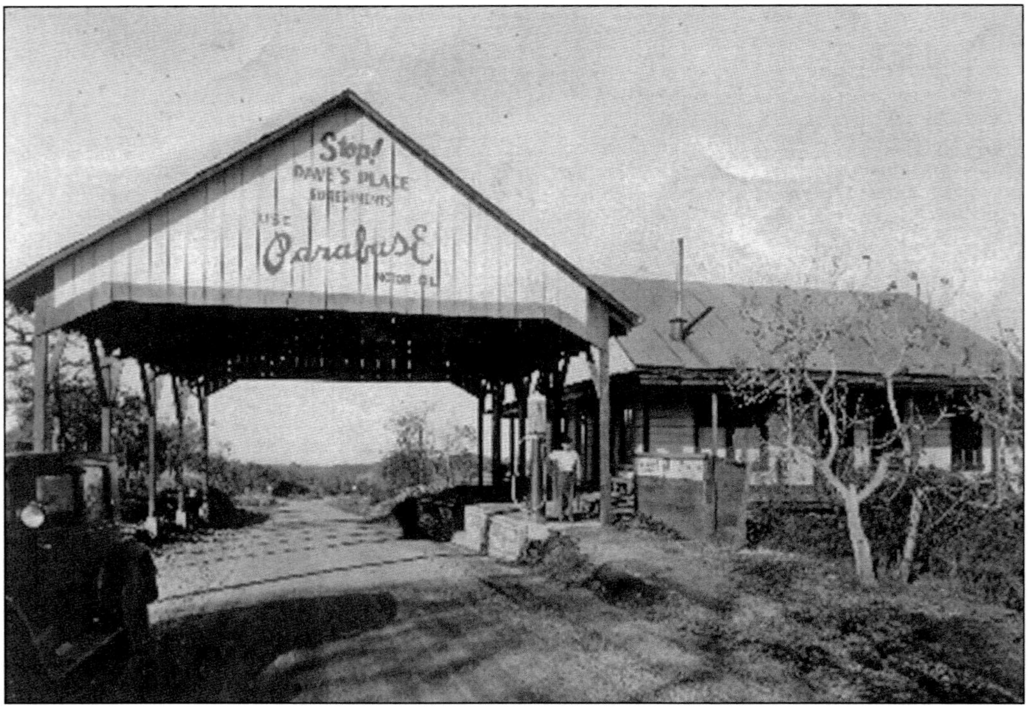

Pictured is Dave Kerr's place, which once stood on the Ione-Jackson Road, near the halfway crossing. This photograph was taken several years after the railroad was built.

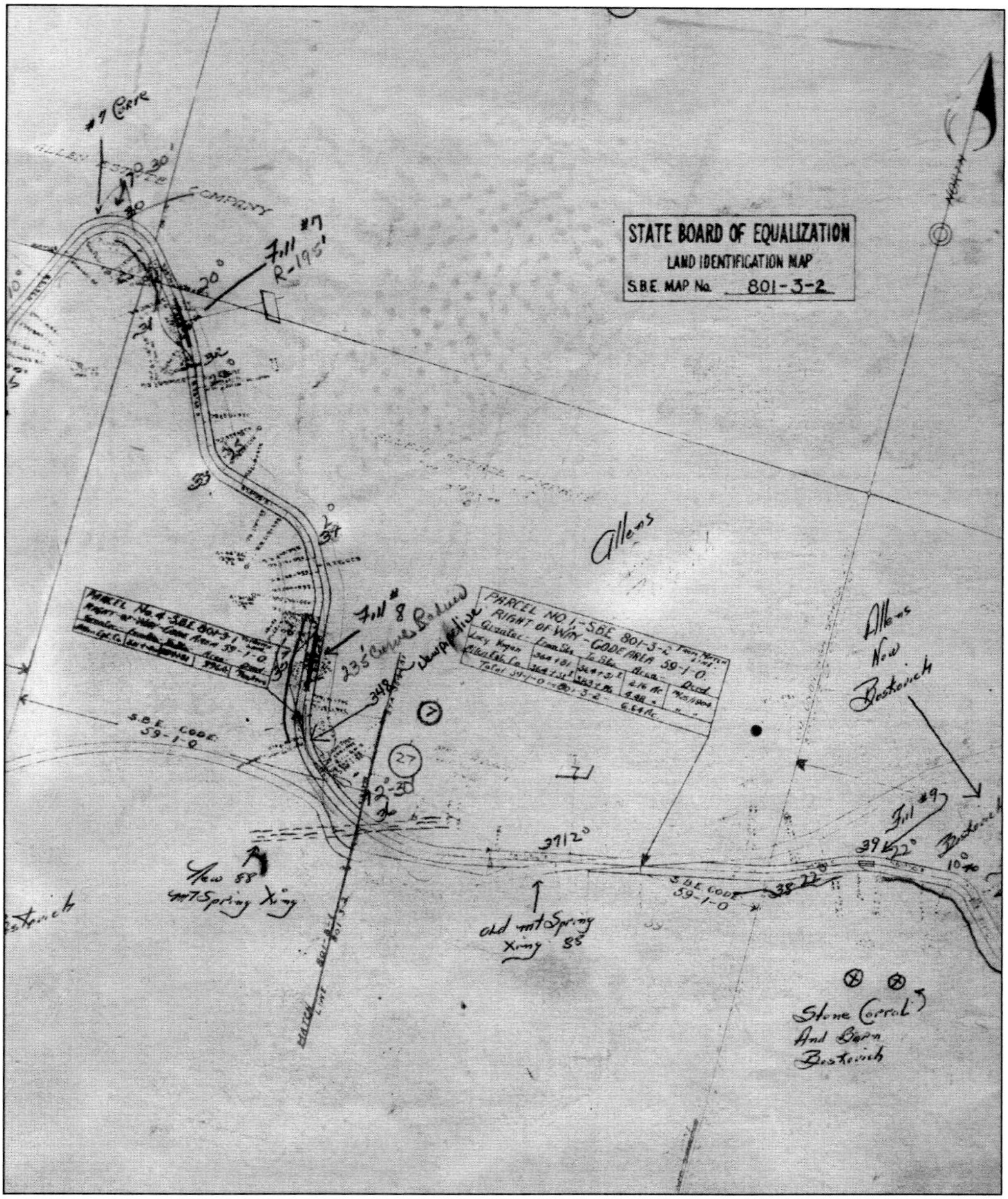

Once the construction workers had finished laying track to the Mountain Springs crossing of the Ione-Jackson Road, both the topography and the weather turned in their favor. By the first of March 1905, the weather became warm and dry, allowing for work at a rapid pace. The crews here met with only one setback. Work on a 50-foot trestle (shown here as Fill No. 8) was suspended for one day when one of the carpenters fell from the trestle to the ground below and broke the bones in his left foot. The newspaper noted that he was lucky he was not killed. The railroad shown on this section of the survey map was completed by the end of March 1905.

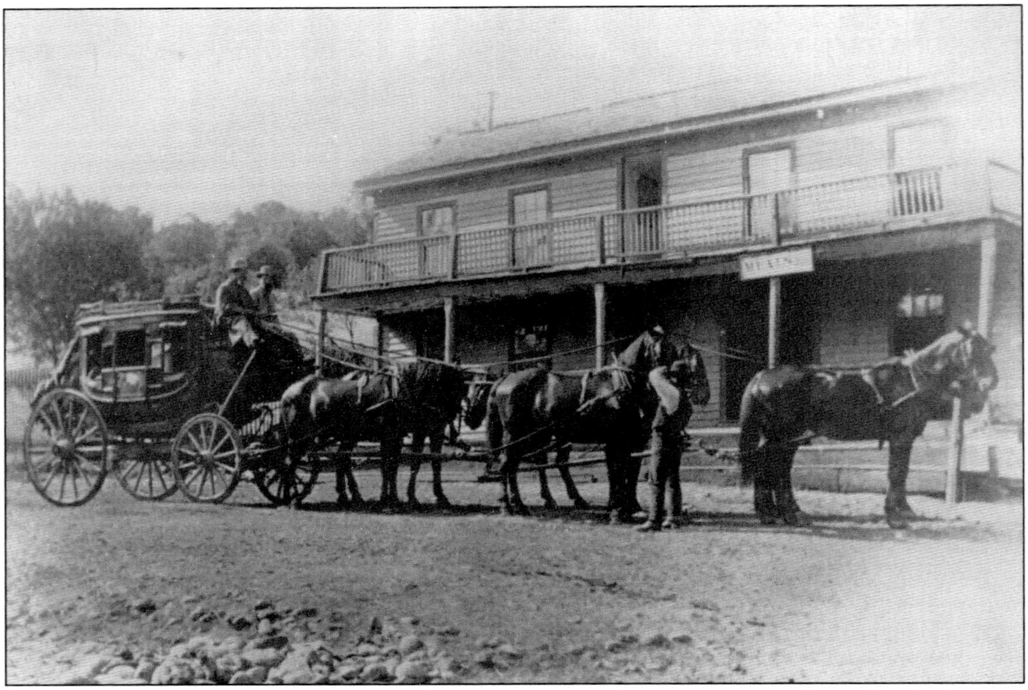

In this photograph, a stagecoach stops at the Mountain Springs House, a short distance east of the halfway crossing on the Ione-Jackson Road. When grading crews reached this point, the railroad company rented a barn here to serve as a temporary depot. For a time, camp No. 2 was set up here, but was later moved up the line to the Stone Corral.

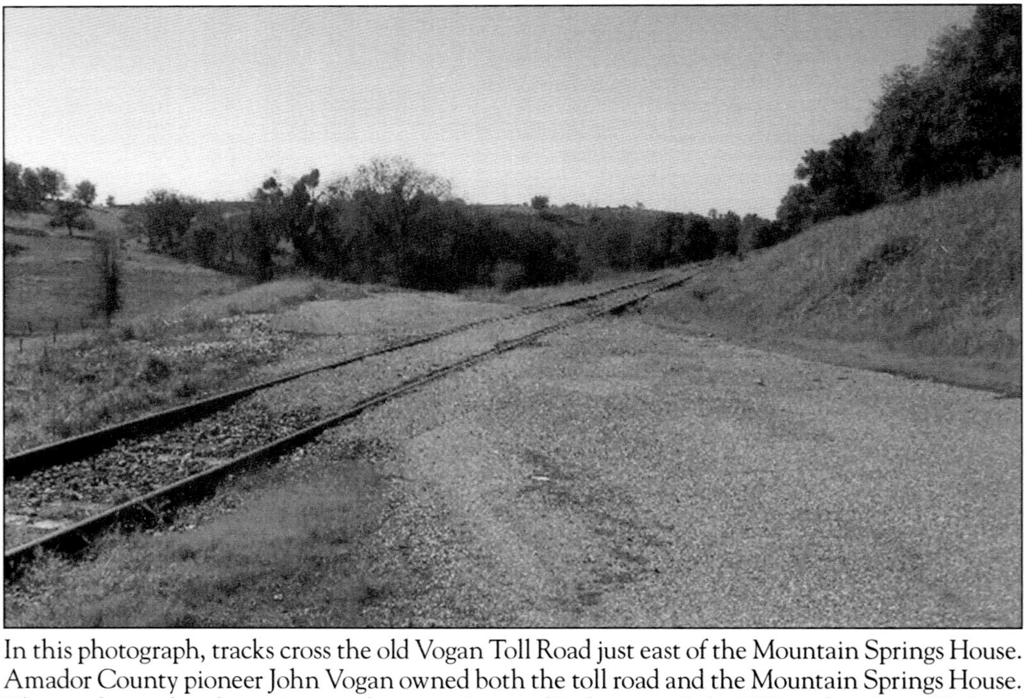

In this photograph, tracks cross the old Vogan Toll Road just east of the Mountain Springs House. Amador County pioneer John Vogan owned both the toll road and the Mountain Springs House. This road served as the main route between Ione and Jackson until the 1930s, when State Highway 88 was built and the road was rerouted to the north. (Author's collection.)

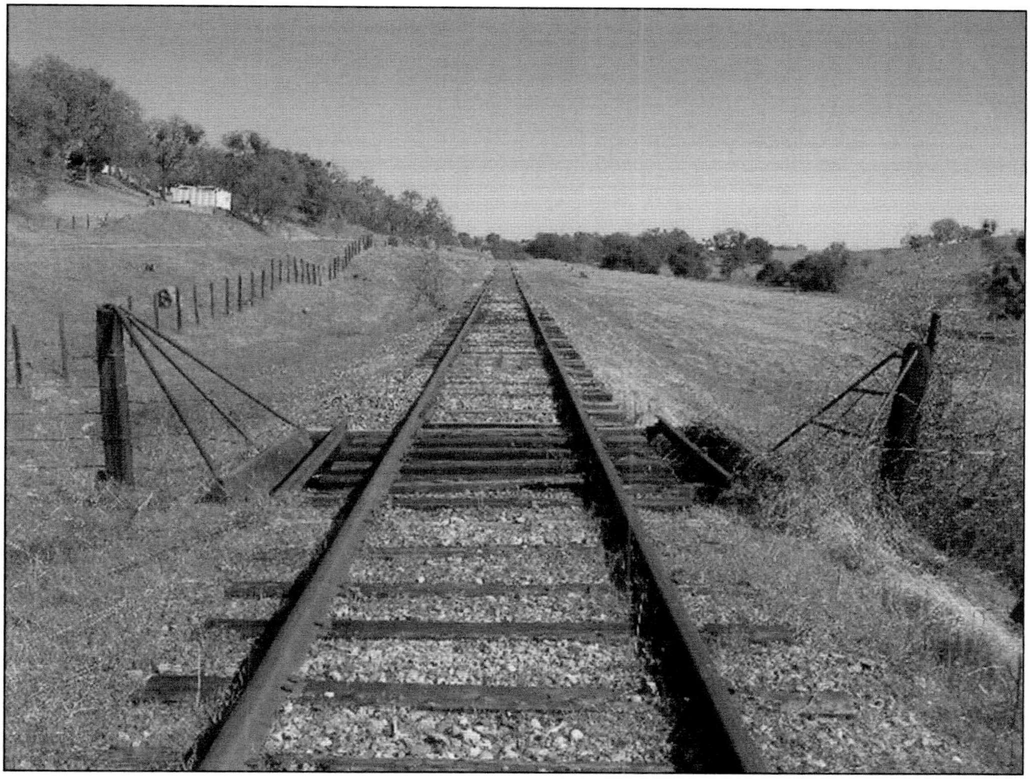

Most of the land traversed by the Ione & Eastern Railroad was open country occupied by farms and livestock ranches. When the right-of-way was obtained, the railroad company also entered into legal agreements with ranchers to build cattle guards at locations designated by the landowners. The one pictured here straddles the tracks just east of the Vogan Toll Road crossing. (Author's collection.)

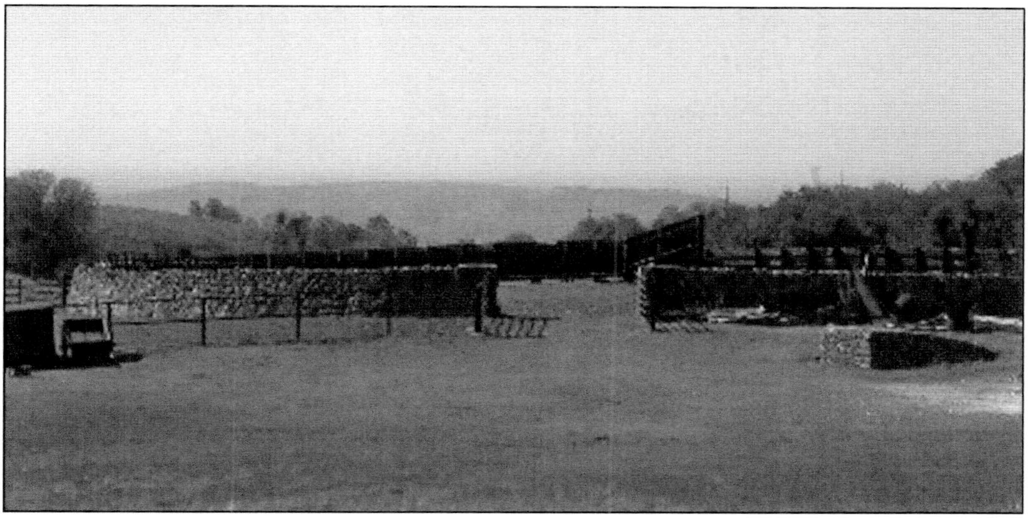

Railroad crews working between Mountain Springs and Martell moved camp No. 2 from the Mountain Spring House to near the Stone Corral on what was known as the Old Robinson Ranch. Even today, this corral is a landmark for visitors traveling the rails in speeder cars. (Author's collection.)

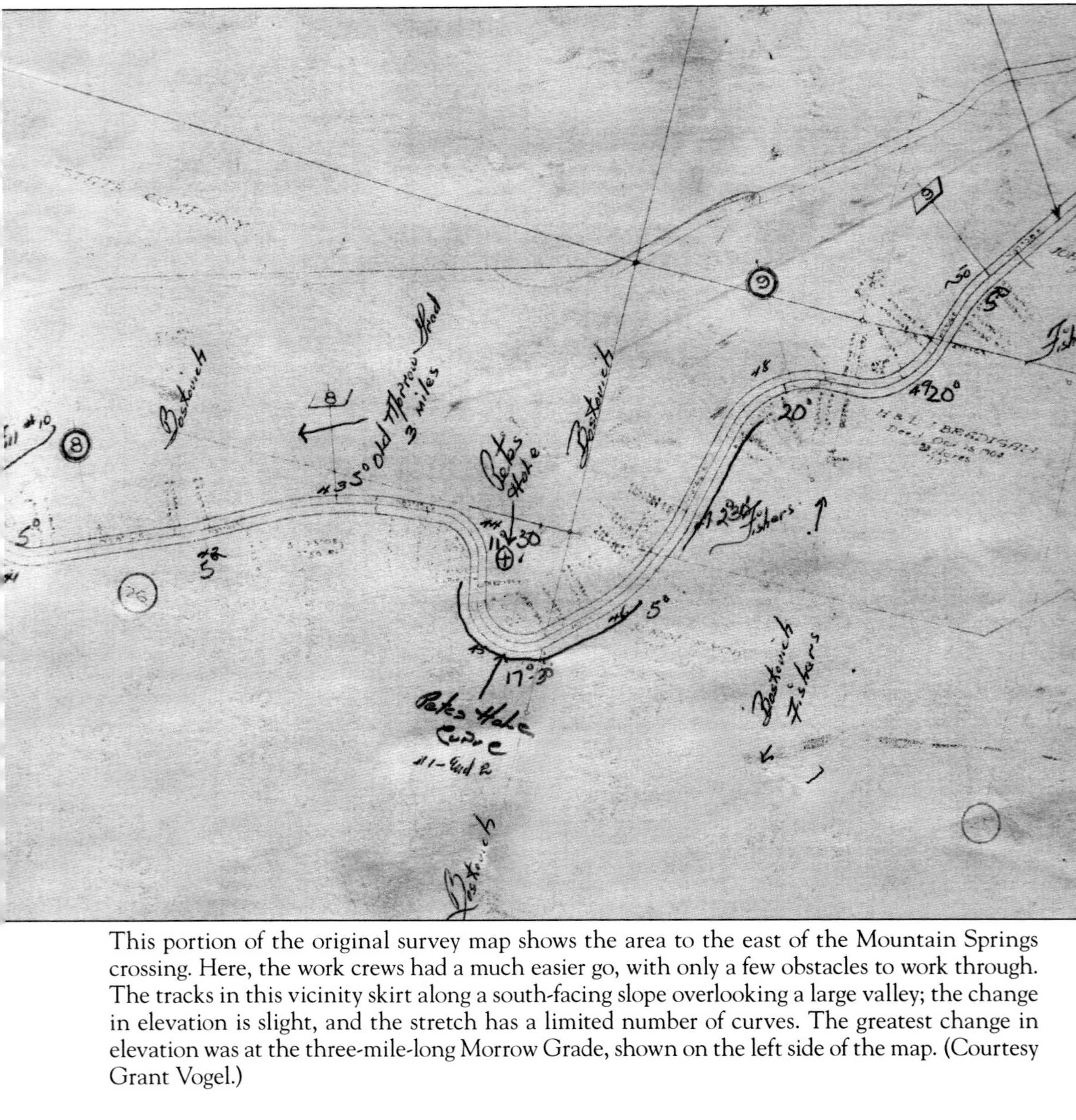

This portion of the original survey map shows the area to the east of the Mountain Springs crossing. Here, the work crews had a much easier go, with only a few obstacles to work through. The tracks in this vicinity skirt along a south-facing slope overlooking a large valley; the change in elevation is slight, and the stretch has a limited number of curves. The greatest change in elevation was at the three-mile-long Morrow Grade, shown on the left side of the map. (Courtesy Grant Vogel.)

Many of the features along the railroad were named for landowners who gave right-of-way to the Ione & Eastern. Pictured here is Harriet Esther Tanner Morrow. Her property was adjacent to the railroad where the Morrow Grade is located, hence the name.

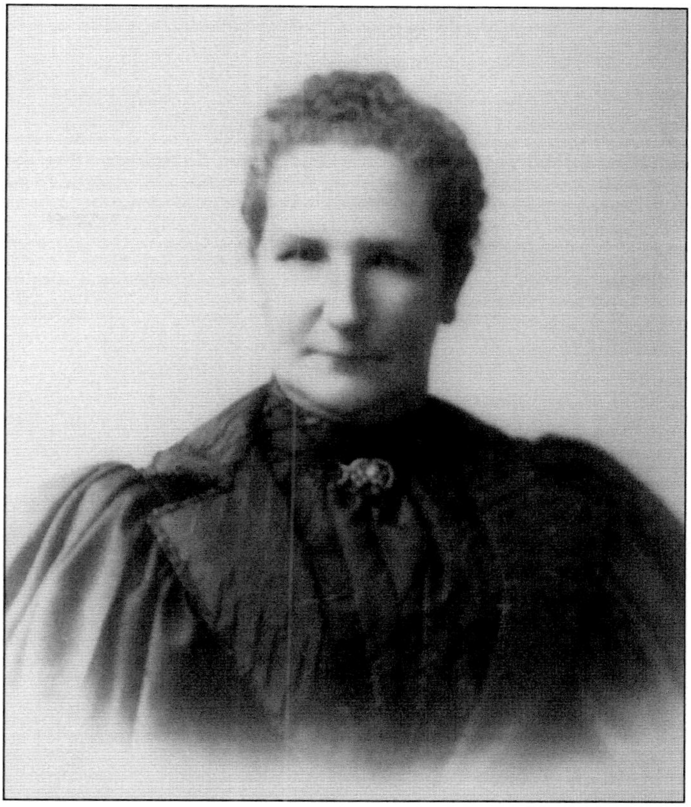

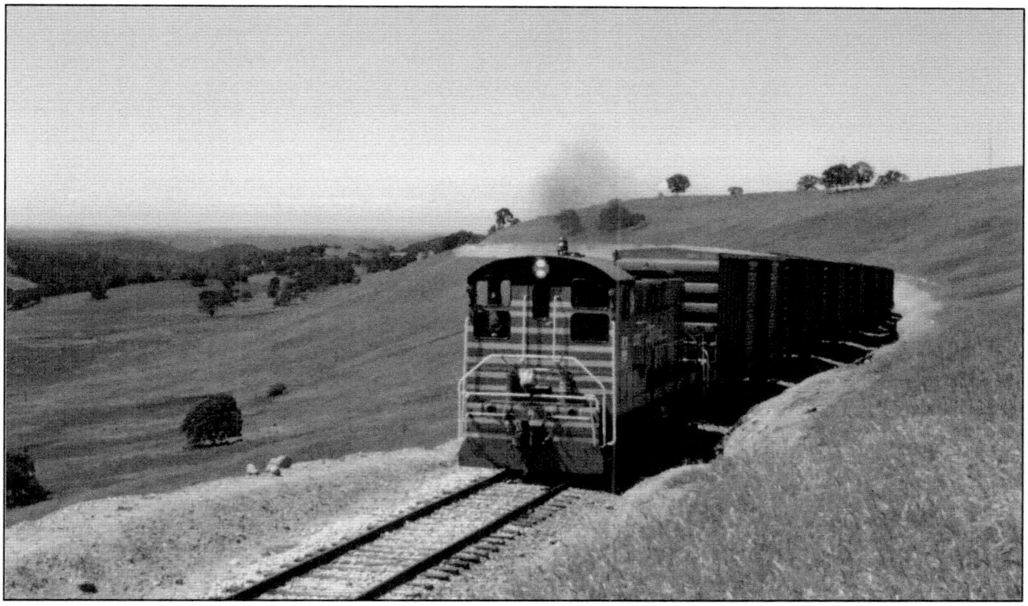

In this 1993 photograph, engine No. 10 pulls a string of cars up the Morrow Grade. Work crews scraped a cut along the hillside for nearly four miles, stretching from just east of the Mountain Springs House to where the rails crossed the Ione-Jackson Road near the Cyclone Station. Additionally, several stretches were built up with soil and gravel to avoid the rail bed giving way during wet weather.

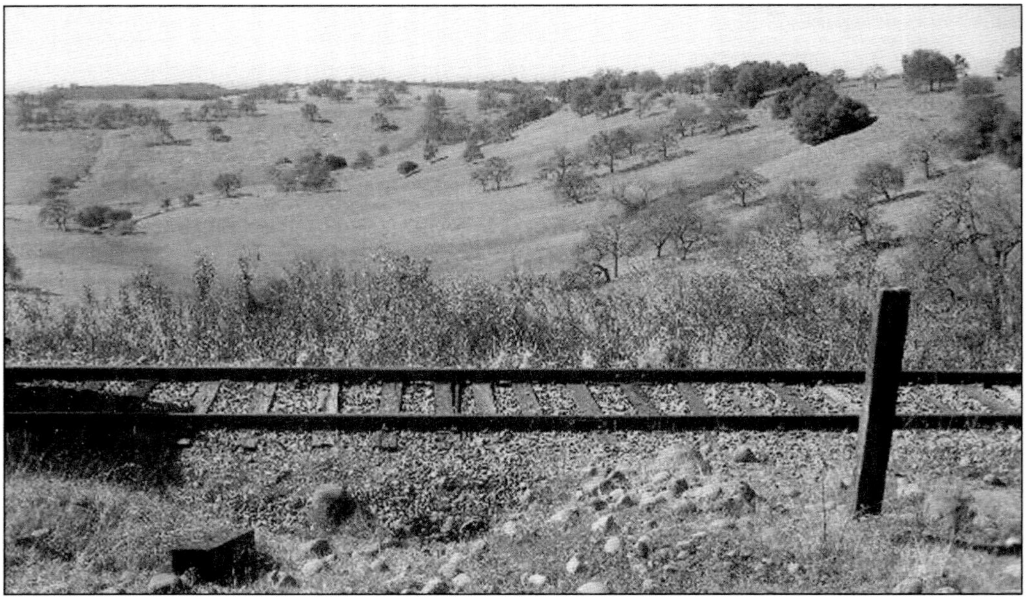

Every railroad seems to have several humorous stories associated with it, and this railroad is no exception. The low spot in the foreground was known as Pete's Hole because a railroad worker fell into a sinkhole on this spot. It is not known if Pete was injured in the fall, but one cannot help but chuckle to think that the event left its mark as a feature on the line. (Author's collection.)

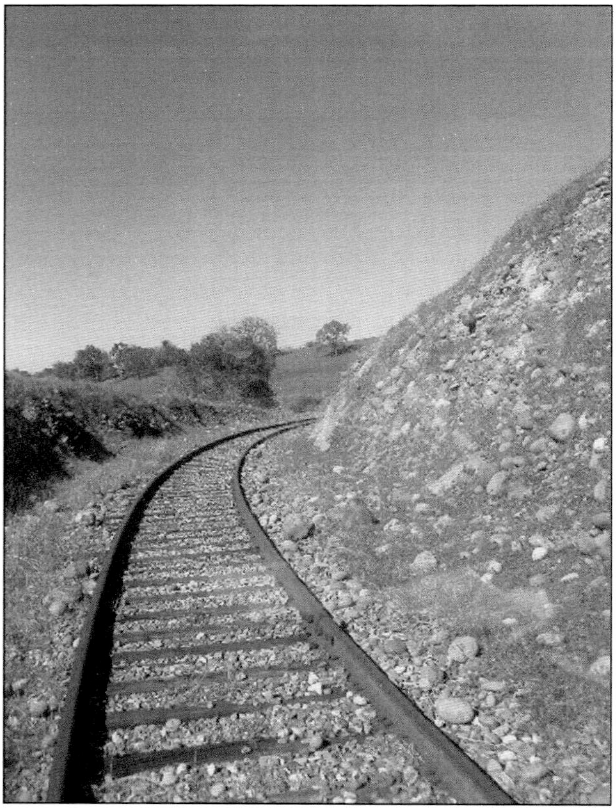

When crews reached a point several miles east of the Mountain Springs House, their work slowed a bit when they had to cut a curve through the hillside. The cut is known as Pete's Hole Curve. The newspaper reported that 90 men were working to accomplish this by hand. This photograph shows the rocky nature of the ground through which the curve was cut. (Author's collection.)

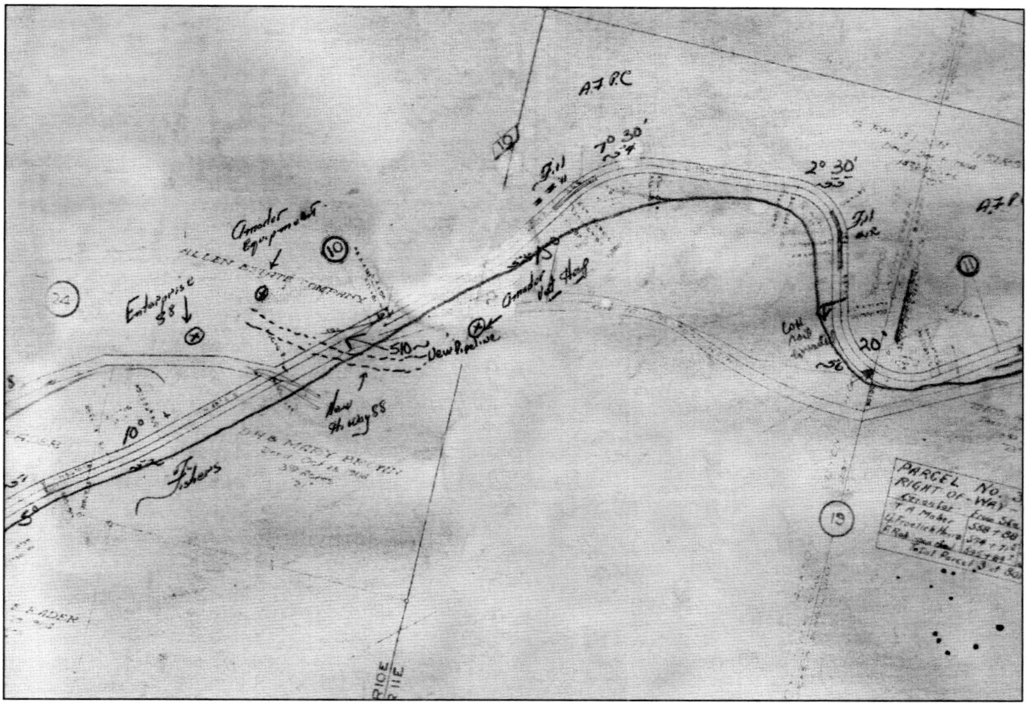

By the time the work crews had laid track at the road crossing shown on this map, they were on the home stretch to reaching Martell. A significant place not marked on this map was the Cyclone Station, which sat not too far from the intersection of the road and the rails. Camp No. 2 was moved here while the crews worked the final leg of the line. (Courtesy Grant Vogel.)

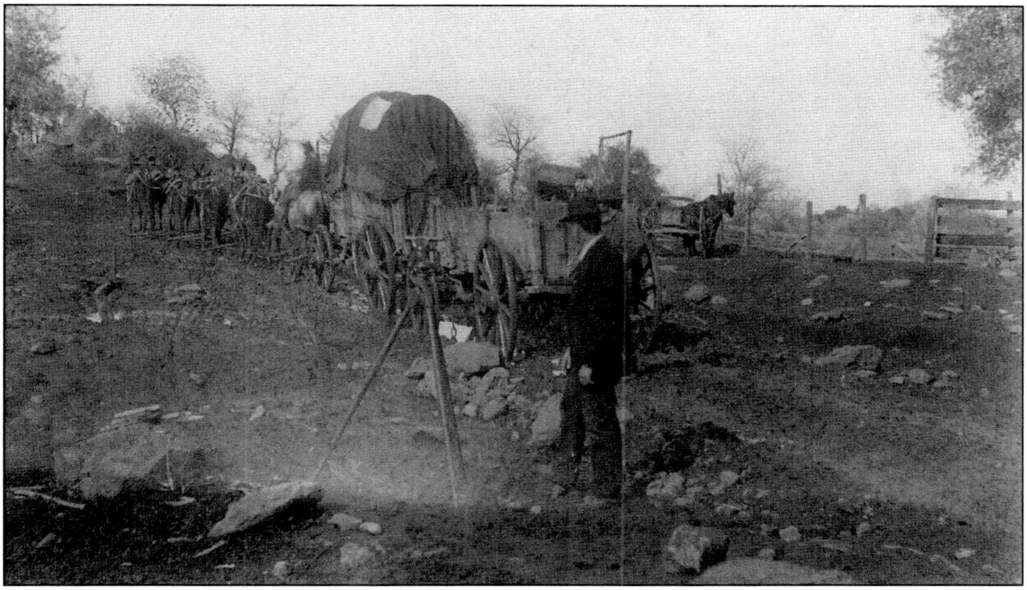

A handwritten note on the back of this photograph states that it was taken in the vicinity of the Cyclone Station. The surveyor in the photograph is unidentified; however, the stature of the man and the hat he is wearing appear similar to those of H.E.C. Feusier, who surveyed the route of the Ione & Eastern. Feusier was a well known engineer, working for a time for the US Geological Survey.

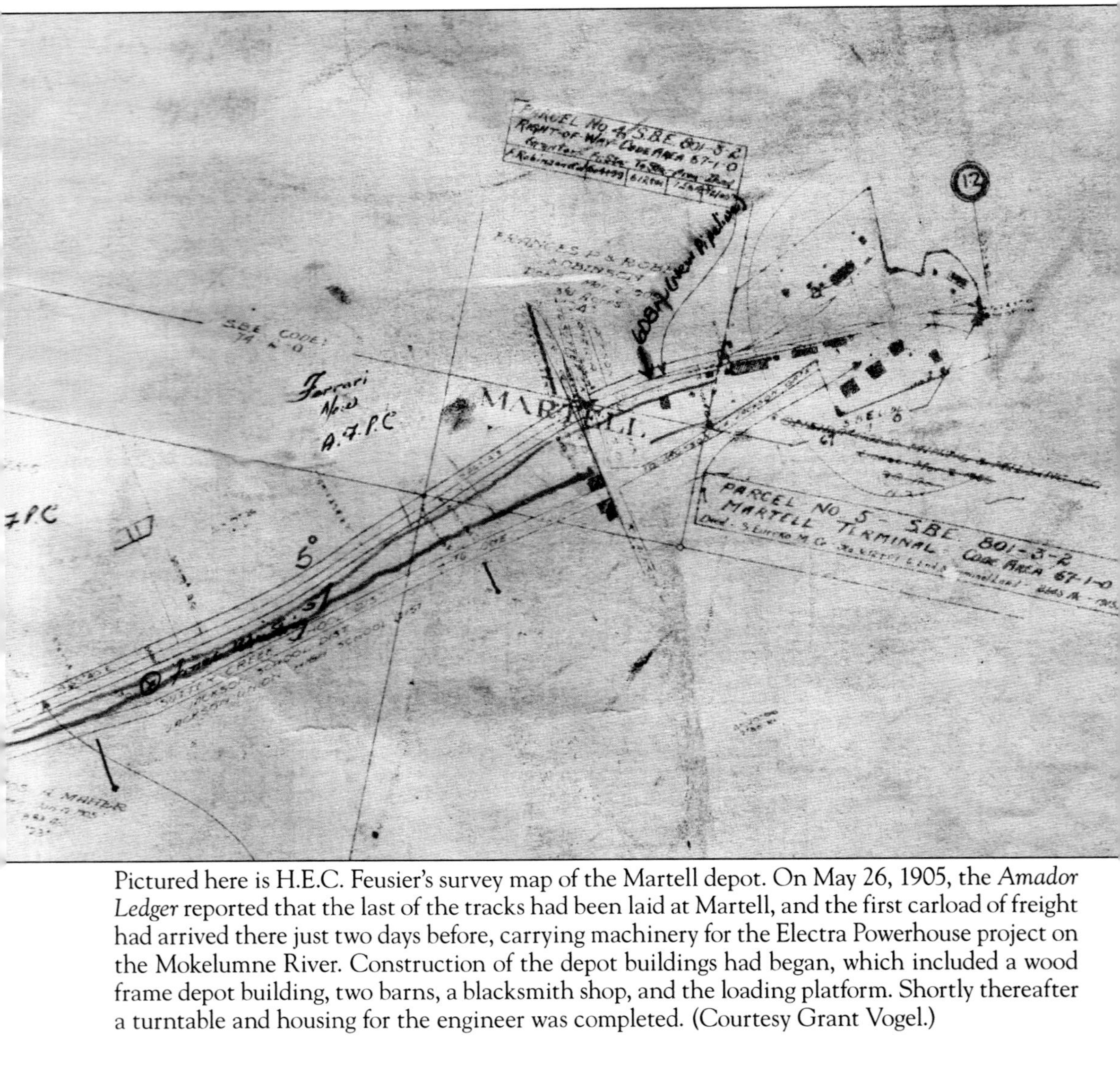

Pictured here is H.E.C. Feusier's survey map of the Martell depot. On May 26, 1905, the *Amador Ledger* reported that the last of the tracks had been laid at Martell, and the first carload of freight had arrived there just two days before, carrying machinery for the Electra Powerhouse project on the Mokelumne River. Construction of the depot buildings had began, which included a wood frame depot building, two barns, a blacksmith shop, and the loading platform. Shortly thereafter a turntable and housing for the engineer was completed. (Courtesy Grant Vogel.)

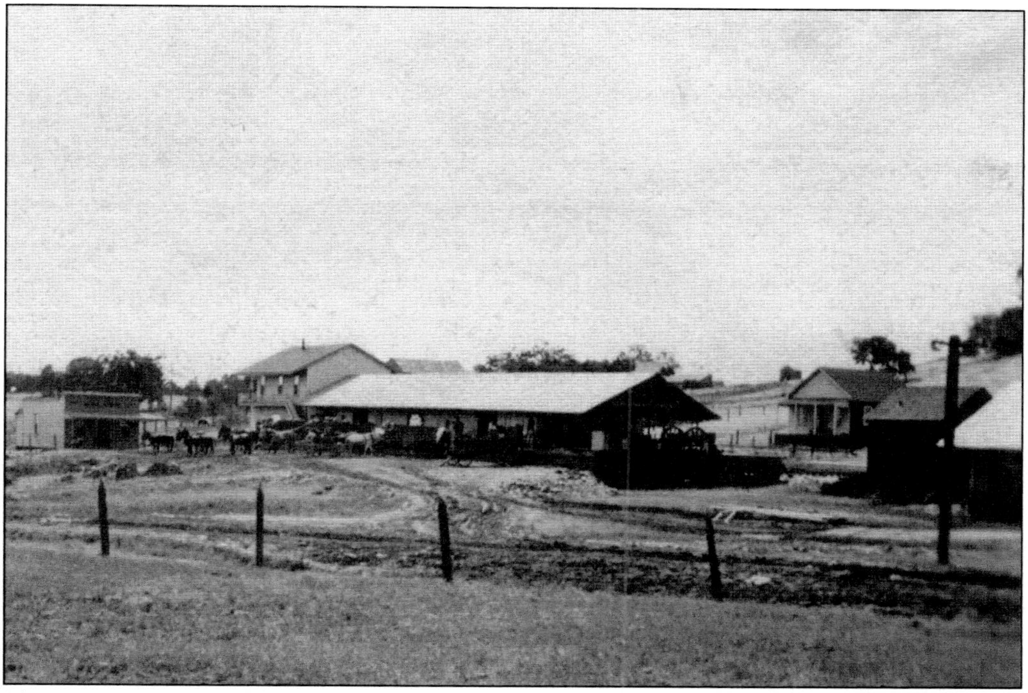

This picture was taken at Martell shortly after the railroad was completed. The depot building is the two-story structure left of center. The long building attached to the depot is a freight shed, where goods were stored until they were loaded onto wagons.

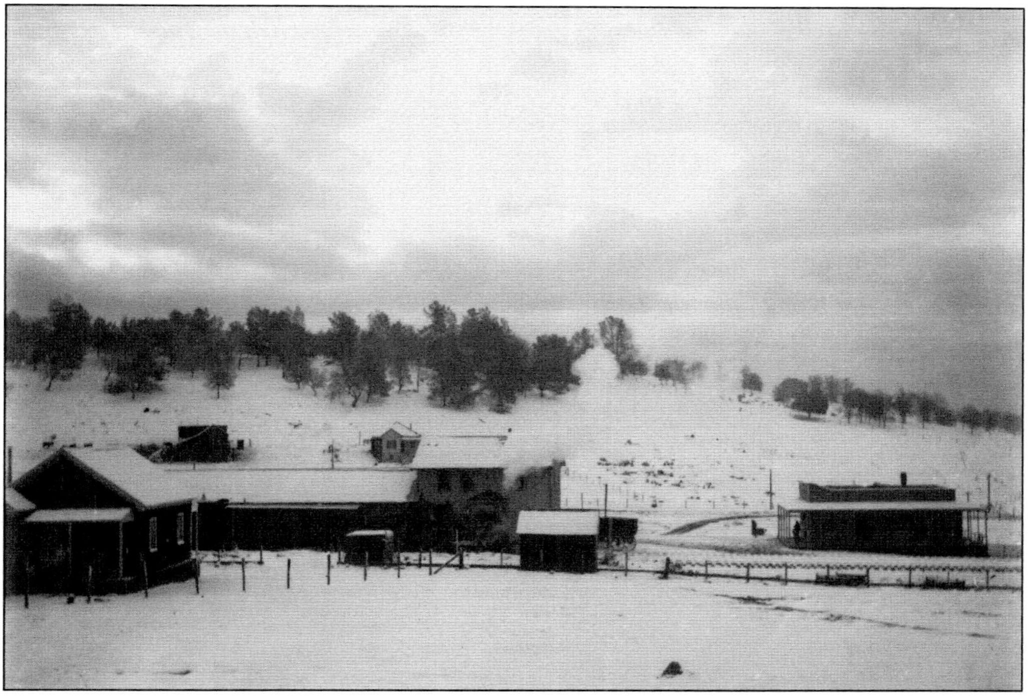

This snowy view of the Martell depot was taken in the winter of 1905–1906. It presents an opposite view of the site from that shown above. The tracks cannot be seen because of the snow-covered ground. Note the locomotive blowing steam while it sits next to the depot building.

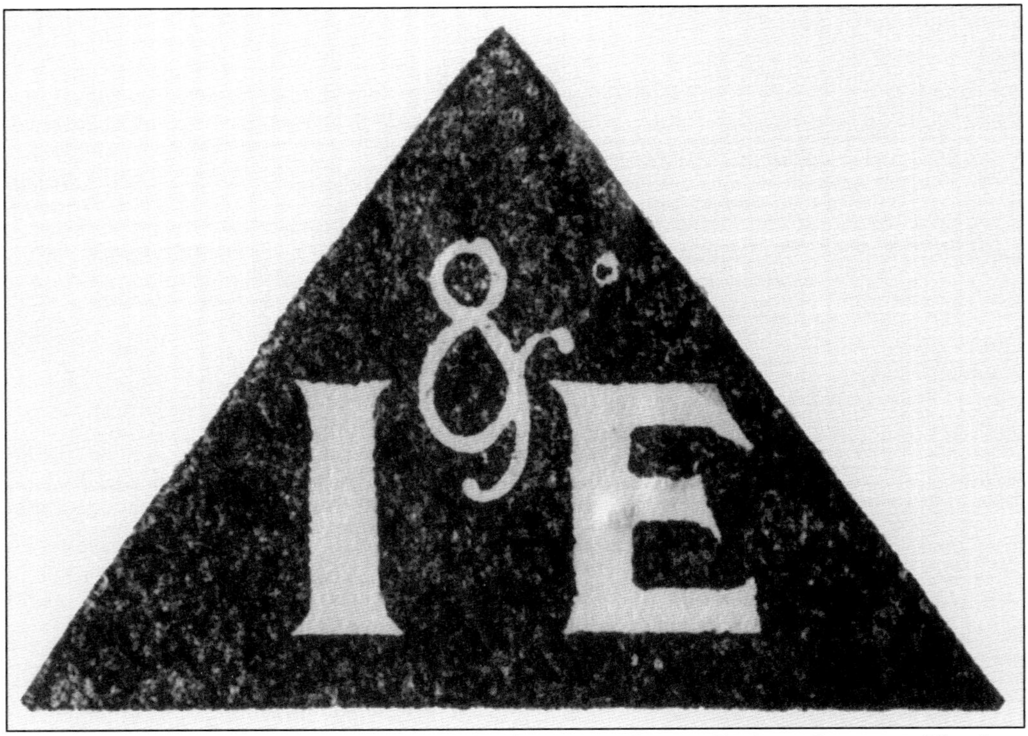

Pictured is a rare image of the logo adopted by the Ione & Eastern Railway Company. This logo was printed on invoices and bills of lading for the railroad and served to identify the line until it changed hands in 1908 and was renamed the Amador Central Railroad. (Author's collection.)

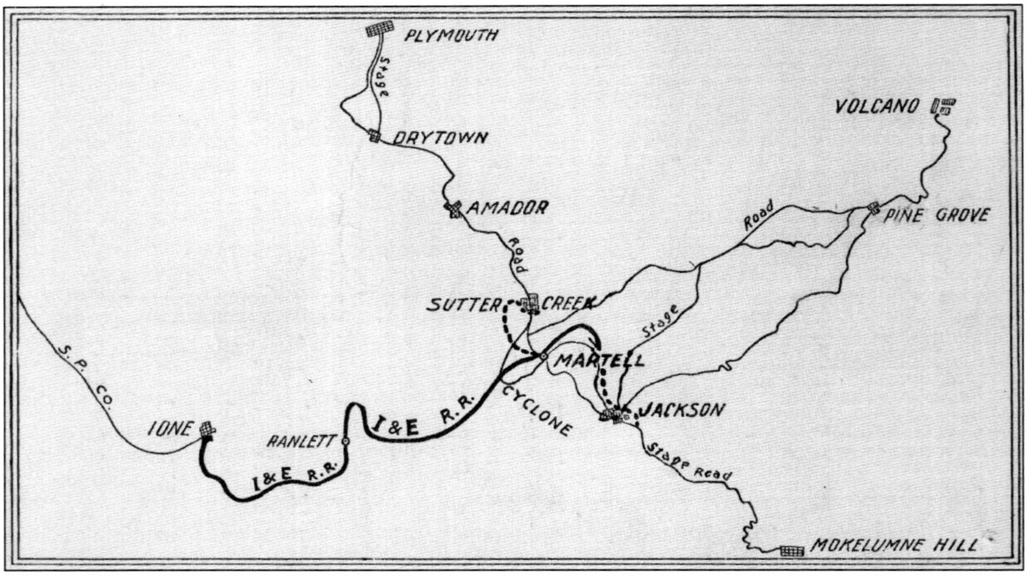

In 1905 when the railroad was completed, the Ione & Eastern Railway Company printed small handbills displaying this map to inform its prospective customers of the service it provided, including station stops and connections to Southern Pacific and to stagecoach lines. The dotted lines on the map depict proposed extensions of the railroad to stations in Jackson and Sutter Creek.

Four

TICKETS, PLEASE!

Why is it that the words *romance* and *railroad* are often found in the same sentence? The crowded train platform has been the scene of both romance and adventure films, where the viewer sees lovers waving as they part, and the far view of a train clacking down the tracks, carrying travelers to some unfamiliar destination. Likewise, the railroad has been used as the stage for action films, where notorious characters threaten the life and limb of passengers before the hero arrives to save the day. Since tracks were first laid, the railroad has held an air of mystery and intrigue. Many often gaze in admiration as they watch the train pass, wondering what it would be like to find a seat on it and leave behind the monotony of everyday life.

When the railroad came to Amador, it offered the excitement of travel to faraway places, but the building of the Ione & Eastern opened up new opportunities within the community. In 1905, when the Ione Academy opened, it was the first high school in the county. The railroad set special fares so that students from all areas of Amador could attend. Gold bullion and the large cash payrolls of mining companies were no longer subject to highwaymen who held up the stages that carried the valuables.

Amador's short line also experienced worldwide notoriety on several occasions. When Dr. F.N. Staples was accused of murdering his wife, his departure from the Martell depot was a big news item. Likewise, when Emma LeDoux murdered an ex-husband, stuffed him in a trunk, and shipped it to Martell, the railroad became a key player when employees discovered the body. It gained its most notoriety when it brought rescue workers to the most famous episode in Amador's history, the Argonaut Mine fire.

Whether riding the coaches of an excursion train, sending off the goods of a hard day's work, or awaiting the help of heroes from a faraway place, all the residents of Amador County found pleasure in and reaped the benefits of their railroad.

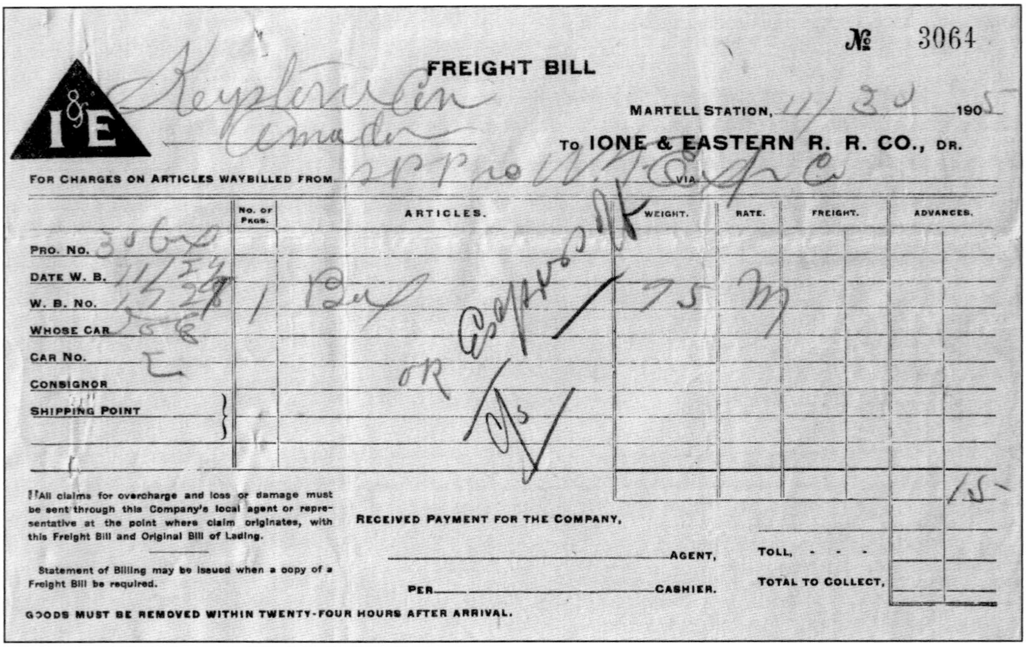

№ 3064

FREIGHT BILL

MARTELL STATION, 11/30 1905

Keystone Min
Amador

To IONE & EASTERN R. R. CO., DR.

FOR CHARGES ON ARTICLES WAYBILLED FROM ____ VIA ____

	No. of Pkgs.	ARTICLES.	WEIGHT.	RATE.	FREIGHT.	ADVANCES.
PRO. NO.						
DATE W. B.						
W. B. NO.	1	Box	75	M		
WHOSE CAR						
CAR NO.						
CONSIGNOR						
SHIPPING POINT						

All claims for overcharge and loss or damage must be sent through this Company's local agent or representative at the point where claim originates, with this Freight Bill and Original Bill of Lading.

Statement of Billing may be issued when a copy of a Freight Bill be required.

RECEIVED PAYMENT FOR THE COMPANY,

____ AGENT, TOLL, - - -

PER ____ CASHIER. TOTAL TO COLLECT, 15

GOODS MUST BE REMOVED WITHIN TWENTY-FOUR HOURS AFTER ARRIVAL.

The Ione & Eastern Railroad began shipping freight as soon as the station was constructed at Ranlett. Much of this freight was bound for the mines, as shown by this November receipt of goods transported for the Keystone Mine. Goods came into the Ione Station via the Southern Pacific and were transferred to the Ione & Eastern. They were then off-loaded at Ranlett and delivered to their destination by wagon.

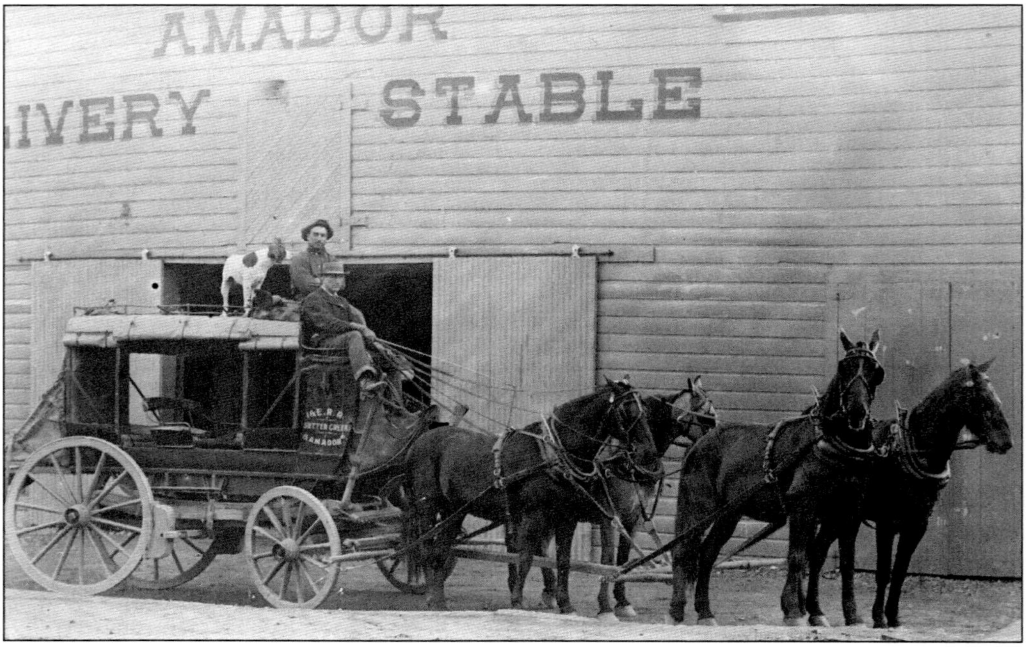

The Ione & Eastern, like other railways, offered travel connections to other towns not accessed by the rails. By the time the line was completed, the company had purchased two freight and stage lines to accommodate their passengers. In this photograph, a stage for the Ione & Eastern sits in front of the livery stables at Amador City.

Passenger service did not start immediately after the Ione & Eastern was completed; however, it was only a short time before this was initiated, and by the Fourth of July in 1905, the railroad ran an excursion train from Martell to Ione for the holiday celebration there. By September, two daily passenger trains were running. This 1906 timetable shows both passenger and mixed trains available to riders.

IONE & EASTERN RAILROAD

Effective January 1, 1906 — TIME TABLE No. 1, Subject to Change — Effective January 1, 1906

DAILY BETWEEN IONE AND MARTELL

FROM IONE — TO IONE

Mixed No. 4	Pass'r No. 2	Mls.	STATIONS			Pass'r No. 1	Mixed No. 3
10.00 a. m	†3.30 p.m.	0	Lv.	Ione	Ar.	9.05 a.m.	3.00 p.m.
				5			
10.50 a. m	3.55 p.m.	5	Lv.	*Ranlett	Lv.	8.45 a.m.	2.20 p.m.
				5			
11.40 a. m	4.20 p.m.	10	Lv.	*Brown or Cyclone	Lv.	8.25 a.m.	1.45 p.m.
				2			
12.00 N.	4.30 p.m.	12	Ar.	Martell	Lv.	8.15 a.m.	1.30 p.m.

READ UP

†Leave 3.30 or on arrival of S. P. Trains.

*Trains stop only on signal, or to leave passengers.

Stages for Jackson, Sutter Creek, Amador City and Mokelumne Hill connect with passenger trains at Martell.

Trains Leave the Following Points Daily:

San Francisco, Foot of Market St., to Ione .... 8.40 a. m.
Sacramento to Ione.. 10.10 a. m.
Ione to San Francisco.. 9.25 a. m.
Ione to Sacramento.. 9.25 a. m.

This new scenic road gives easy access to the following famous mines of the Great Mother Lode:

Zeile	**Wildman Con.**
Argonaut	**Burlington**
Kennedy	**South Spring Hill**
Oneida	**Keystone**
South Eureka	**Bunker Hill**
Central Eureka	**Fremont**

And Others

Martell Station had, for some time, been an important crossroads stop in Amador County and thus seemed the likely place for a railroad station. Several members of the Martell family and friends are pictured below: Louis Martell (holding horse in front of cart), his wife Delia and daughter Dell (both in cart), Anne Martell (sitting with parasol), Mayme Martell (standing in foreground), and Johnie Conanica (shoeing horse).

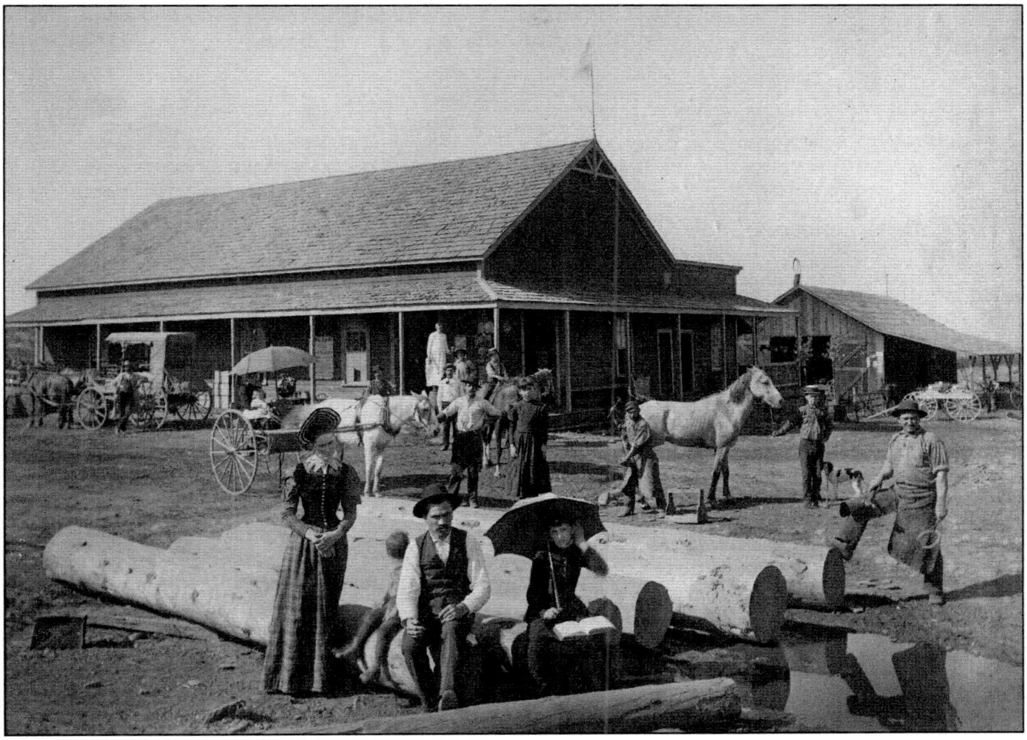

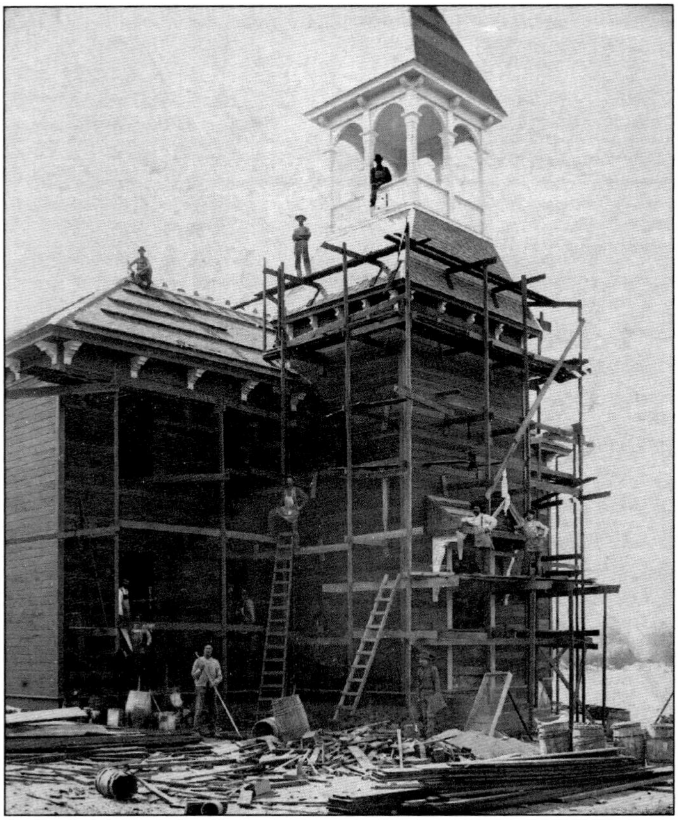

In 1902, businessmen of Ione organized the Ione Academy, the first high school in Amador County. Classes were held in the Baptist Church in Ione, until the building shown at left was completed and the school opened on September 5, 1905.

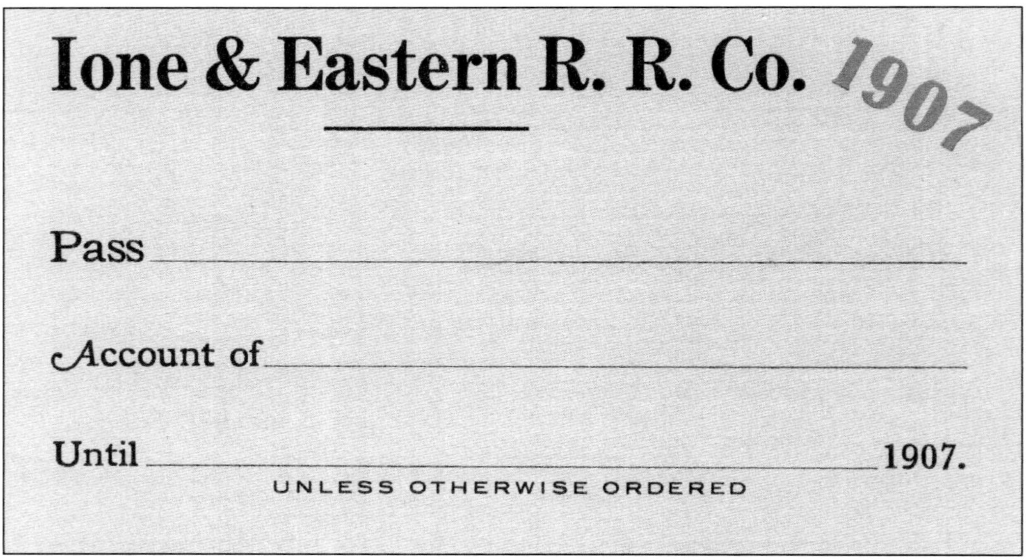

Ione & Eastern R. R. Co. 1907

Pass

Account of

Until 1907.

UNLESS OTHERWISE ORDERED

After the railroad was completed, the ability to travel to Ione by rail afforded the opportunity of a higher education to students from all areas of the county. Months before the school was completed, the Ione & Eastern posted announcements in the local newspapers that students would be given a special rate for a round-trip monthly pass, such as the one pictured above. The cost for the pass was noted as the "extremely low figure" of $10 per month from Martell, and $15 per month from Amador City, Sutter Creek, and Jackson.

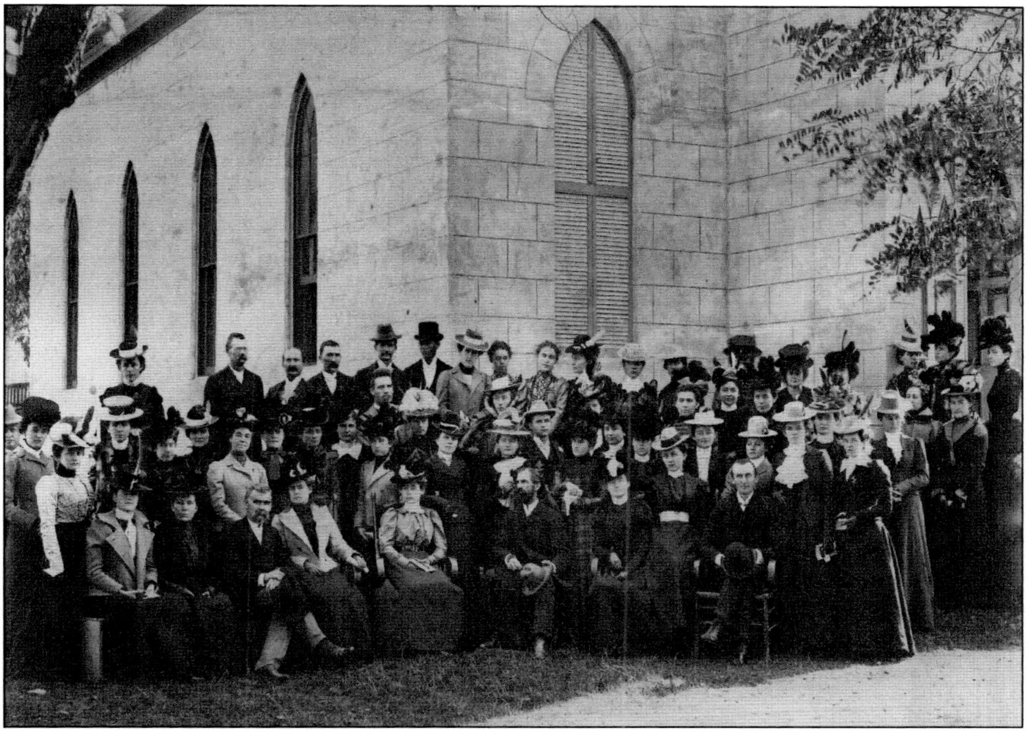

Amador educators also benefited from the new rail service. In response to state requirements, teachers in local jurisdictions were required to attend an annual conference known as the Teacher's Institute. These were held in various towns about Amador. Upon completion of the Ione and Eastern, special fares between Martell and Ione were offered to the participants. In this photograph, the group gathers in front of the Methodist Church in Ione.

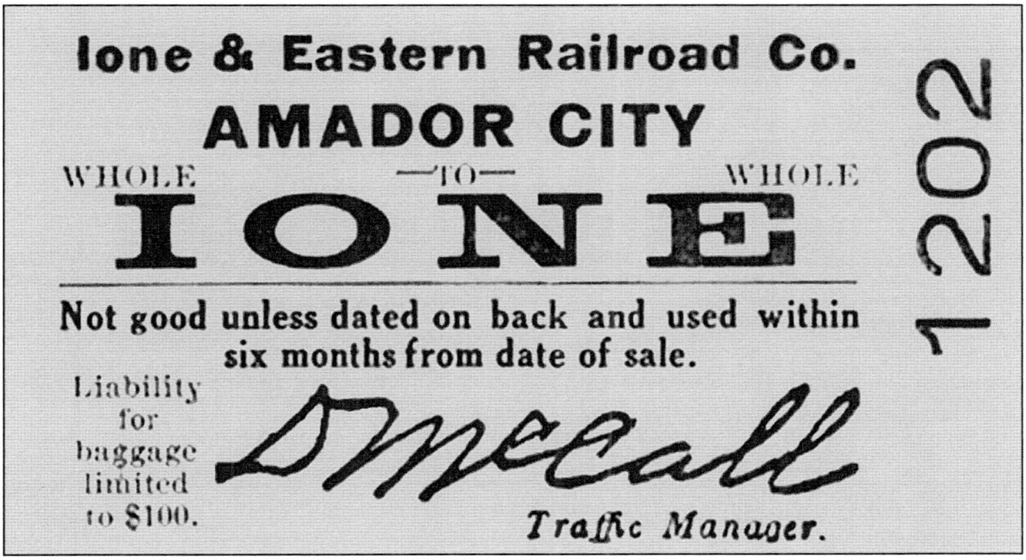

Students and other passengers needing to travel by stage to either Ione or Martell to catch the train were issued a ticket like the one pictured here. The ticket was good for the round trip between the two travel points. Tickets were printed for each outlying town. Passengers wishing to change or extend their journey beyond these points were required to purchase another ticket.

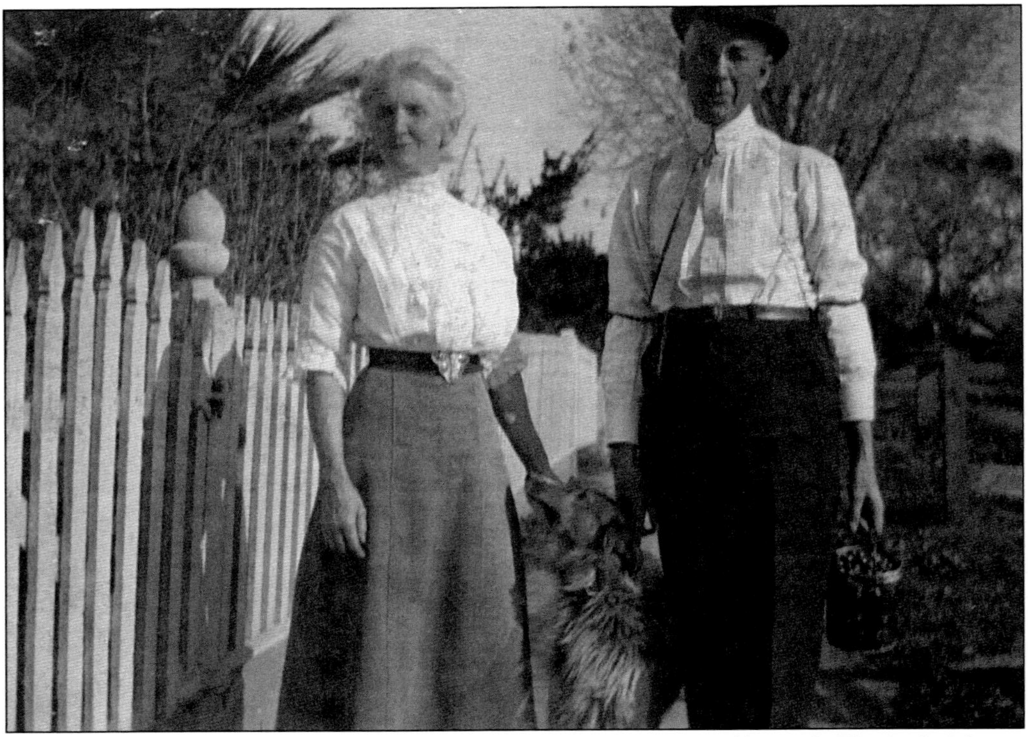

Pictured are longtime Ione residents John Francis "Frank" Martin and his wife, Elizabeth. Martin went to work for the Ione & Eastern soon after it was built and continued as an employee when it became the Amador Central Railroad. He worked as the ticket agent at the Ione Station until he retired.

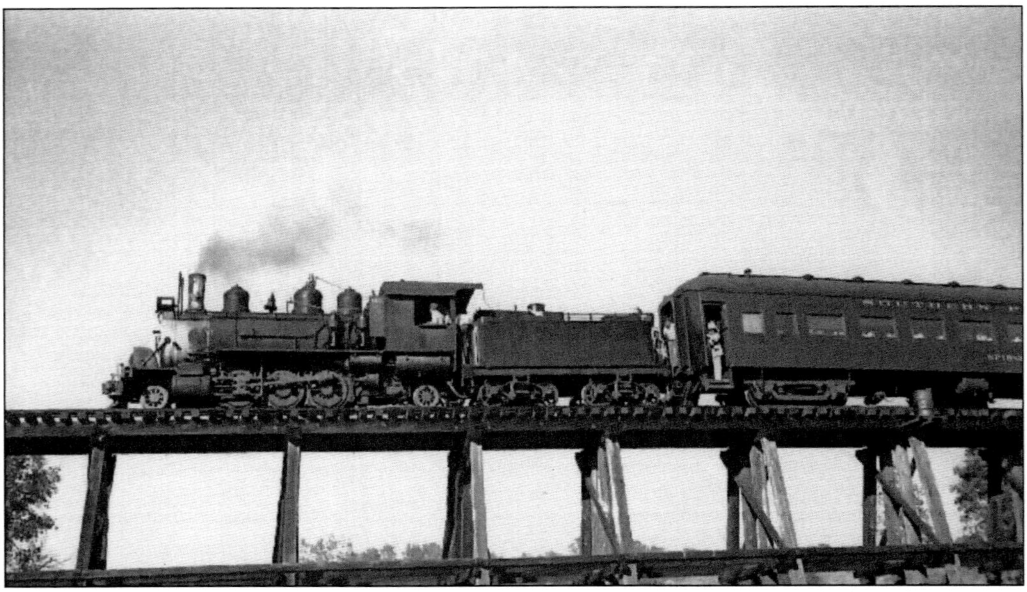

Martin and other ticket agents soon found themselves very busy. It did not take long for the Ione & Eastern to realize that residents were ready and willing to travel by rail and take advantage of the connection with the Southern Pacific out of Ione. In this photograph, Amador Central No. 7 pulls a Southern Pacific passenger car toward Ione.

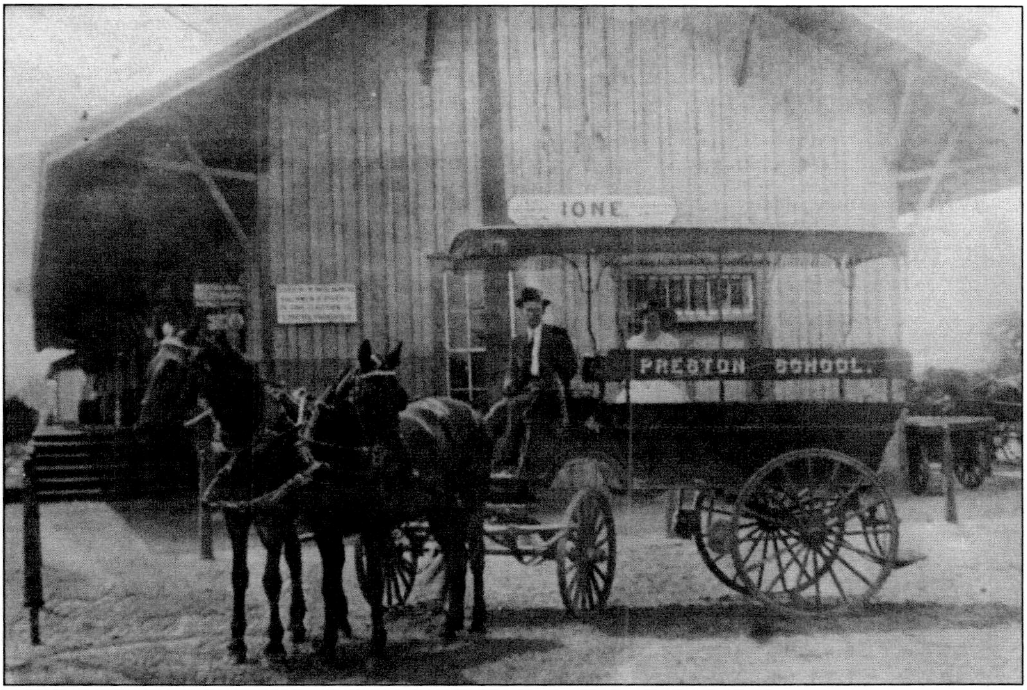

The Preston School of Industry, a reformatory school for juvenile offenders in Ione, also enjoyed the benefits of the railroad. The inmates, known as "wards," arrived in Ione by rail and were then taken to the school. Likewise, visitors and workers at the institution took advantage of rail travel. In this photograph, a shuttle wagon from Preston sits at the Ione depot with a passenger on board.

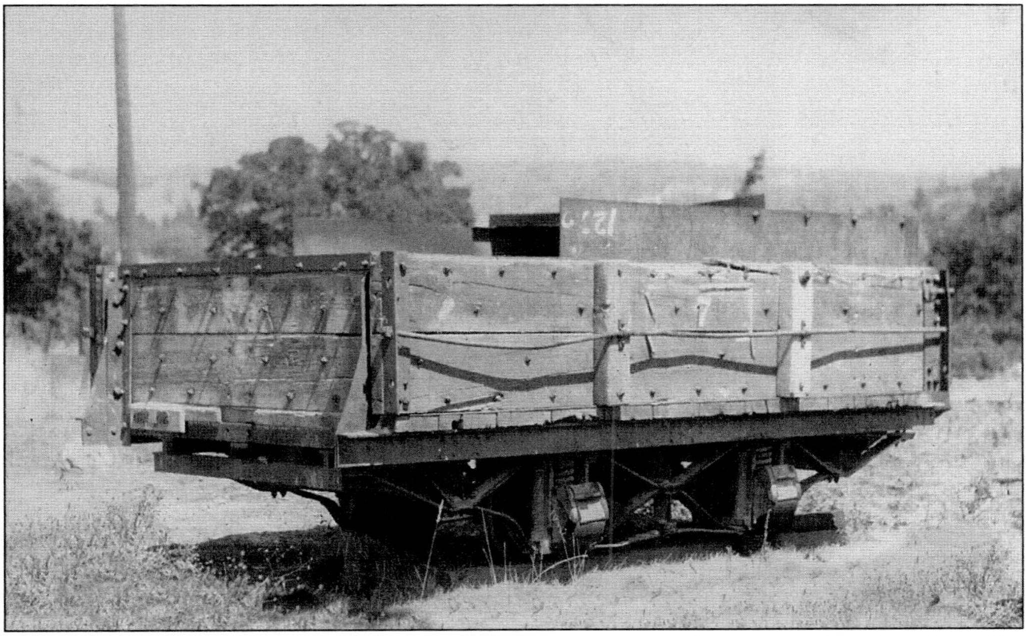

When passenger service began on the Ione & Eastern, accommodations were less than desirable. In September 1905, passengers on an excursion train to Sacramento rode via open flat car. When they arrived in Sacramento they looked as if they had been through a hurricane. The flat car pictured here was the first one used on the railroad.

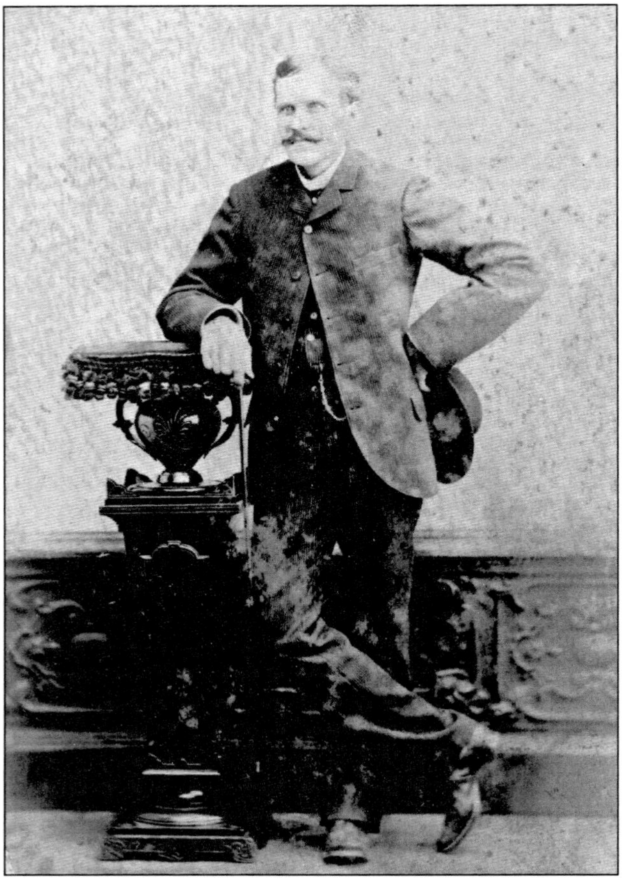

In November, the Ione & Eastern received its first passenger coach (below). The new car was 40 feet in length and could carry 30 seated passengers. The enclosed coach was an improvement over the open flatcars, which were involved in several mishaps. In one incident, just before reaching Martell, the wheels of the car left the rails when there was a problem with a switch. The car overturned, spilling out the passengers; however, none received any serious injuries, as the train was moving at a slow pace while approaching the station. This first coach was built by local contractor C.E. Fournier (left), who remodeled an observation car, enclosing it and adding seats and other accoutrements.

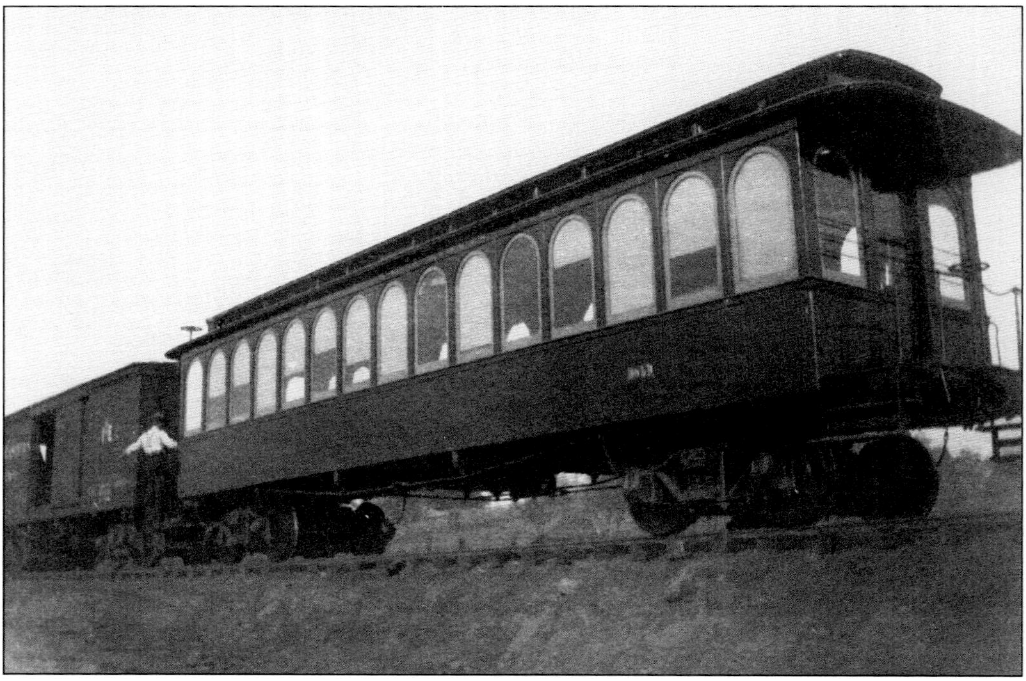

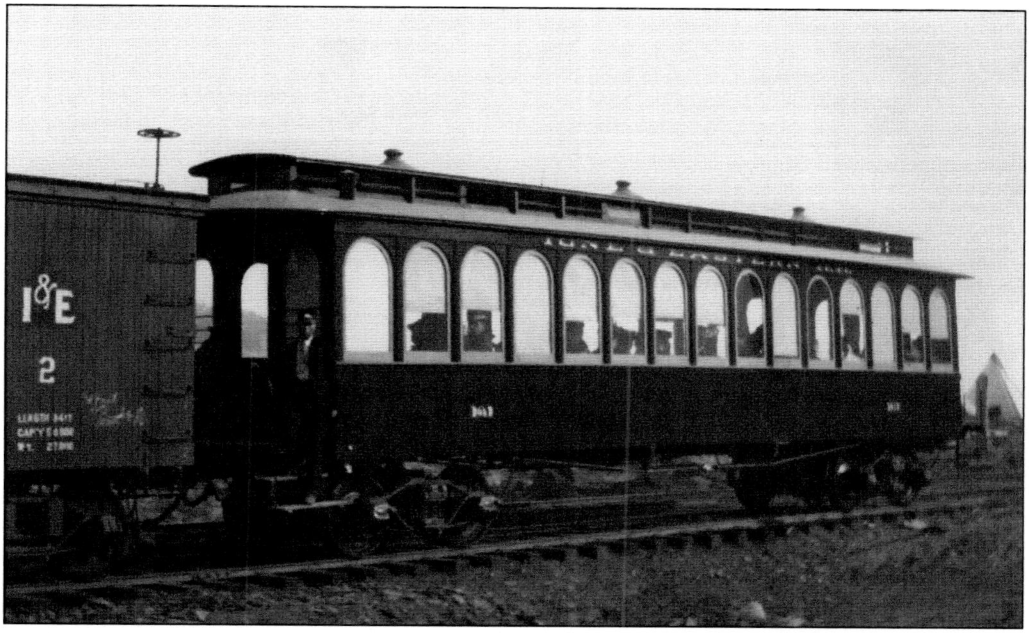

Within a short time, a second passenger coach was running on the Ione & Eastern. This coach, similar to the first, was also built by Fournier. Both coaches were used on mixed train runs, where both freight and passengers were carried. In this photograph, coach No. 2 sits behind boxcar No. 2. The man on the steps of the passenger coach is Ione & Eastern conductor W.J. Williams.

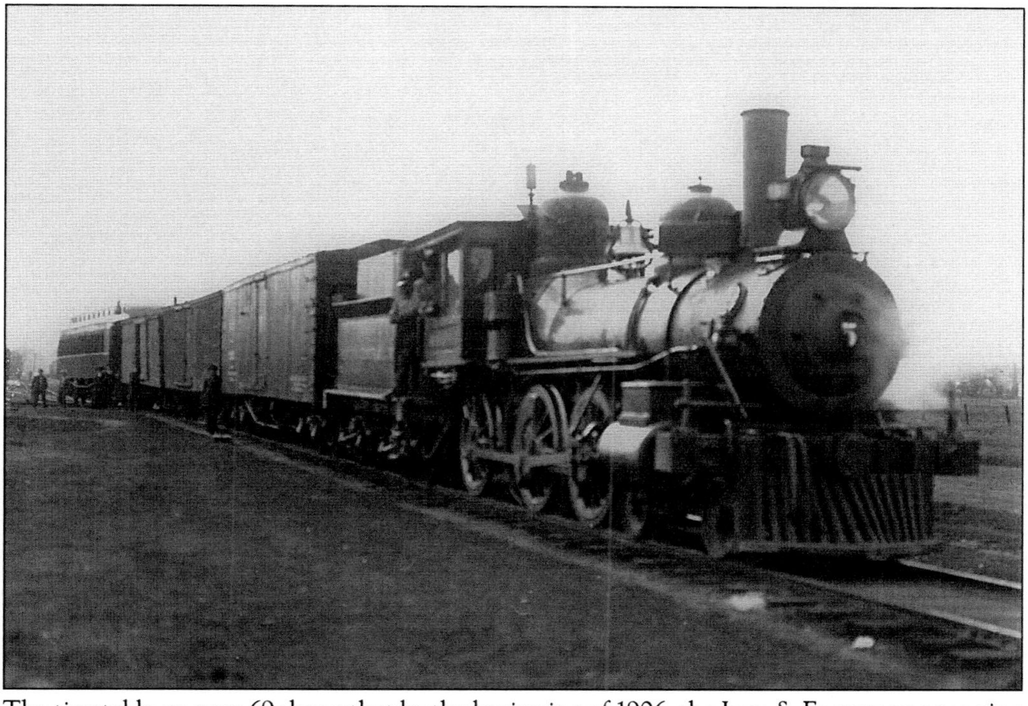

The timetable on page 69 shows that by the beginning of 1906, the Ione & Eastern was running two mixed trains per day, hauling both freight and passengers. In this photograph, taken after 1910, Amador Central engine No. 5 pulls a mixed train out of Martell. Most early photographs of this railroad show that the passenger coaches were hooked at the rear of the train.

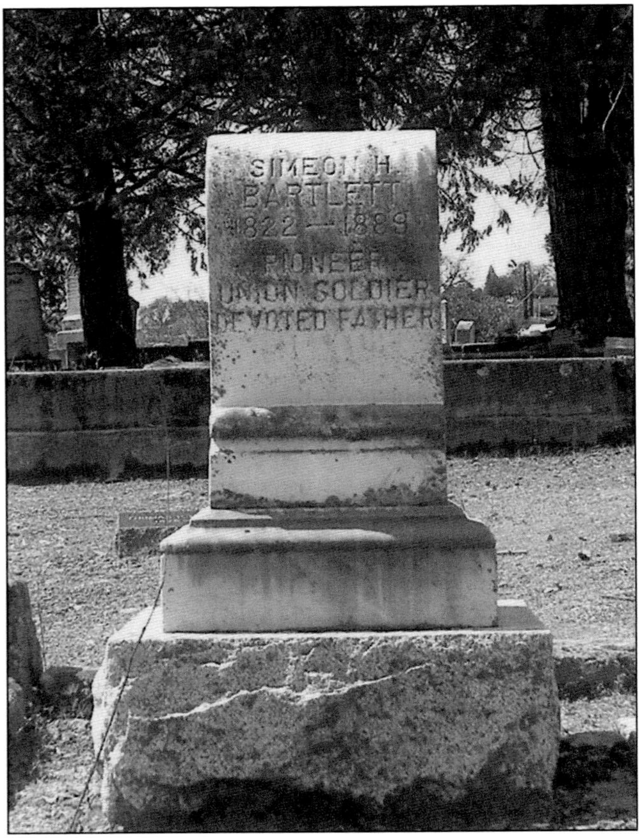

The Ione & Eastern provided services to the community beyond the transportation of passengers and freight. The first decade of the 20th century brought a resurgence in patriotism and a desire that all graves of Civil War veterans be marked. The Ione & Eastern shipped headstones delivered from Washington, D.C. free of charge, including the one pictured here that marks the Jackson grave of Simeon Bartlett.

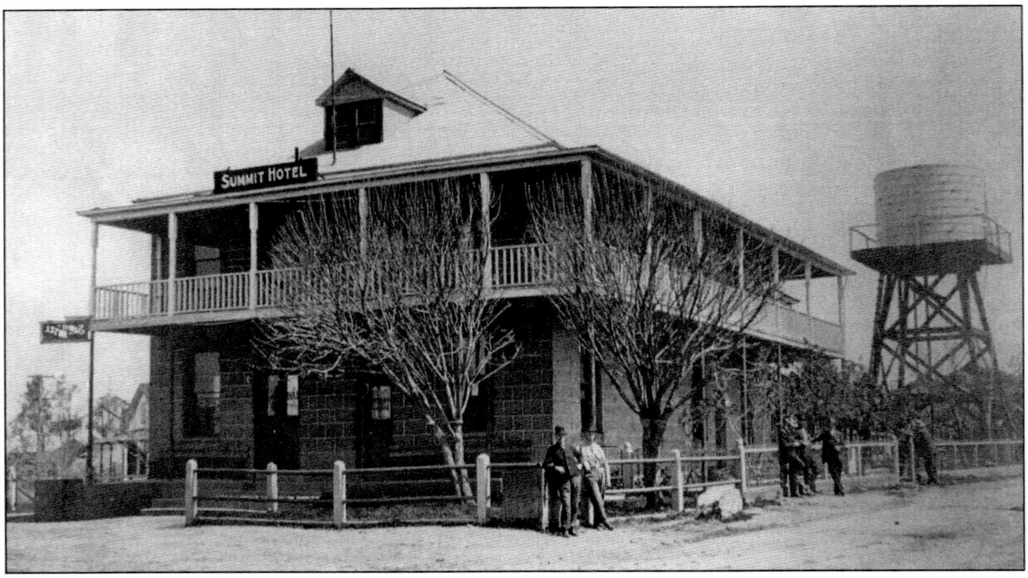

Most railroads have their associations with nefarious characters, and the Ione and Eastern was no exception. One of these was Agostine Borello. In 1908, he burned the Summit House, a hostel that stood a short distance from the Martell depot, to the ground. Three days after the fire he was arrested at the depot while attempting to flee the county. This photograph was taken after the hotel was rebuilt.

The building of the Ione & Eastern opened up a new genre of entertainment for Amadorians, the traveling circus. In April 1906, circus train cars were hooked to an Ione & Eastern locomotive and pulled into Martell. The circus was held in Jackson, to the delight of many. The *Amador Ledger* reported that 3,000–4,000 people attended the circus, coming from as far away as 20 miles.

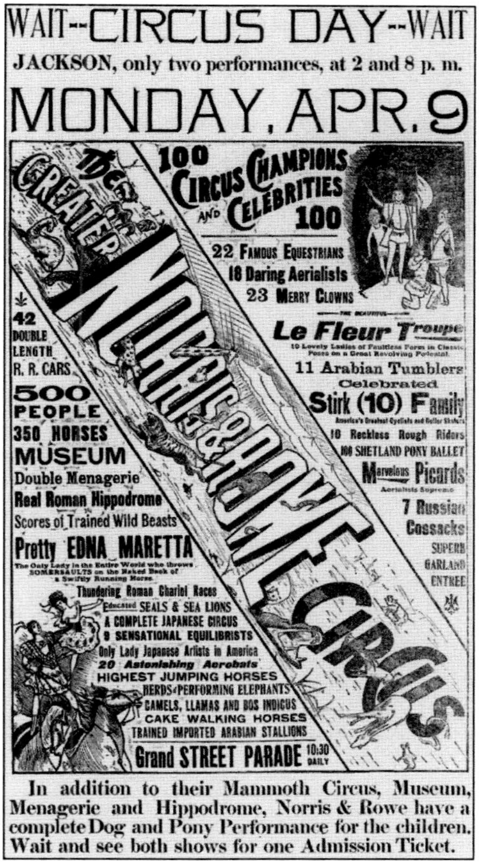

Pictured below is the Amador Central ticket office at the Ione depot in 1912. Originally built as a depot for the Amador Branch Railroad, it later cleared freight and accommodated passengers of both lines. The men in the photograph are, from left to right, brakeman Byron Miller, fireman Mark Spinetti, mechanic Charles Engstrom, general manager John A. McPerson, Ione agent Frank Martin, engineer Jack Thomas, and conductor Ralph Miller.

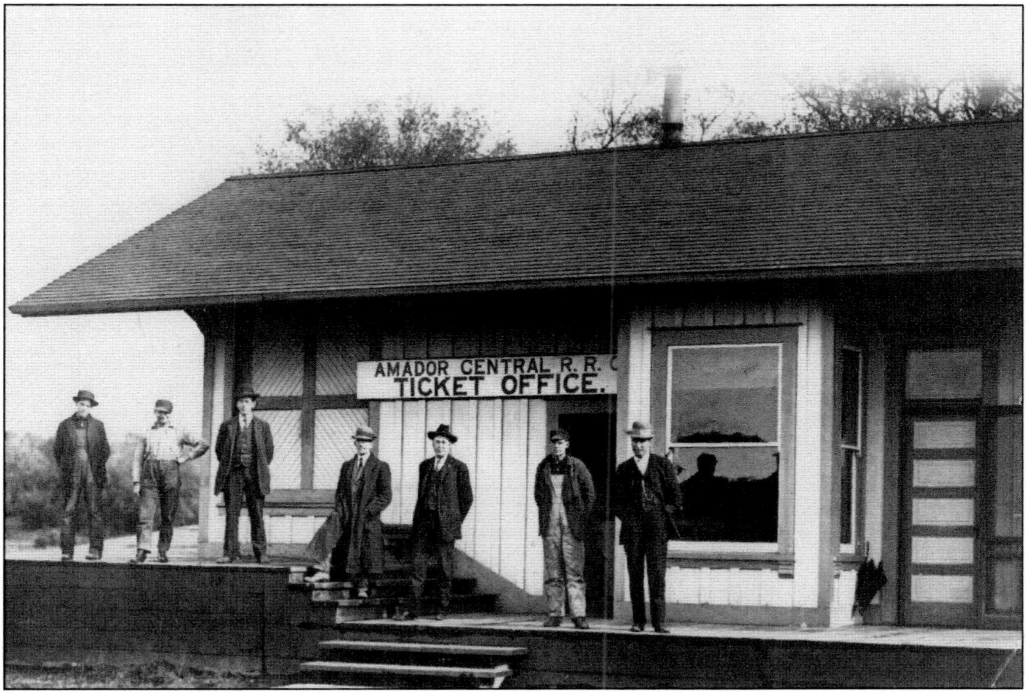

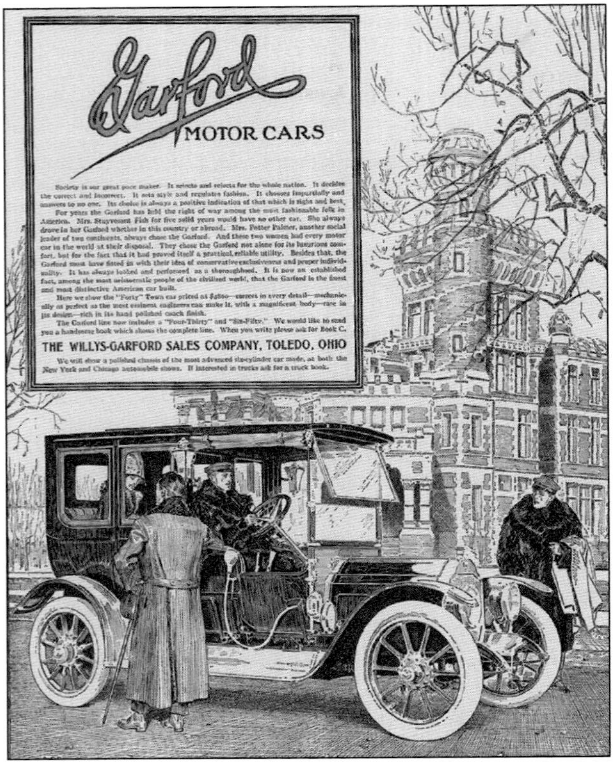

After the advent of the automobile, many railroads experimented with adapting gasoline vehicles to rail travel. In 1915, the Amador Central put into use a 1909 Studebaker Garford, similar to the one pictured in this advertisement. This vehicle employed its original rear rims, onto which were shrunk tires from a Shay engine that had first been machined down to a suitable thickness. The front wheels and axle were taken from a Buda push car. (Author's collection.)

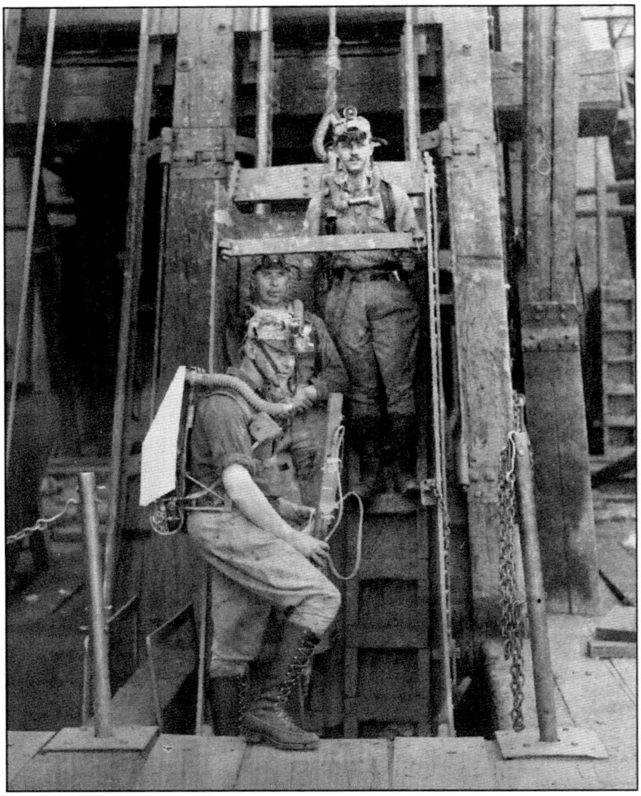

The Amador Central became a valuable resource when disaster struck at the Argonaut Mine in Jackson. In 1922, a fire broke out trapping 47 miners. The railroad was credited with bringing rescue workers and equipment to the site in record time. This photograph was taken during the rescue effort.

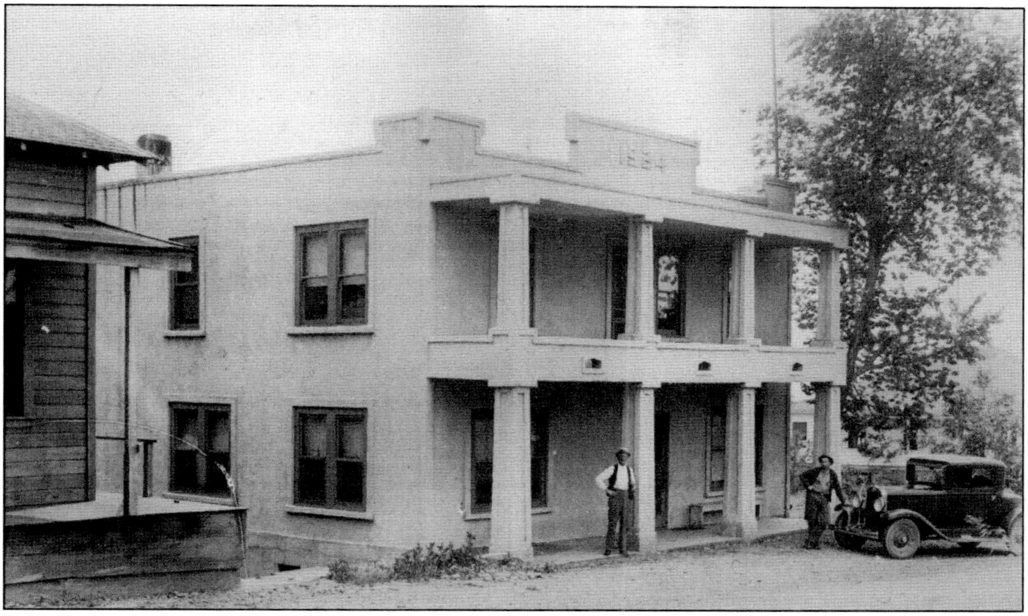

Traveling businessmen and visitors to Amador County would often need to overnight after arriving at Martell on the train. Nearby the Martell Station was the Casazza Boarding House, built in 1924. The hotel served mainly as a home to men working at nearby mines, renting rooms on a weekly or monthly basis. It would, however, house travelers when rooms were available.

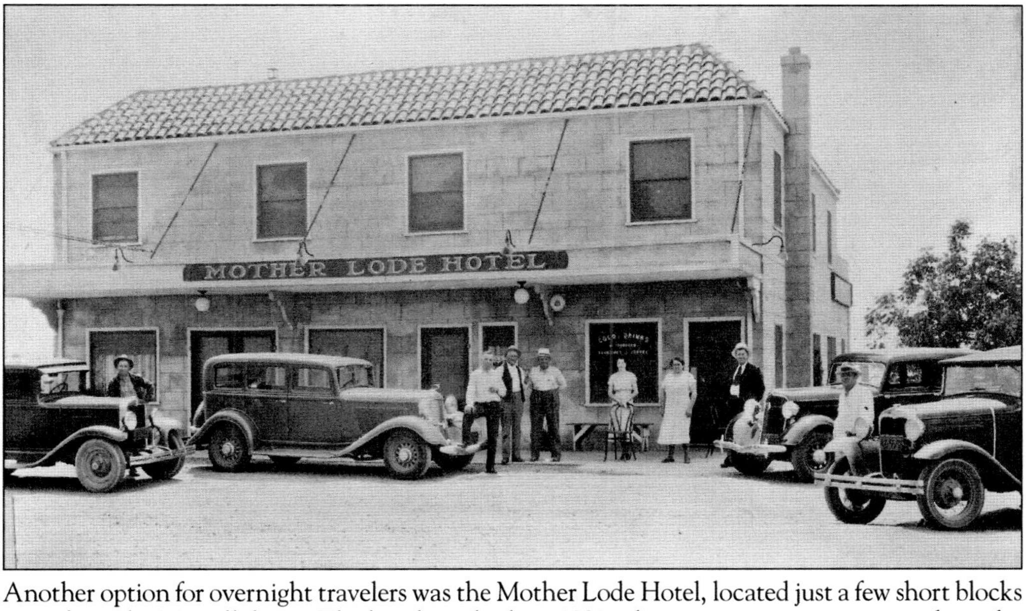

Another option for overnight travelers was the Mother Lode Hotel, located just a few short blocks away from the Martell depot. The hotel was built in 1931, when improvements were made to the Mother Lode Highway, now designated State Route 49. The site soon became a popular stopping place for travelers by both automobile and train.

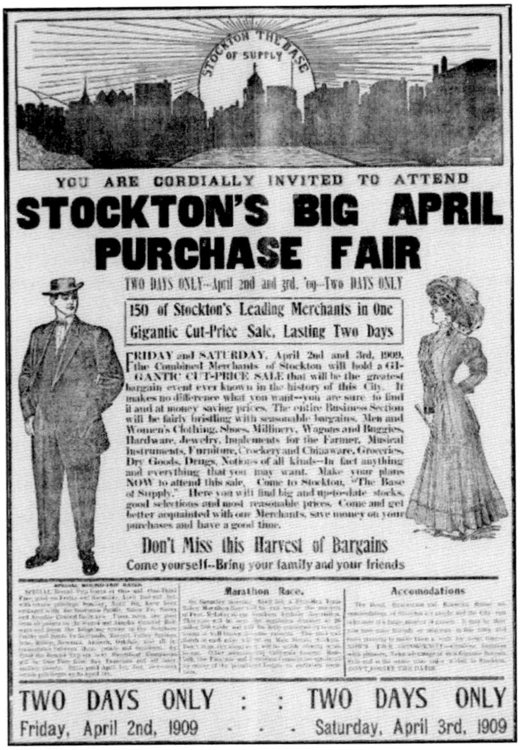

The Amador Central Railroad found that passengers were willing to travel outside Amador County to attend special events and shopping opportunities, such as the Purchase Fair shown in this advertisement. For this event, the railroad offered a special round-trip fare that was one-third the regular cost to passengers. (Author's collection.)

The steady increase of passenger travel prompted the Amador Central to redesign their tickets. Unlike the earlier tickets issued by the Ione & Eastern that designated only two points of travel, tickets issued by 1920 displayed all points along the line. The right side of the ticket shown below is the passenger's ticket, and the left side the conductor's stub.

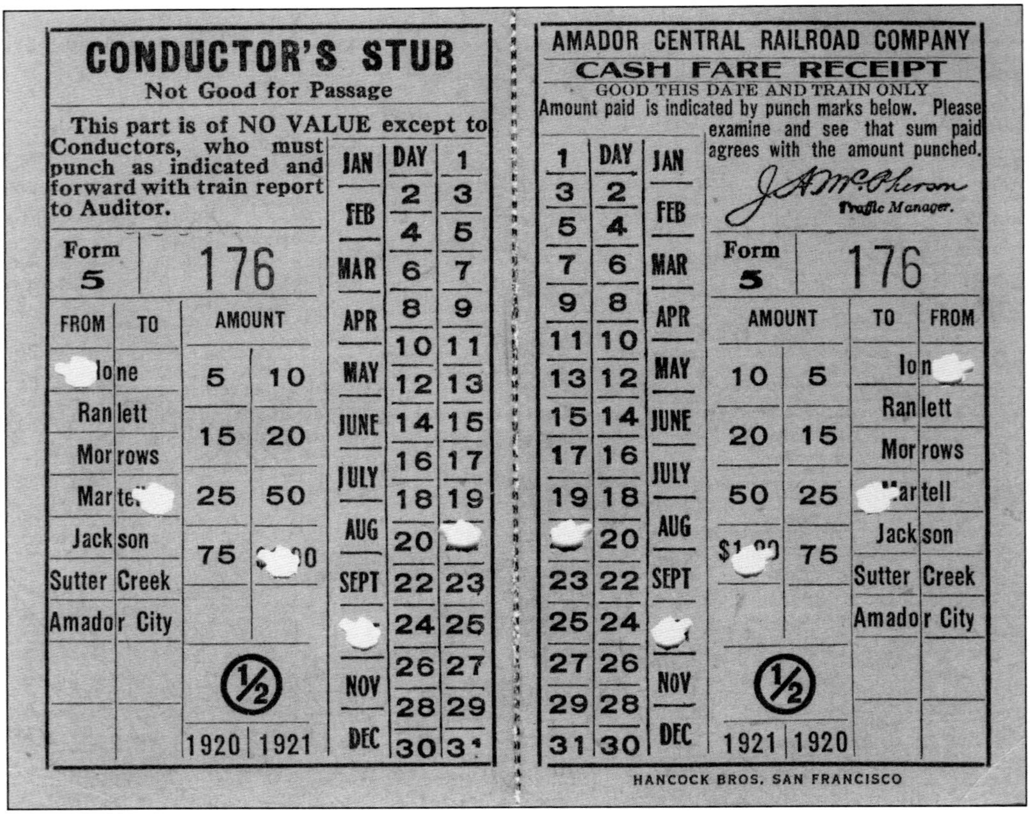

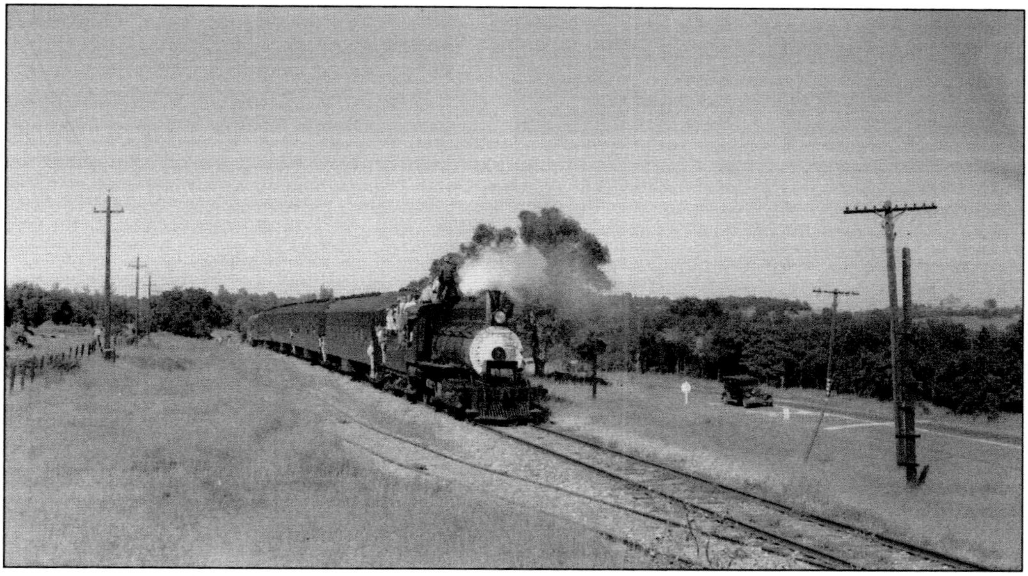

In May 1948, a memorable excursion took place on the Amador Central. The California-Nevada Railroad Historical Society left San Francisco, bound for Martell. When they reached Ione with ten coaches, three were dropped, and seven were hooked to engine No. 7. Shortly after leaving the station, a passenger tripped the emergency fuel switch and stopped the train. The engine had to be re-primed, which took nearly an hour. Then, a short distance out of Ione, the incline became too much for the engine; two more coaches were dropped and diesel engine No. 8 added to the pull. Fortunately, the rest of their day turned out to be an enjoyable experience. The photograph above shows the excursion train before the diesel engine was attached. Below, the two engines pull the visitors to Martell.

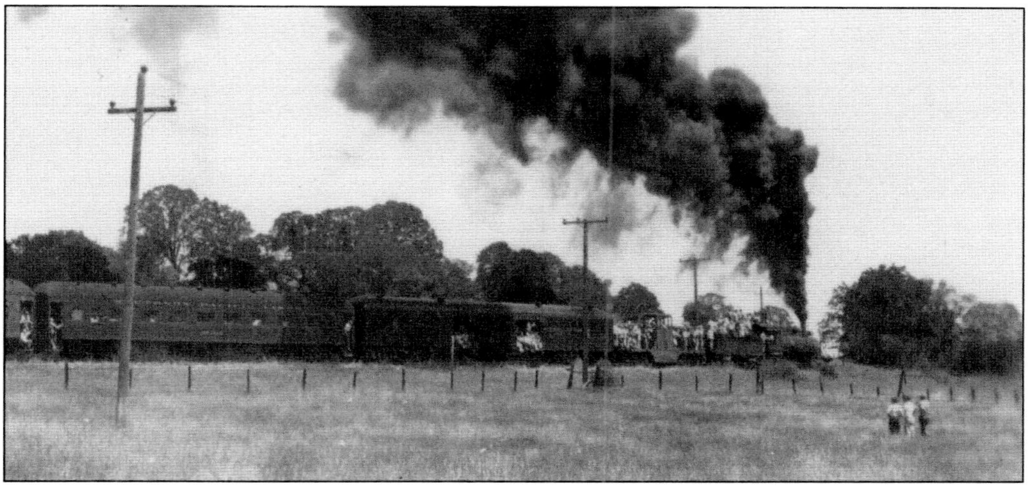

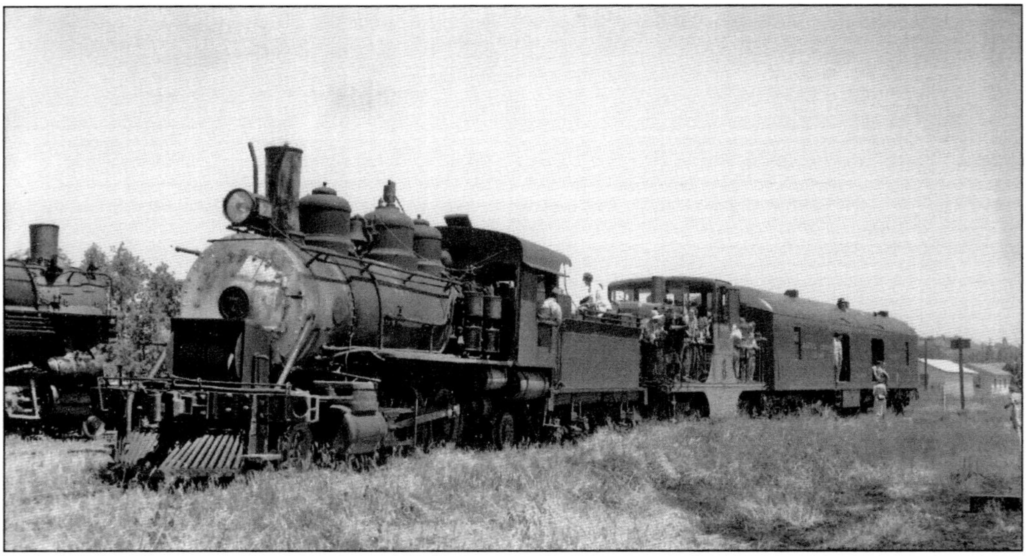

In this photograph, taken during the 1948 California-Nevada Historical Society excursion, passengers unloaded from the dropped coaches have found room on engine No. 8, while waiting for the engines to hook up to the remaining passenger coaches. This photograph was taken just outside of Ione.

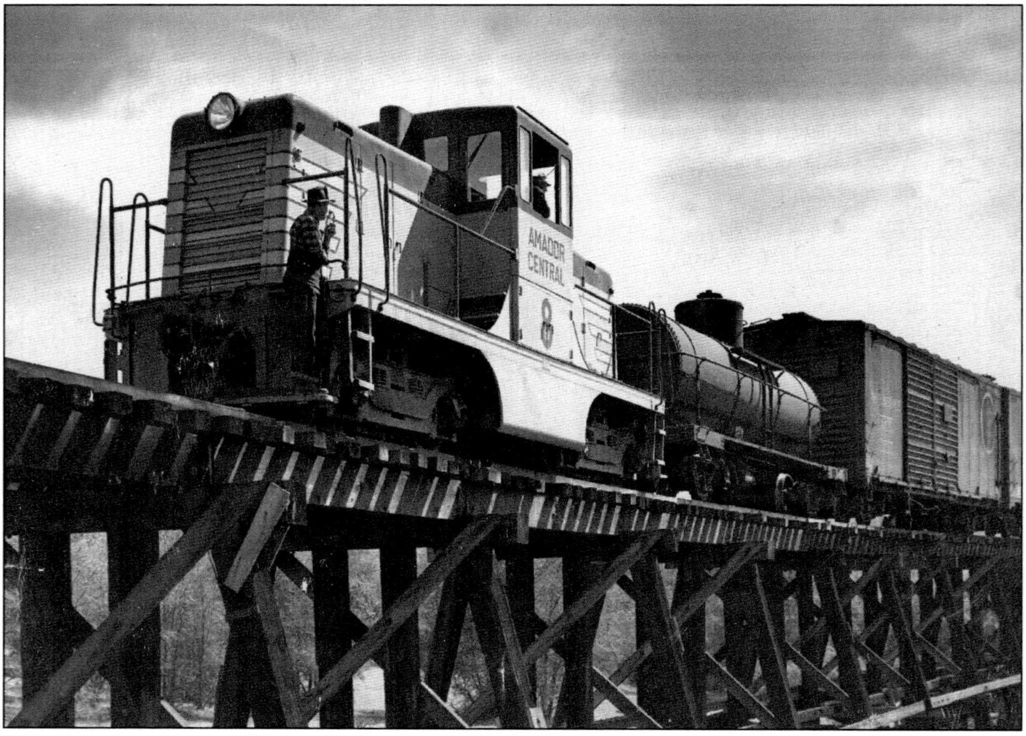

The Amador Central Railroad suspended passenger service on November 10, 1932. Economic hardships brought on by the Great Depression slowed ridership, and the number of passengers dwindled to a fraction of what they were in earlier decades. Although mixed train service was a thing of the past, the railroad continued to haul freight. This photograph of engine No. 8 pulling freight cars was taken in 1945.

Five

Iron and Steel

The rolling stock of a railroad is its most important asset, for without the locomotives and cars, the rails would be nothing more than a ribbon of steel atop wooden supports, stretching across landscapes. The ability to move goods and passengers at a quick pace in a safe manner is the mainstay of making a railroad profitable. Over its 100-year lifetime, the motive power of the Amador Central suited its needs and served it well.

The Amador Central employed 13 regular engines. Of these, eight were steam locomotives, and the remaining five were diesel powered. They numbered from No. 1 to No. 12, with two engines being assigned No. 9. Only two of these, No. 2 and No. 3, were built specifically for the Ione & Eastern Railroad. The other 11 were purchased from other railroad companies. Many went on to serve on other lines, while some were scrapped. Only two of the steam engines remain intact. The No. 7, known as Iron Ivan, is on display in the Ione City Park in Amador County. The other, the first No. 9, is on display at the National Railroad Museum in Green Bay, Wisconsin. For a time, the Amador Central also used a small tank engine for switching. It was one of three tanks that had been repaired in the Martell shops for the Nevada Consolidated Copper Company. It was not the intent of the railroad to purchase the engine, but it was put to use when one of the trestles on the line burned. It was loaded on a flat bed truck at Martell and taken to Ione to do the switching between that depot and the burned-out trestle.

Maintenance of the rolling stock and the right-of-way were a constant. The Amador Central maintained the rolling stock via its shops at Martell. Over time, many improvements were made, including replacing the wooden turntable and most of the rails. Today, a good portion of the rail line remains intact and is used by speeder clubs on a regular basis.

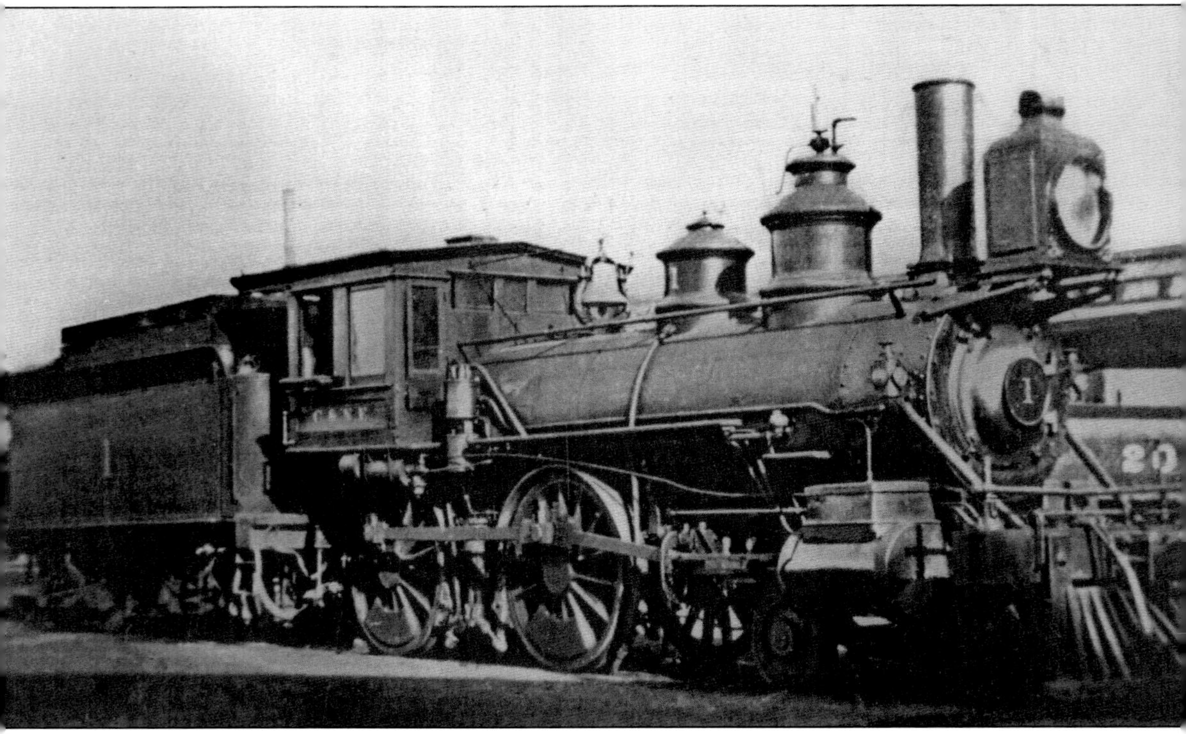

The first locomotive used on the Ione & Eastern Railroad was this Portland 4-4-0. It was purchased from the Southern Pacific Railroad for $500 and first used to haul materials during construction of the Ione & Eastern. It first served on the Northern Pacific Railroad as No. 205 and later as No. 885. It was then put into service on the California & Northeastern Railway, where it served under No. 1 (as pictured here), and was used by their subsidiary, the Far Western Lumber Company. It then became the property of Southern Pacific. This locomotive served on the Ione & Eastern until about 1910, when it was sold to the Pacific & Eastern Railway. (Courtesy Jim Fredrickson.)

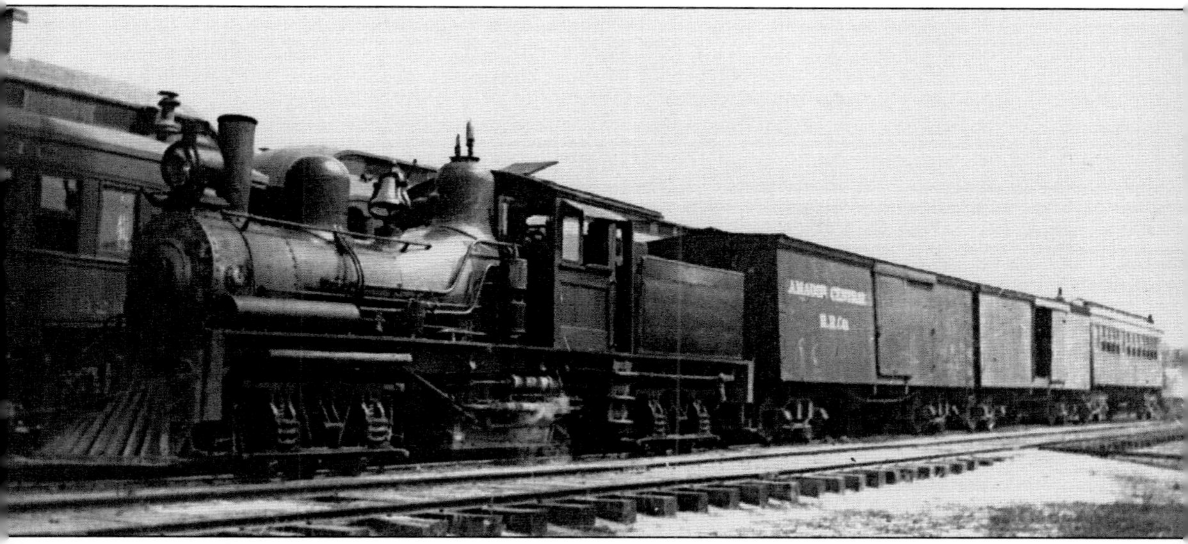

In January 1905, the Ione & Eastern put into service its second locomotive. It was a Shay 3tr, built in 1904 for Charles Erickson, who was the contractor for the Ione & Eastern. He later became owner of the Amador Central Railroad. Prior to the engine's arrival in Ione it was converted to an oil burner when problems were encountered with its operation. Employment of the engine was delayed when it broke down in Lodi on its way to Ione and had to be sent to San Francisco for repairs. The engines on the Shay, three in number, were on the right side of the boiler and connected to a tumbling rod that transmitted power to the wheels by a bevel cog system. The engine weighed 65 tons and was built for pulling rather than for speed. This engine continued in service on the line until well after it became the Amador Central Railroad. Around 1912, it was sold to Metropolitan Redwood Lumber Company and subsequently scrapped in 1942.

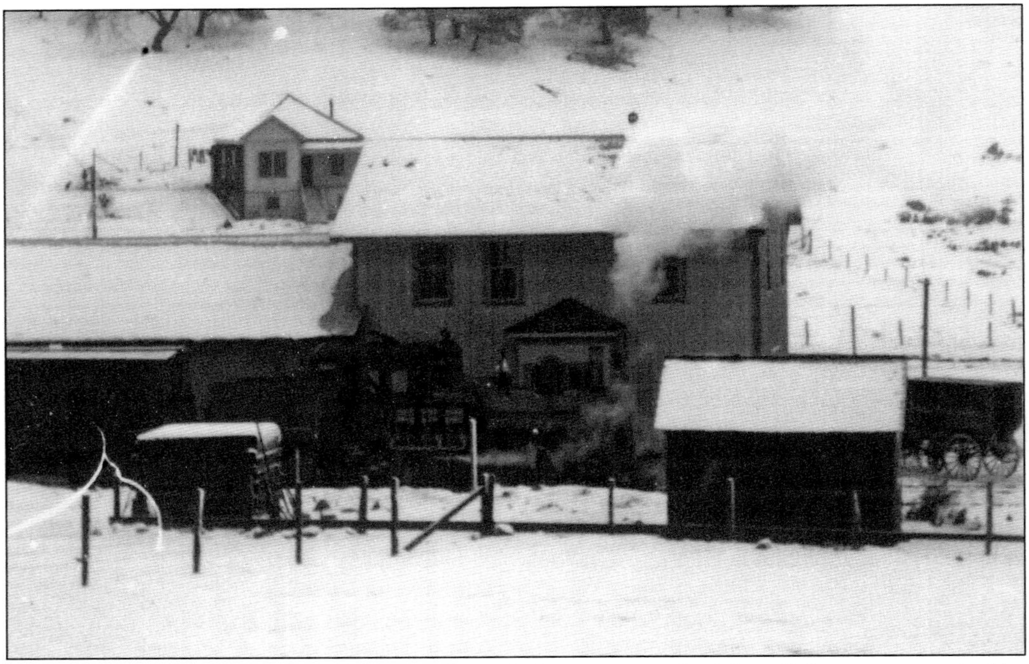

In this photograph, engine No. 2 blows steam while waiting at the Martell depot, surrounded by a blanket of snow. When this locomotive was finally fixed and put to work, the *Amador Ledger* reported that it cost the railroad company $2,000 to have it repaired, and a lawsuit was filed to recover the costs.

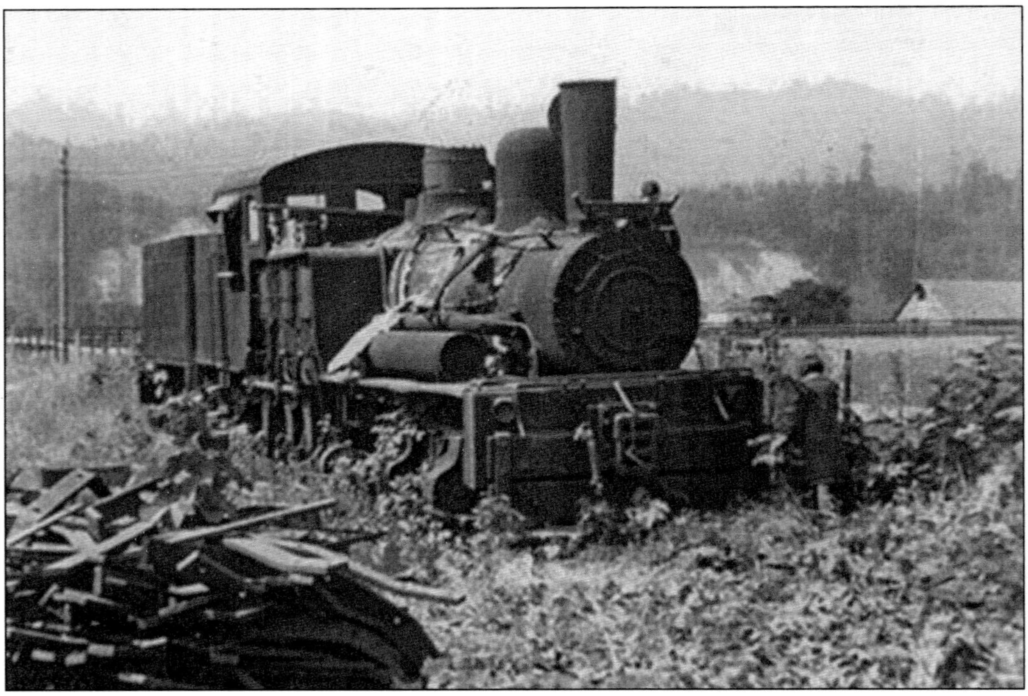

When retired, many locomotives were "set out to pasture." Here, the Ione & Eastern No. 2 sits abandoned and subject to the elements after being turned out by the Metropolitan Redwood Company. Some of its parts are missing, scavenged for use on other locomotives.

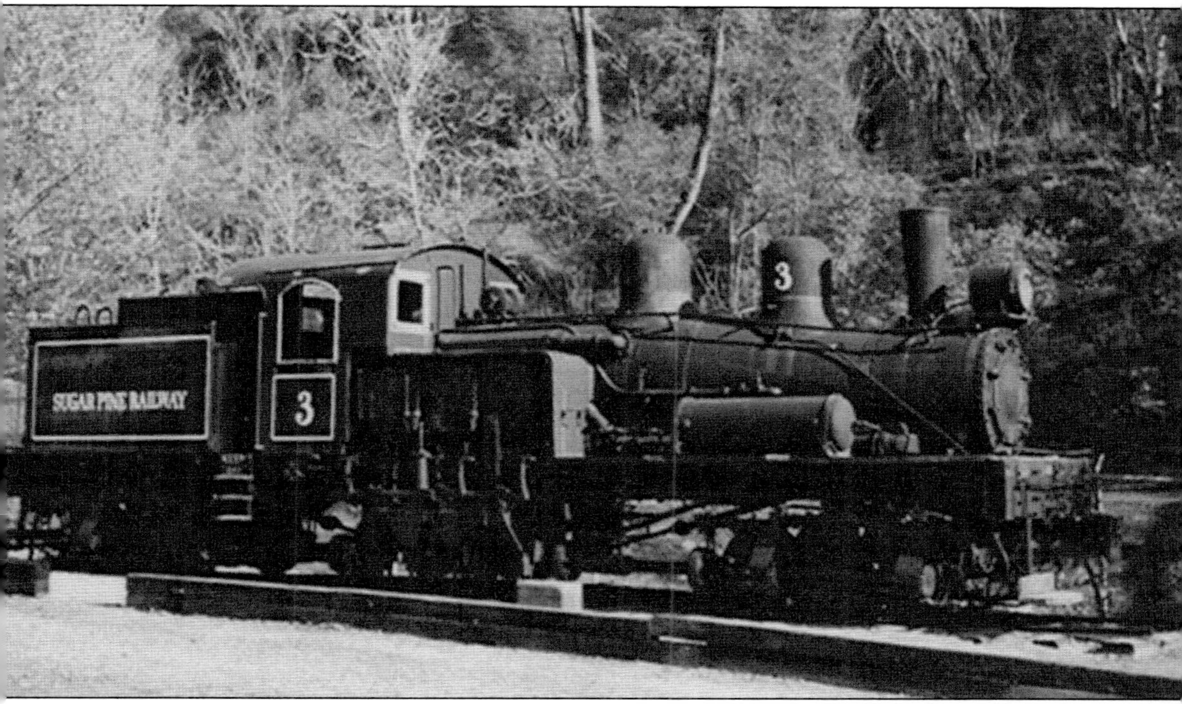

The third locomotive built specifically for the Ione & Eastern in 1905 was a Shay 2tr, similar to the one pictured here, which is on display in Sonora, California. It ran on the line until 1920, when it was sold to the Great Western Power Company in Plumas County, California. Great Western partnered with the Red River Lumber Company to harvest massive amounts of timber, clearing land to build the Lake Almanor reservoir and dam. This engine created a sensation when it rolled into Ione, with many residents turning out at the station to hail its arrival. It was eventually scrapped; rumor has it that the remains of this engine may be buried under California State Route 70, near the Bucks Creek Powerhouse in Plumas County.

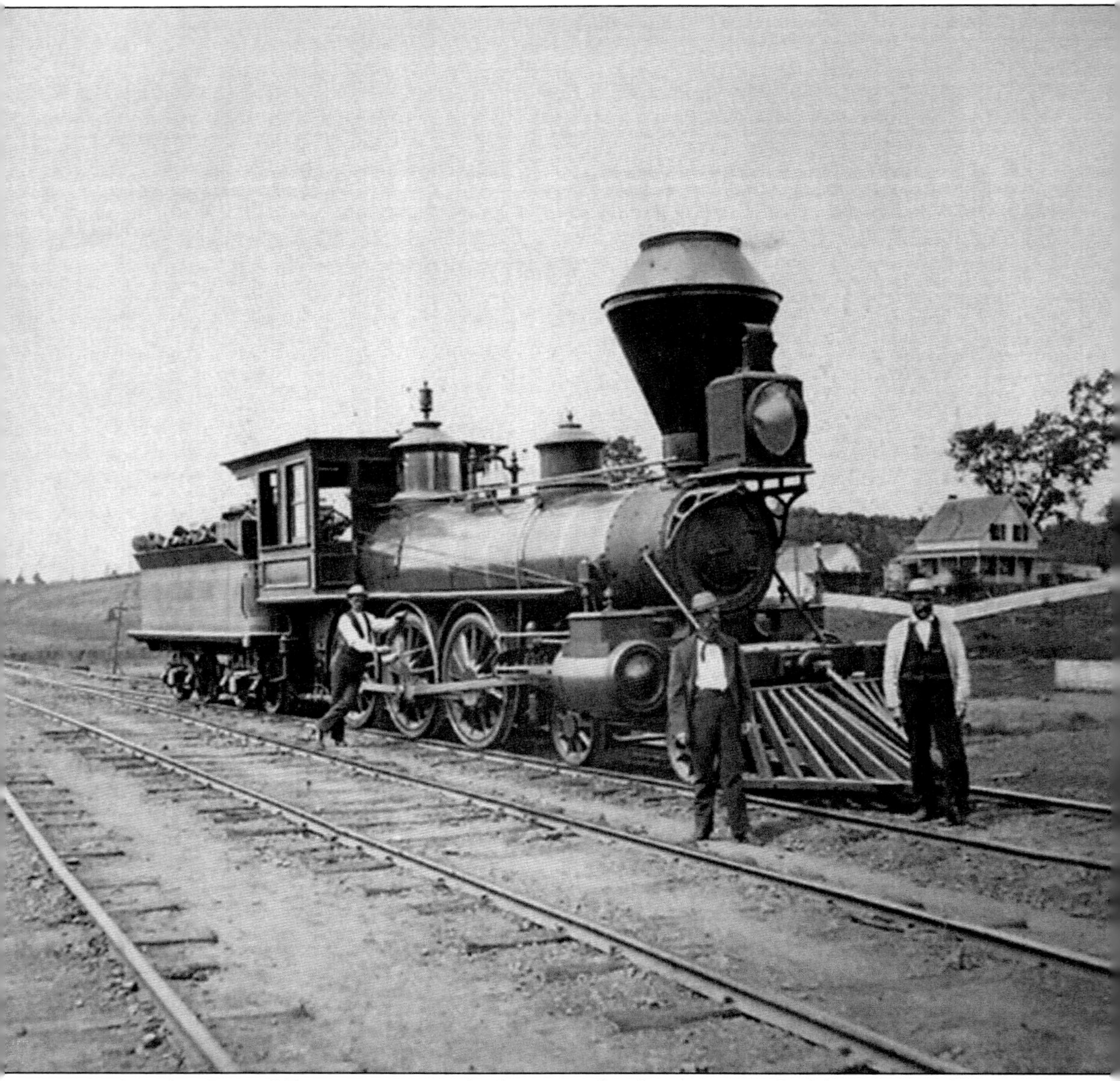

Amador Central Engine No. 4 was built in 1866 by the McKay and Aldus Iron Works as a 4-6-0 for the Central Pacific Railroad, where it served as No. 21 and was known at the "Tamroo." It was similar to the one pictured here, the "Majestic." It was then sold to Southern Pacific, where it was numbered 1524, rebuilt to a 0-6-0, and renumbered 1055. In 1909, it was purchased by the Amador Central Railroad, where it was used until about 1917. It was then sold to Stone & Webster Construction, and then to the Modesto & Empire Traction Company, where it served as Engine No. 2 until it was scrapped.

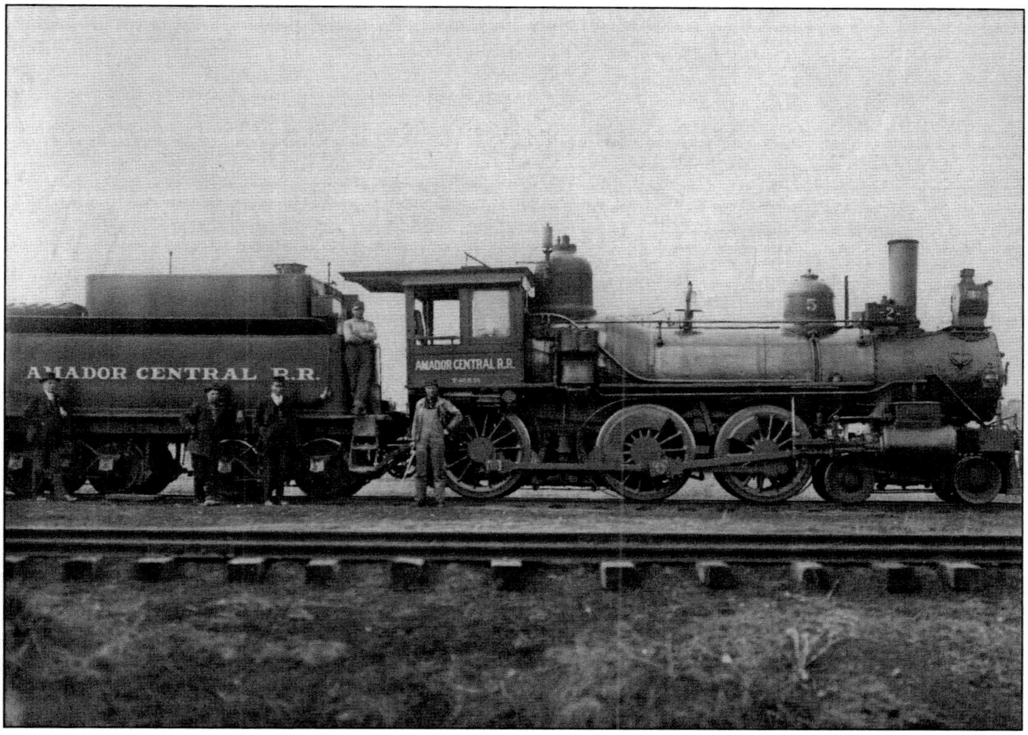

The Amador Central purchased its fifth locomotive in 1910. The top photograph shows engine No. 5 as it appeared when first put into service. It was a Schenectady 4-6-0, manufactured in 1875 for the Central Pacific Railroad, where it served as engine No. 189. It then served on the Southern Pacific Railroad as engine No. 1554 and was later No. 2023. When it was purchased in 1910, the Amador Central had enough business to run all five of its engines on a regular schedule. No. 5 ran on the line until 1945, when it was scrapped. Over time, modifications and improvements were made to the locomotive, as seen below.

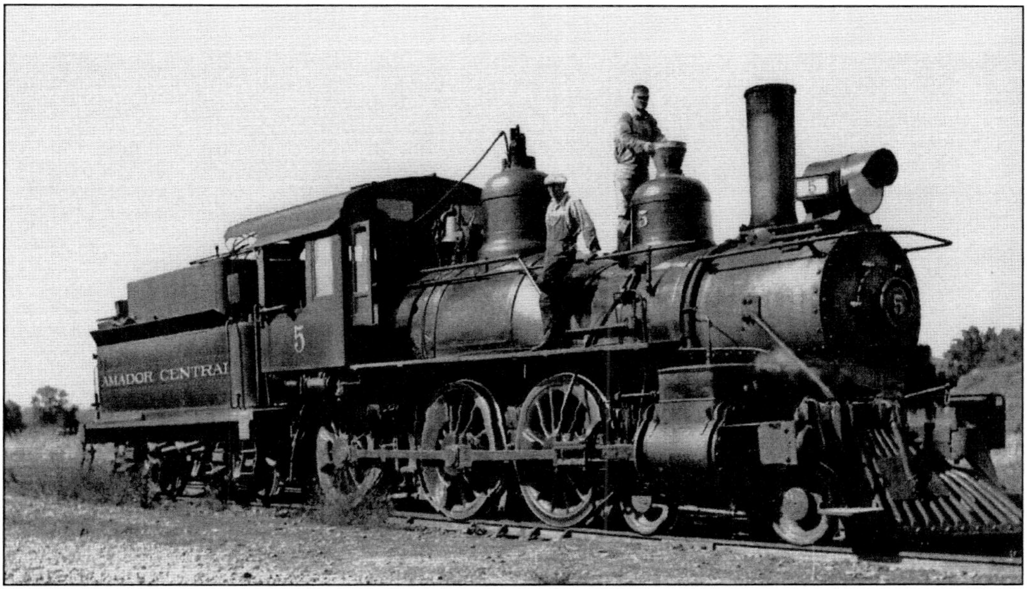

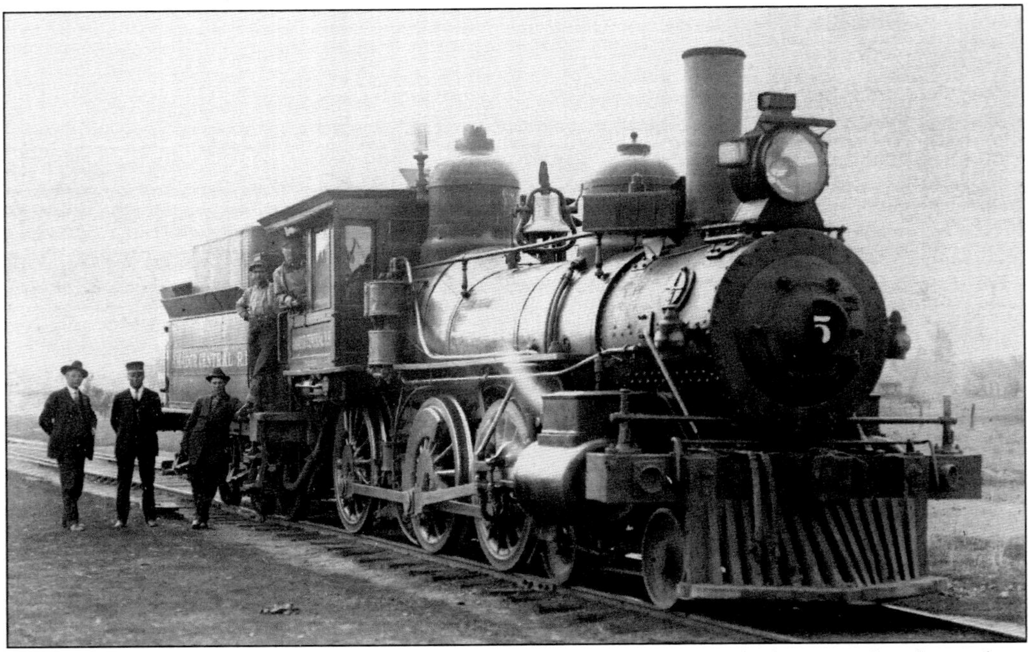

Men who worked on the railroad were proud of their profession and often posed to have their pictures taken with the locomotives. Shown in this photograph are, from left to right, Ione ticket agent Frank Martin, conductor Ralph Miller, brakeman Byron Miller, fireman Mark Spinetti, and engineer Jack Thomas. The photograph was taken at the Ione rail yard in 1910, shortly after the engine was purchased.

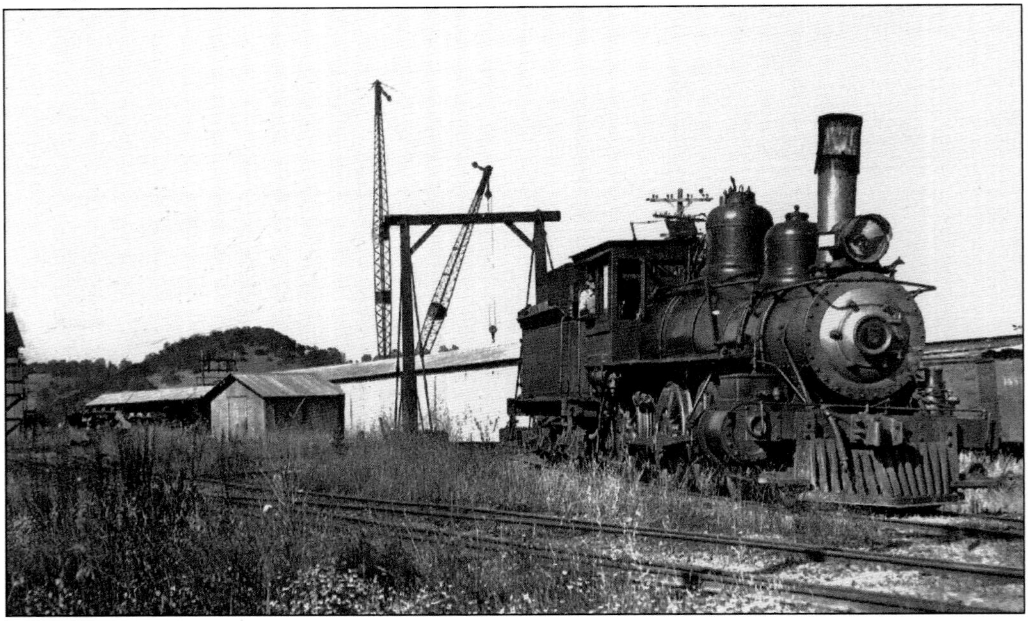

In this photograph, No. 5 sits at the Martell yard with a cover over its stack. Although it appeared that the railroad was doing well financially at the time this engine was purchased, it was not. Throughout 1909, local papers reported that the line had a very heavy freight business; however, in May 1909, Charles Erickson borrowed money from the Union Trust Company, putting up two locomotives as collateral.

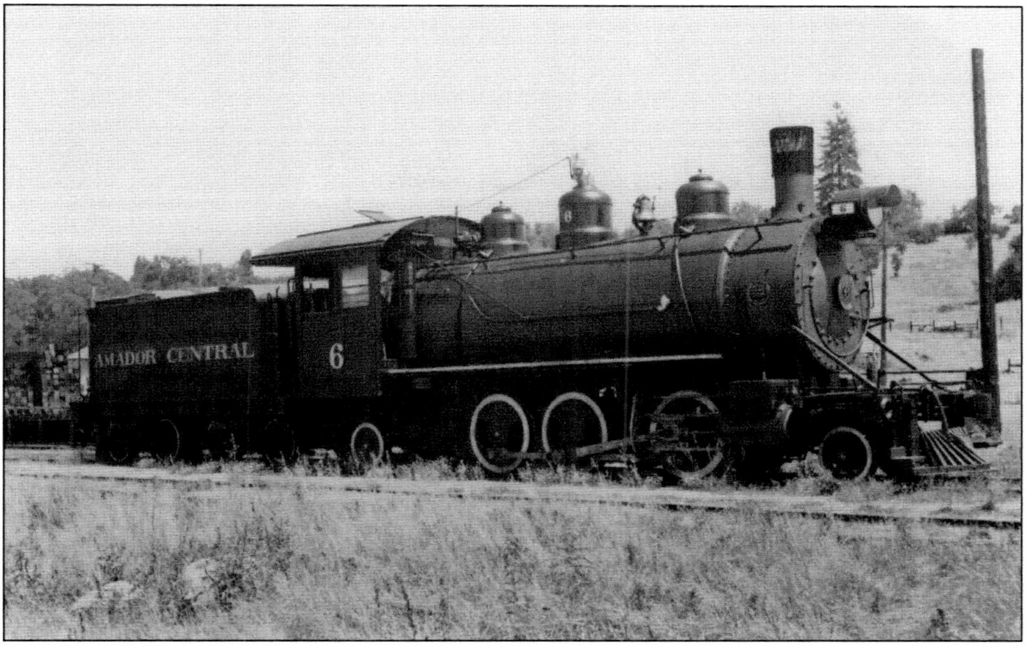

These two photographs give different side views of Amador Central engine No. 6, a 1906 Baldwin 2-6-2. This engine was purchased and put into service on the Amador Central line in about 1912. It was originally built for the Klamath Lake Railroad, serving as No. 1 on that line. The Napa Valley Electric Company leased the No. 6 during World War II, in a deal that helped bring much needed revenues to the Amador Central Company during tough economic times. The Amador Central may have restricted the use of this engine to pulling freight; it was ill suited for passenger trains because of nosing problems with the reciprocation rods, which created stability problems. The engine was scrapped in 1945. The top photograph was taken in 1937 at the Martell yard.

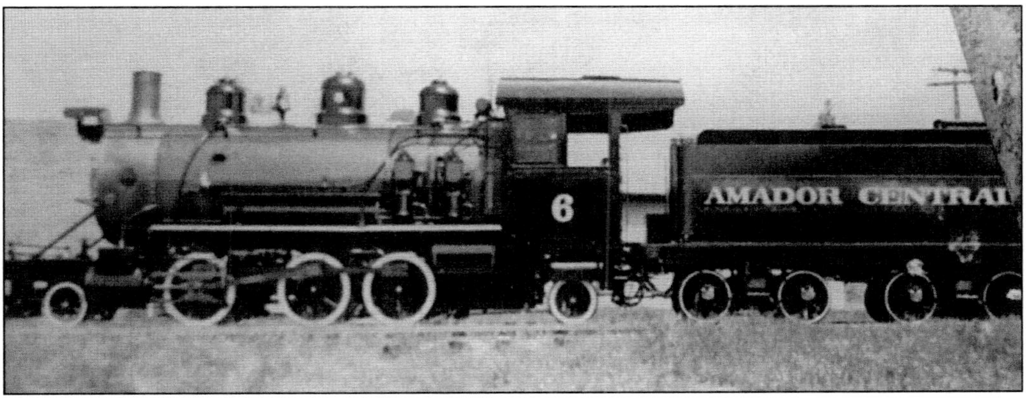

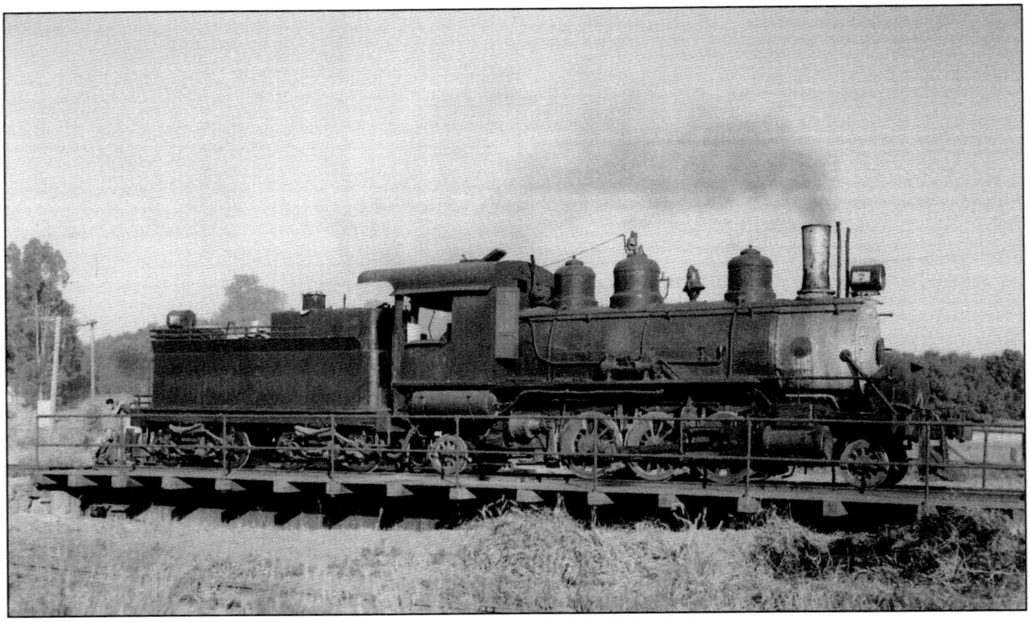

Many a railroad, including the Amador Central, can boast having an old No. 7 locomotive. Amador's No. 7, affectionately known as Iron Ivan, was built by the Baldwin Locomotive Works in 1901 for the McCloud River Railroad. It served on that line, hauling lumber for the Red River Lumber Company, as engine No. 8. Ivan was moved to the Amador Central in 1937 and was subsequently purchased in 1939. This 2-6-2 Baldwin Prairie model was the last steam locomotive used on the Amador Central, working until 1945 when it was retired to standby service and replaced by a General Electric 44-ton diesel, Amador Central No. 8. The top photograph, of Ivan on the turntable at Martell, was taken in 1947. The bottom photograph was taken in 1948.

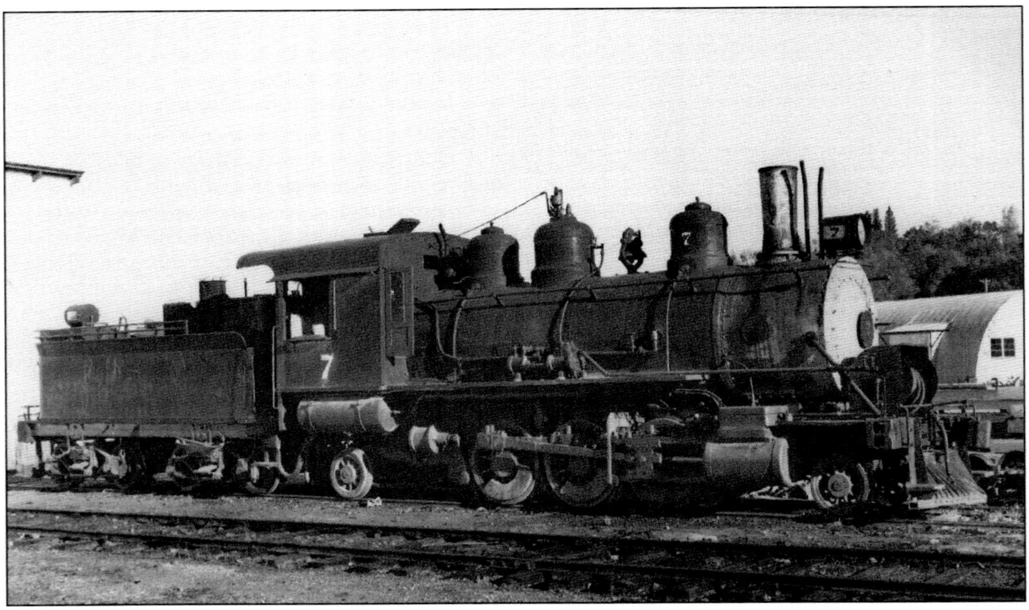

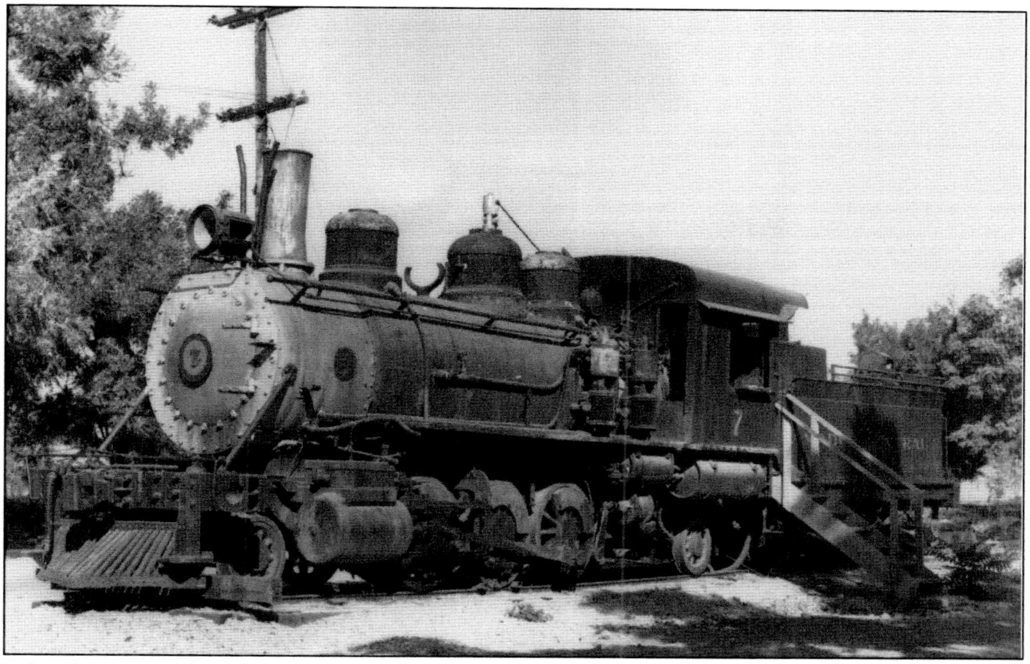

It has been said that Iron Ivan supported the railroad through the difficult years of World War II and likewise, "supported" the rail in another way. When No. 7 was retired from the Amador Central, the engine was stored in the Martell depot. In the 1950s, a large ceiling beam fell onto the locomotive, where it rested on its stack for many years, supporting the roof of the building. In 1961, the Winton Lumber Company donated the locomotive to the Amador Chamber of Commerce, and it was moved to the Ione City Park, where it found a permanent home. In the photograph above, taken in 1962, Iron Ivan sits in the park, open for all visitors to climb aboard. Shortly thereafter, a fence was erected around the engine.

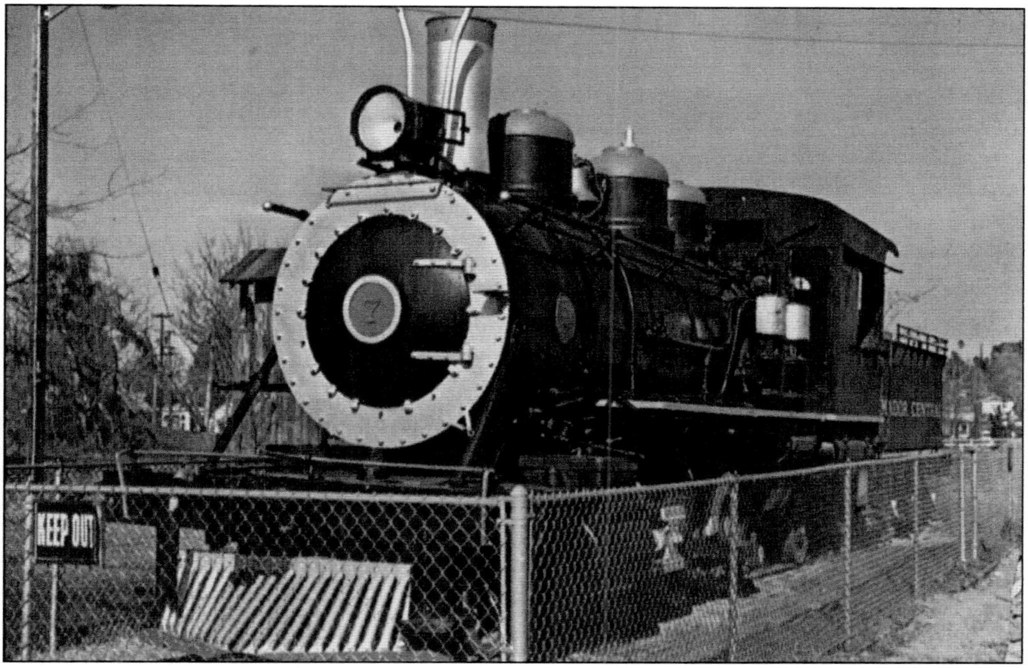

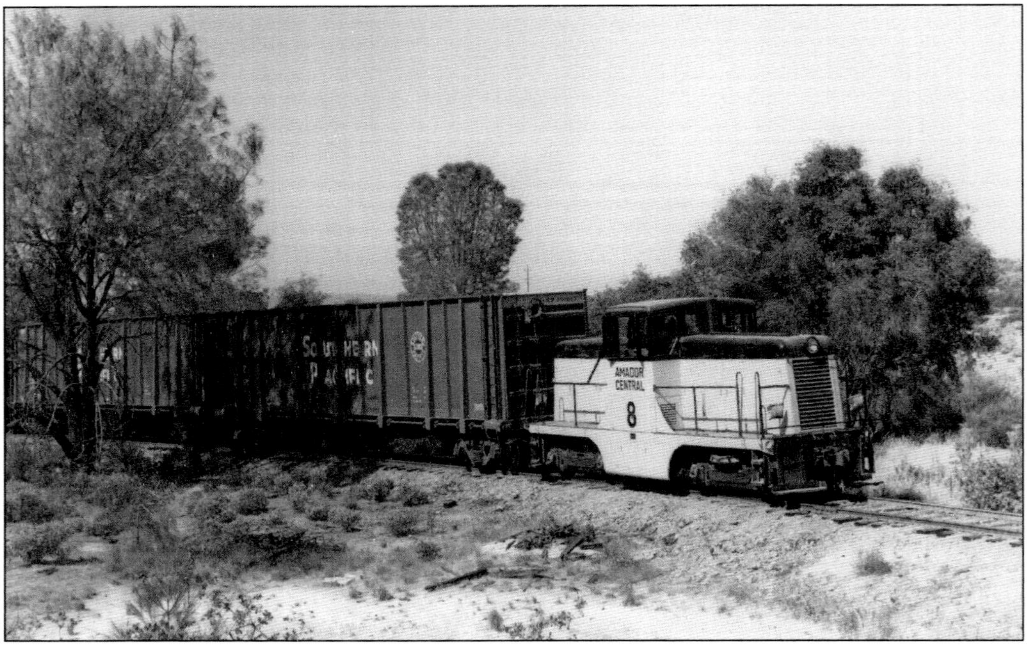

In this photograph is Amador Central No. 8, which replaced Iron Ivan as the main workhorse on the line. This 44-ton, 380-horsepower B-B model diesel was built by General Electric in 1945 and put to work on the Amador Central shortly thereafter. In 1974, it was sold to the Colorado Fuel and Iron Company, where it served as engine No. 32.

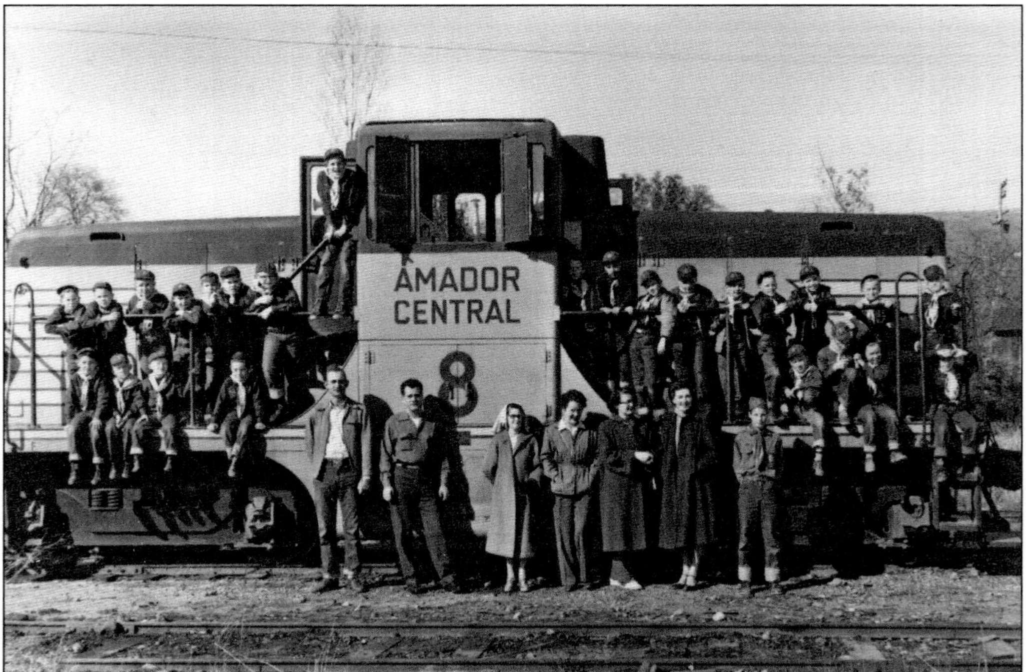

The Amador Central remained a favorite attraction throughout its lifetime to residents of Amador County. In this photograph, local troops of Cub and Boy Scouts, along with their chaperones, stop during a field trip to pose on engine No. 8.

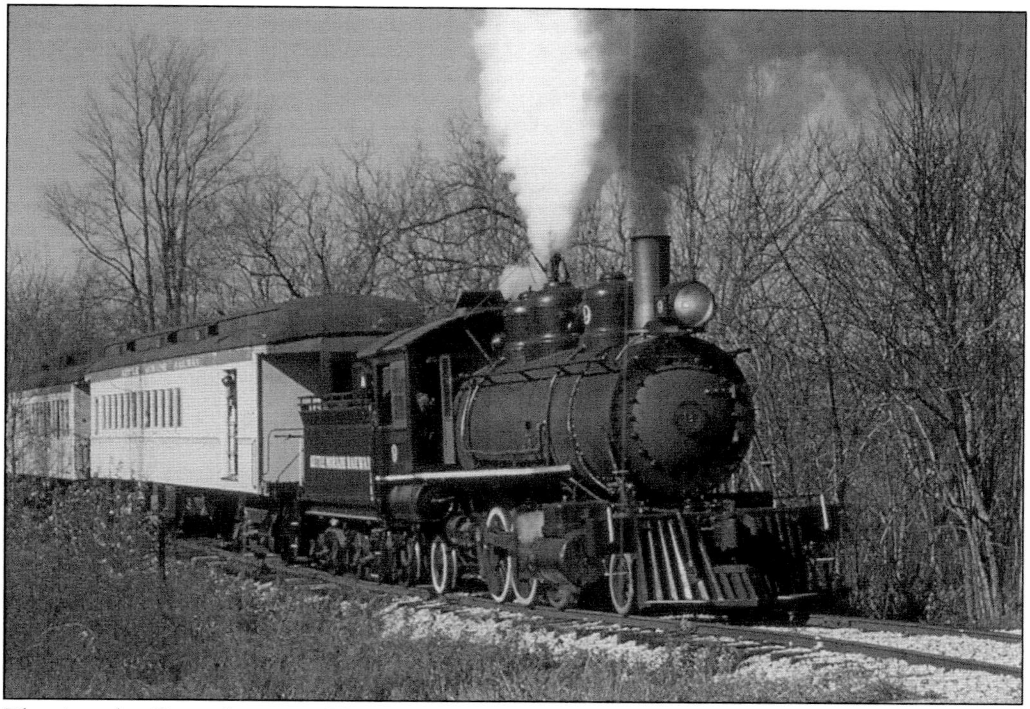

The Amador Central ran two No. 9 engines. The first (above) was a Baldwin 2-6-2, built in 1901. It served alongside Iron Ivan on the McCloud River Railroad. In 1939, it was sold to the Yreka Western Railroad. Then, in 1944, it was purchased by the Amador Central, where it ran until 1945; at that time, it was sold to the Nez Pierce Railroad. In 1966, it was purchased by Richard Heinbaugh for the Kettle Moraine Railroad. In 2003, it was donated to the National Railroad Museum. The second No. 9 engine (right) was a Baldwin B-B diesel. It was purchased by the Amador Central in 1965 and stayed until operations ceased in 2004. (Above, courtesy Jeff Terry.)

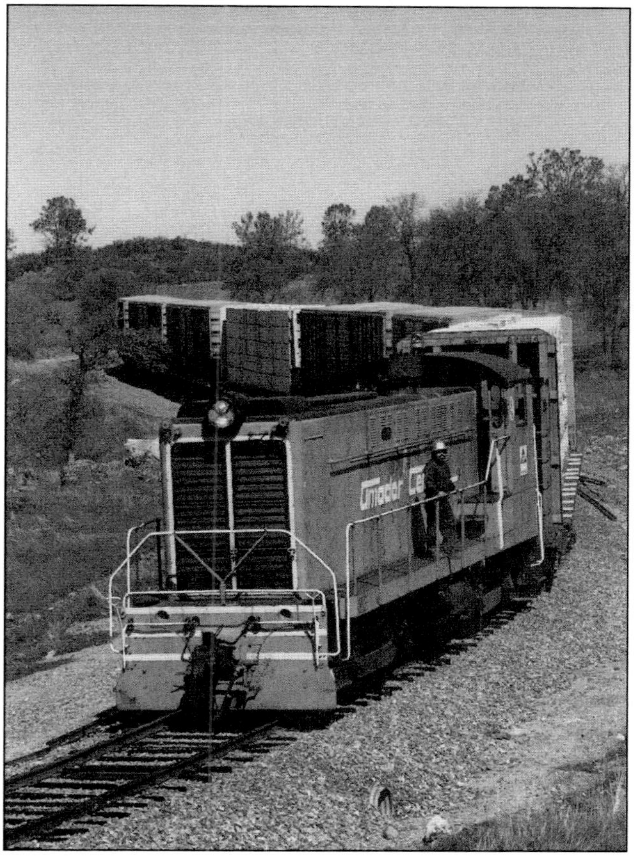

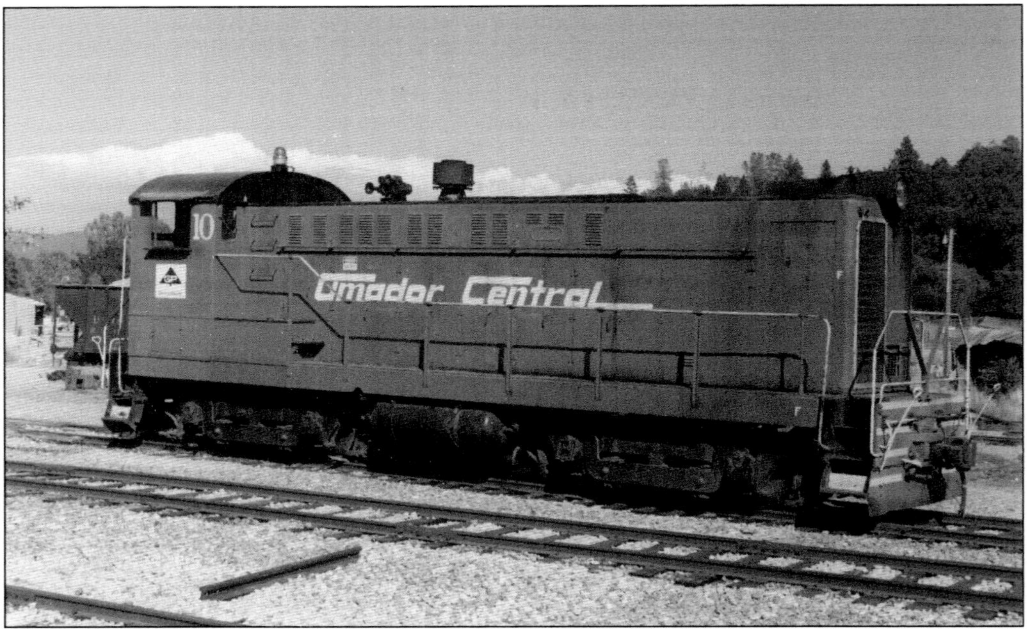

In 1972, the Amador Central purchased its No. 10 engine from the Chrome Crankshaft Company. This Baldwin was built in 1952 for the Texas and New Orleans Railroad, where it was employed as No. 105. It was then sold to Southern Pacific, where it ran as No. 2121, prior to being sold to the Chrome Crankshaft Company. No. 10 worked on the Amador Central until 2004, when the line ceased operations.

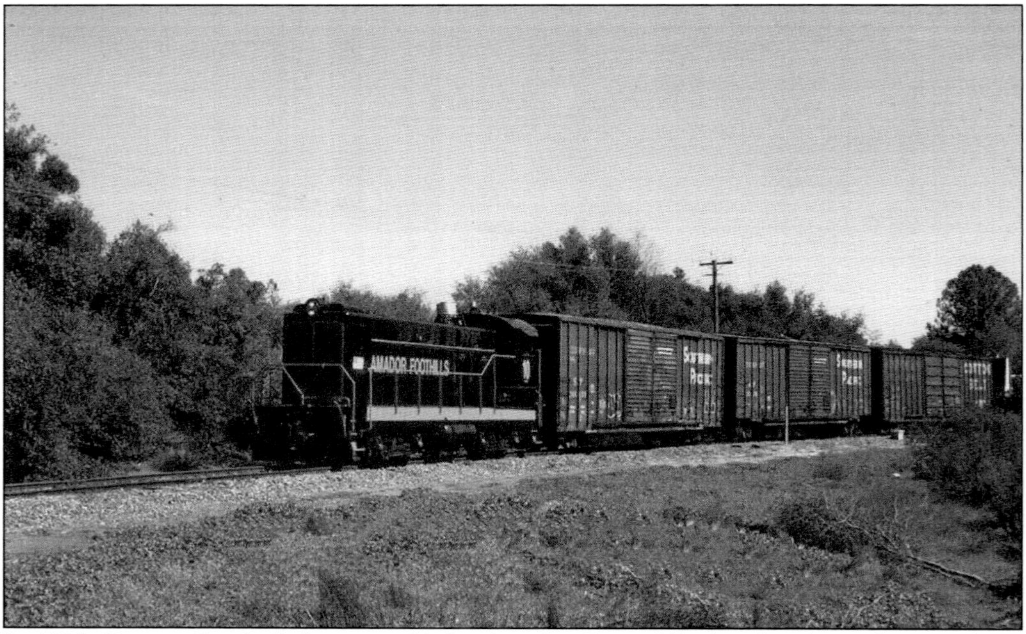

In 1996, Georgia Pacific Industries sold the Amador Central Railroad and its other Northern California operations to Sierra Pacific Industries. Georgia Pacific held the trademark to the railroad name, and thus, the new owners gave it the title of the Amador Foothills Railroad. In this photograph, painted with the name of its new owner, No. 10 pulls a line of Southern Pacific cars towards Ione.

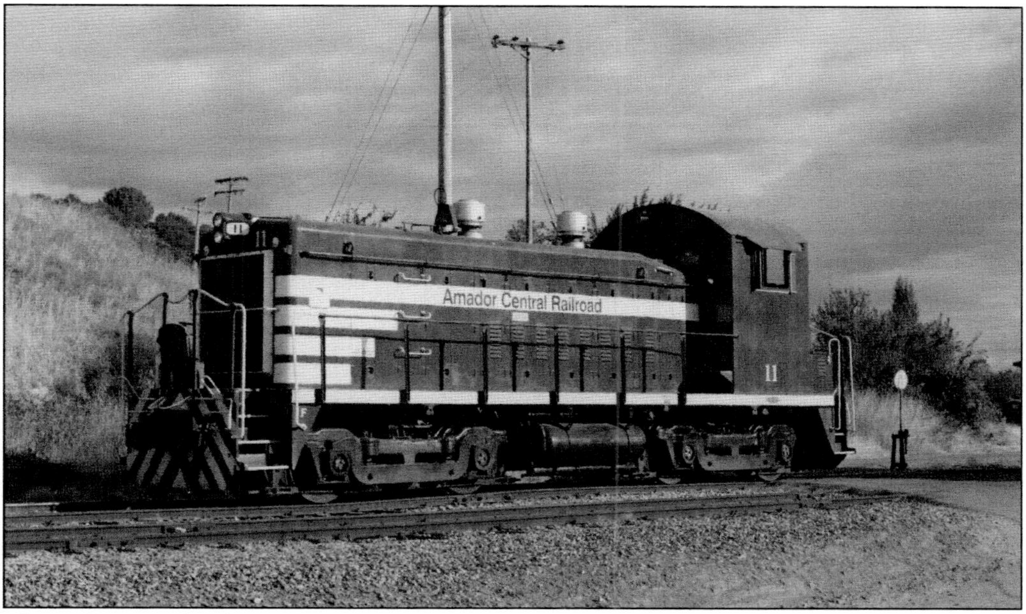

These photographs show Amador Central locomotive No. 11. This SW1200 engine was built in 1963 by the Electric Motive Diesel Company, a subsidiary of Caterpillar, Inc. Prior to running on the Amador Central, it worked on the rails of the Ashley, Drew & Northern Railway in Arkansas, first marked as No.178 and later as No. 1208. After serving the Amador Central, it was sold to the Quincy Railroad, where it worked as No. 5. In the top photograph, taken in 1996, No. 11 sits at the Martell depot. The bottom photograph, taken in 1997, shows the engine pushing cars uphill from Ione.

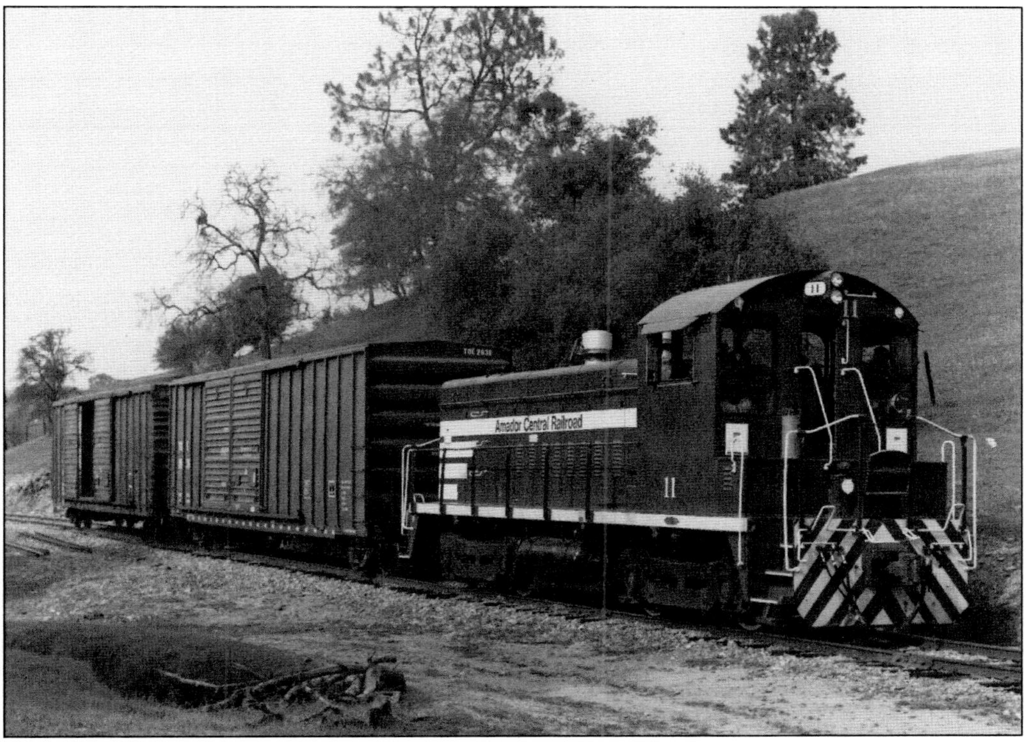

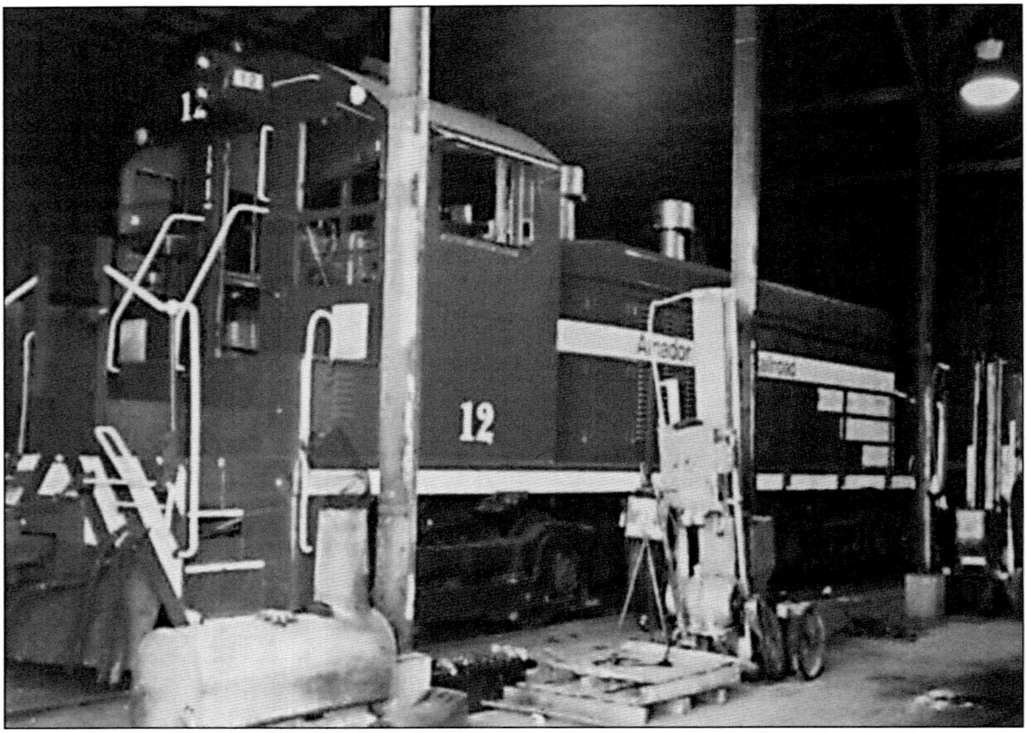

Amador Central No. 12, like No. 11, was built by the Electric Motive Diesel Company. This 1952, SW9 was built for the Arkansas & Louisiana Missouri Railway, which for a time was also owned by Georgia Pacific Industries. It then served on the Chattahoochee Industrial Railroad in Georgia. In 1997, after working on the Amador Central, it was moved to the Quincy Railroad, now owned by Sierra Pacific Industries. On the Quincy it retained the No. 12 designation. The top photograph was taken inside the shop building at the Martell depot. Below, the engine pulls a string of cars while working on the Quincy Railroad.

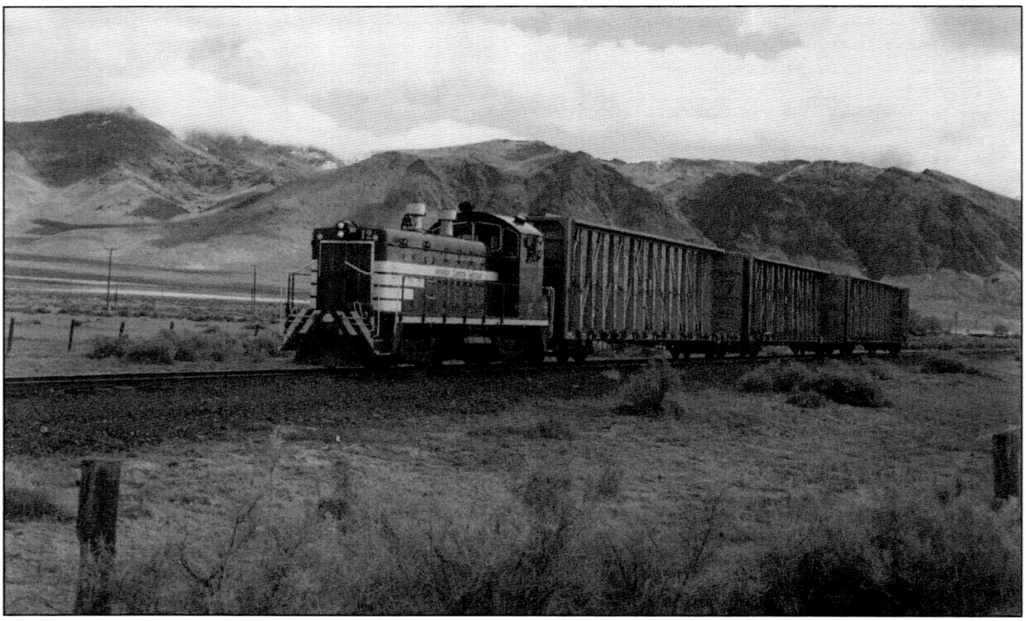

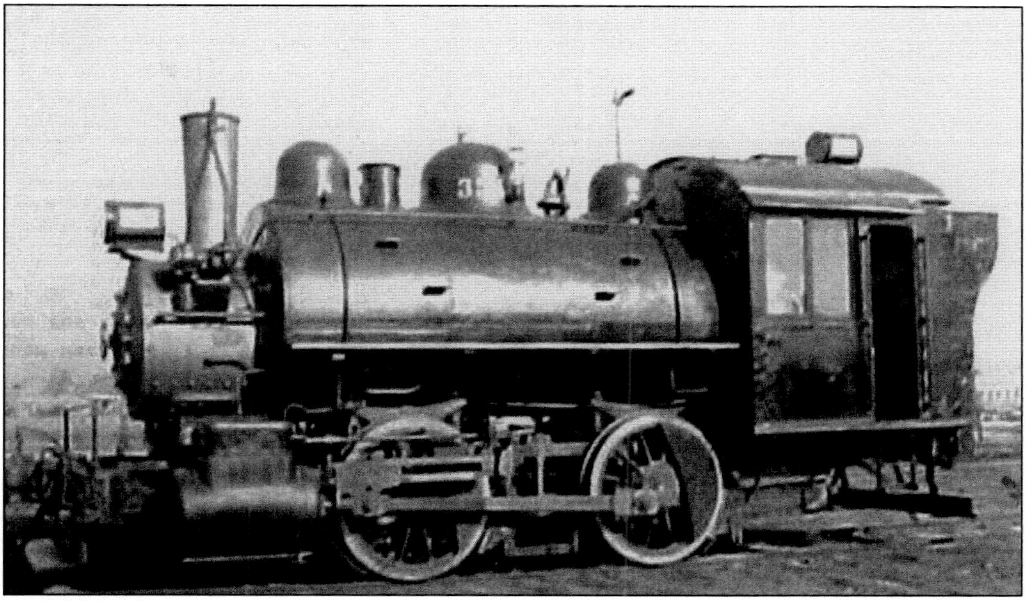

This tank engine, No. 334, served on the Amador Central for only a short time. It originally came from the Nevada Consolidated Copper Company and was rebuilt at the Martell shop, but was not intended for use on the Amador Central. When a large trestle between the firebrick plant and Ione burned, the engine was loaded on a truck and taken to Ione to do the switching between Ione and the burned trestle. It was eventually sold.

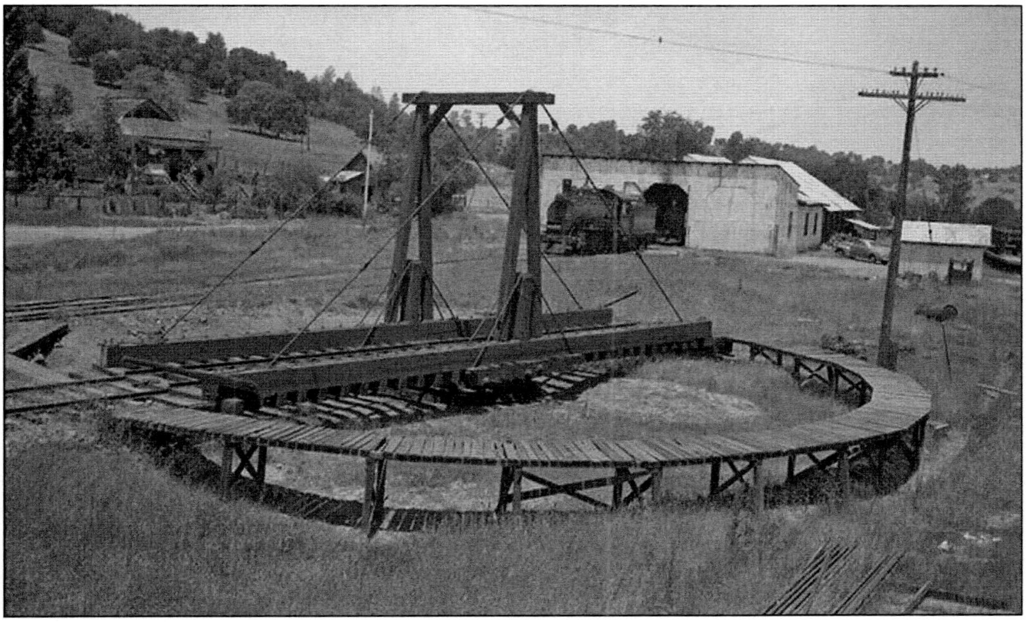

Pictured here is the first turntable built for the Ione & Eastern Railroad. Once an engine was centered over the wooden structure, it took four men to turn the engine for the return trip to Ione. This turntable was replaced with a steel model soon after the Winton Lumber Company purchased the railroad in 1945.

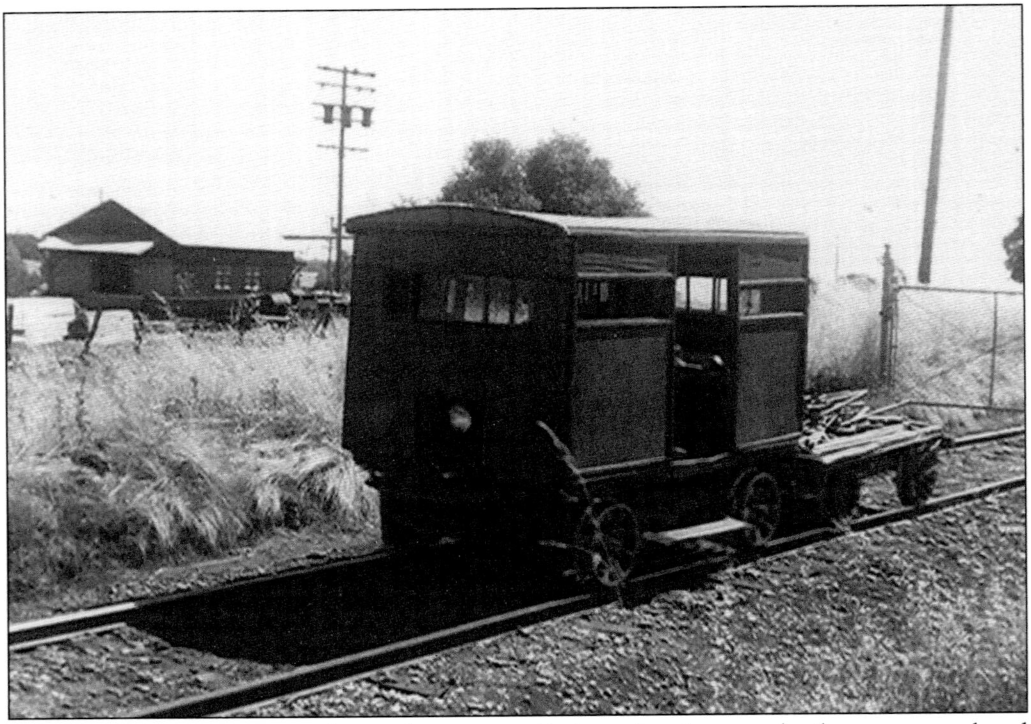

Railroad maintenance is a vital part of operations. Early on, hand-powered railcars were employed along the Ione & Eastern for maintenance. Later, a track work car, sometimes referred to as a speeder, was employed. The car shown in this photograph is parked with a utility trailer at the Martell depot.

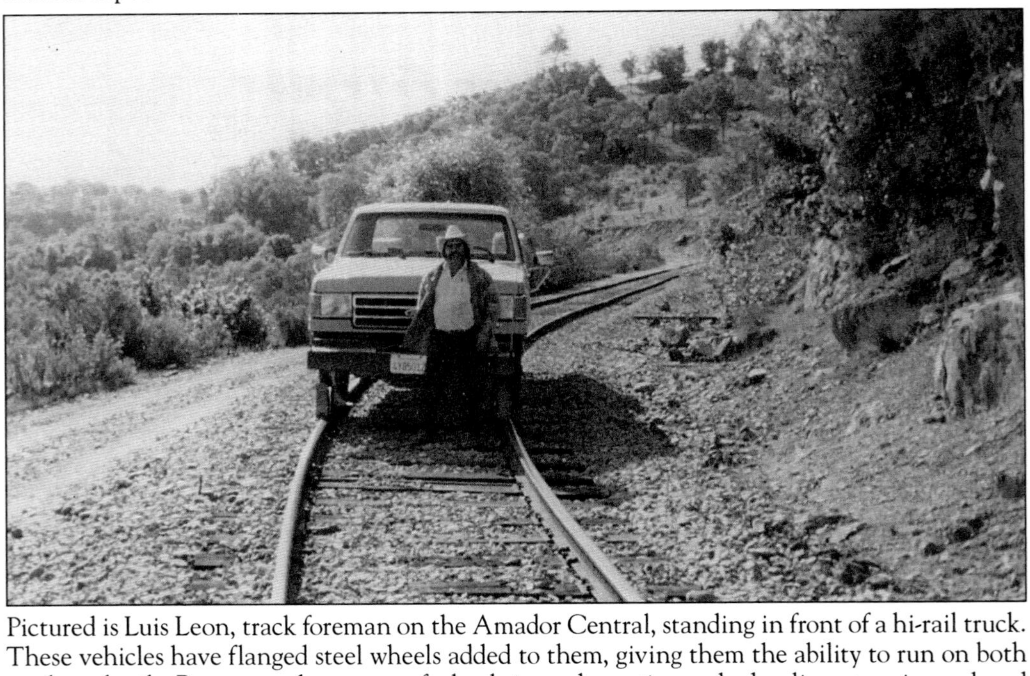

Pictured is Luis Leon, track foreman on the Amador Central, standing in front of a hi-rail truck. These vehicles have flanged steel wheels added to them, giving them the ability to run on both roads and rails. Because only one set of wheels is used at a time, a hydraulic system is employed to lower and raise the rail wheels.

Six

Ups and Downs of Running the Rails

Any business must be properly managed to succeed. From the time the Ione & Eastern was built, through its life as the Amador Central and as the Amador Foothills Railroad, its profitability was mercurial. Both poor decision making on the part of management and external economic trends defined periodic success and repeated failures. From 1905, when the railroad was completed, until World War II, the line experienced many financial ups and downs. It was not until after World War II that Amador Central became more cost-effective and financially sound.

In the beginning, the Ione & Eastern found success in transporting both passengers and freight. The prolific mining industry contributed a great deal to its success. The efficiency and comfort experienced by travelers was a welcome change to traveling by wagon. However, the company spent nearly every penny made, leaving it bankrupt and unable to pay on the bonds issued during construction. In 1908, the company failed. Charles Erickson, the contractor, purchased the line, and the Amador Central Railroad was born.

Over the next three decades, under the management of Erickson, and then his wife, Meta, after his death, the railroad found moderate success. Despite rocky times through the Great Depression and having to suspend passenger service, the company held on. In the mid-1930s, numerous losses from fires put the company under, and it applied to abandon the line. A new Amador Central Railroad Company was organized and took over. This company, too, found moderate success, but also experienced losses from fires. During World War II, when the mines were closed down, the railroad focused on hauling lumber for government contracts, which kept it solvent. Lumber continued to be the main revenue source for the Amador Central over the next five decades. The railroad changed hands three times, and with each sale, the lumber mill at Martell was included. In 1996, the mill was shut down. In 2004, Sierra Pacific Industries applied to abandon the line. A century of railroading in Amador County was about to come to an end.

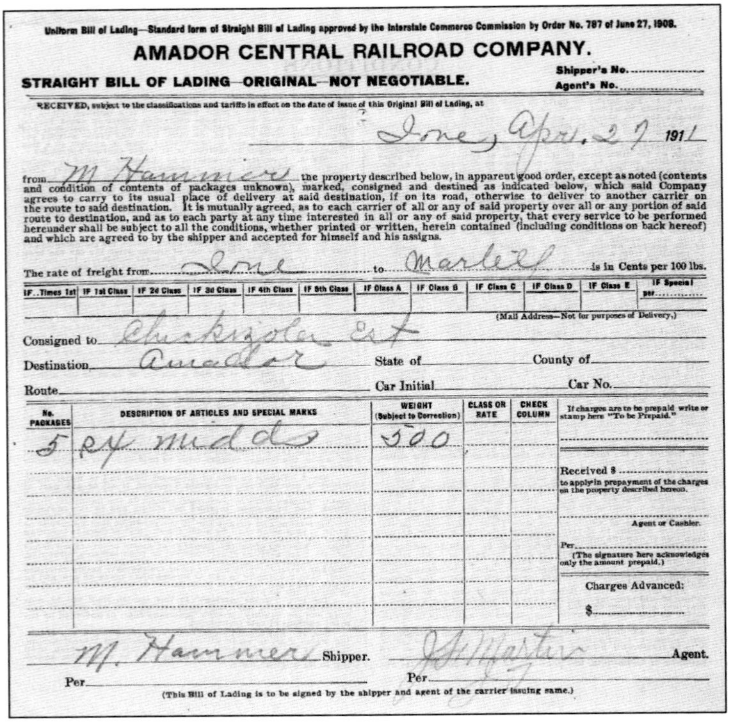
Uniform Bill of Lading—Standard form of Straight Bill of Lading approved by the Interstate Commerce Commission by Order No. 787 of June 27, 1908.

AMADOR CENTRAL RAILROAD COMPANY.

STRAIGHT BILL OF LADING—ORIGINAL—NOT NEGOTIABLE. Shipper's No. .... Agent's No. ....

RECEIVED, subject to the classifications and tariffs in effect on the date of issue of this Original Bill of Lading, at Ione, Apr. 27 1911

from M Hammer the property described below, in apparent good order, except as noted (contents and condition of contents of packages unknown), marked, consigned and destined as indicated below, which said Company agrees to carry to its usual place of delivery at said destination, if on its road, otherwise to deliver to another carrier on the route to said destination. It is mutually agreed, as to each carrier of all or any of said property over all or any portion of said route to destination, and as to each party at any time interested in all or any of said property, that every service to be performed hereunder shall be subject to all the conditions, whether printed or written, herein contained (including conditions on back hereof) and which are agreed to by the shipper and accepted for himself and his assigns.

The rate of freight from Ione to Martell is in Cents per 100 lbs.

IF..Times 1st	IF 1st Class	IF 2d Class	IF 3d Class	IF 4th Class	IF 5th Class	IF Class A	IF Class B	IF Class C	IF Class D	IF Class E	IF Special per........

(Mail Address—Not for purposes of Delivery.)

Consigned to Chickizola Est

Destination Amador State of County of

Route Car Initial Car No.

No. Packages	Description of Articles and Special Marks	Weight (Subject to Correction)	Class or Rate	Check Column	If charges are to be prepaid write or stamp here "To be Prepaid."
5	sx midds	500			

Received $ .... to apply in prepayment of the charges on the property described hereon.

Agent or Cashier.

Per........ (The signature here acknowledges only the amount prepaid.)

Charges Advanced: $........

M. Hammer Shipper. J. G. Martin Agent.

Per Per

(This Bill of Lading is to be signed by the shipper and agent of the carrier issuing same.)

Despite the early success of the Ione & Eastern, in 1908, the company went bankrupt when it failed to pay on bonds issued to Charles Erickson for building the railroad. Erickson purchased the railroad at a foreclosure sale on August 22, 1908, and incorporated the Amador Central Railroad. Within a few short years, the line became very profitable.

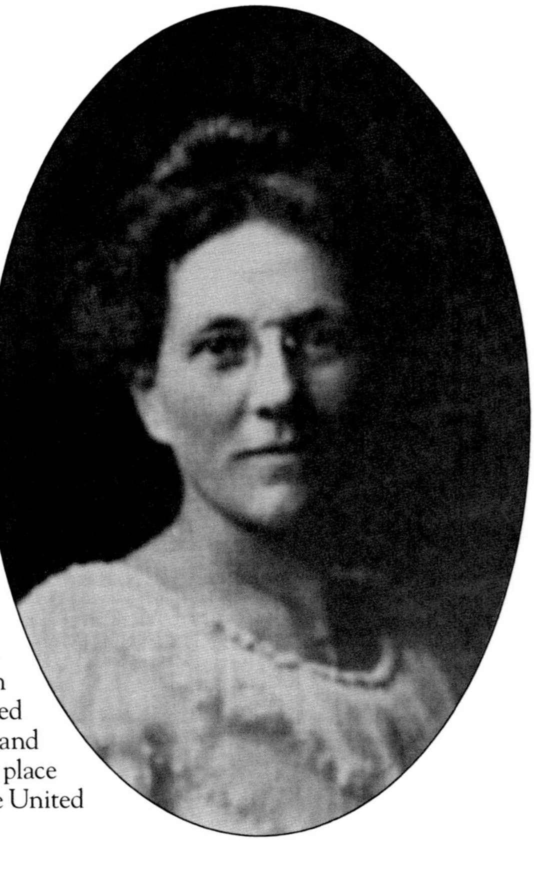

In 1908, with the purchase of the Ione & Eastern, Charles Erickson realized his dream of owning a railroad. However, his dream ended in 1910, when he was struck with appendicitis and died. His wife, Meta J. Erickson (right), took his place at the helm and became the first woman in the United States to serve as the president of a railroad.

Revenues for the Amador Central came from increases in both freight and passenger service. The railroad took advantage of special events in communities outside Amador County, pairing with Southern Pacific to offer special fares. This advertisment, like many others, appeared in a 1910 issue of the *Amador Ledger.*

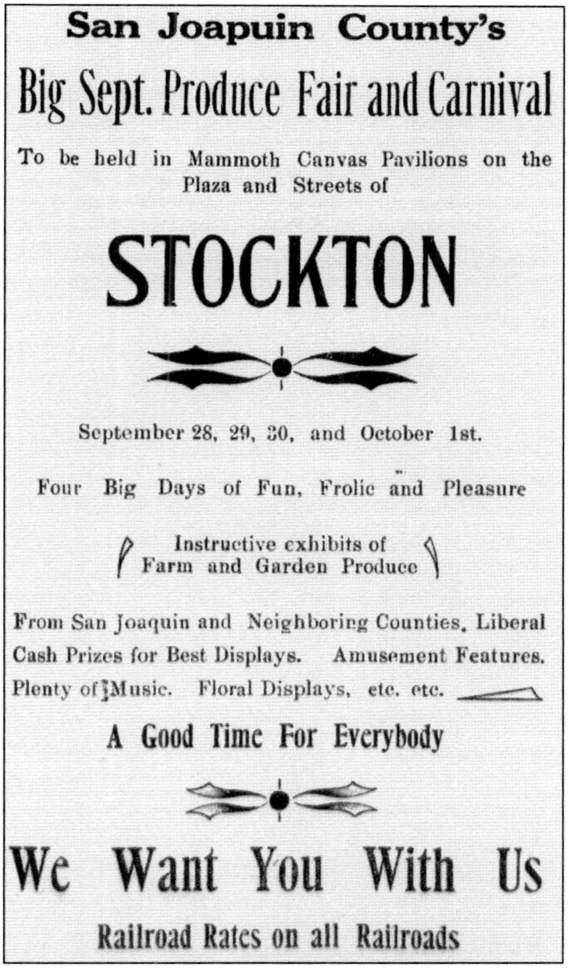

San Joapuin County's

Big Sept. Produce Fair and Carnival

To be held in Mammoth Canvas Pavilions on the Plaza and Streets of

STOCKTON

September 28, 29, 30, and October 1st.

Four Big Days of Fun, Frolic and Pleasure

Instructive exhibits of Farm and Garden Produce

From San Joaquin and Neighboring Counties. Liberal Cash Prizes for Best Displays. Amusement Features. Plenty of Music. Floral Displays, etc. etc.

A Good Time For Everybody

We Want You With Us

Railroad Rates on all Railroads

The railroad also brought in revenues from movie companies. This 1929 photograph was taken at the Martell depot during the filming of *Man Alone*, directed by the "Dean of Hollywood," Hobart Bosworth. He is best known in Amador for using the Argonaut Mine as a backdrop in the days leading up to the disastrous fire that claimed the lives of 47 miners in 1922.

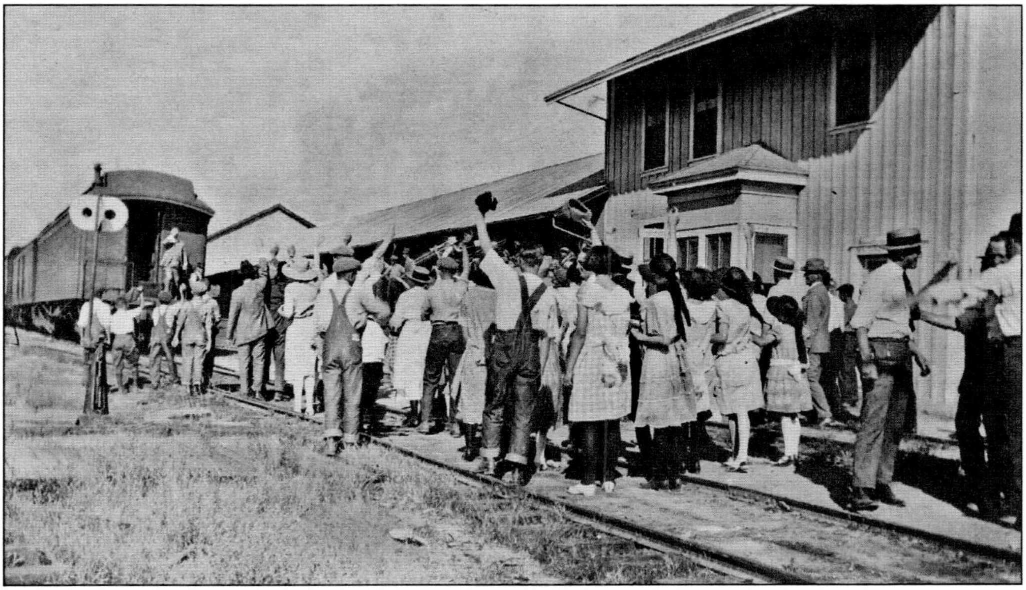

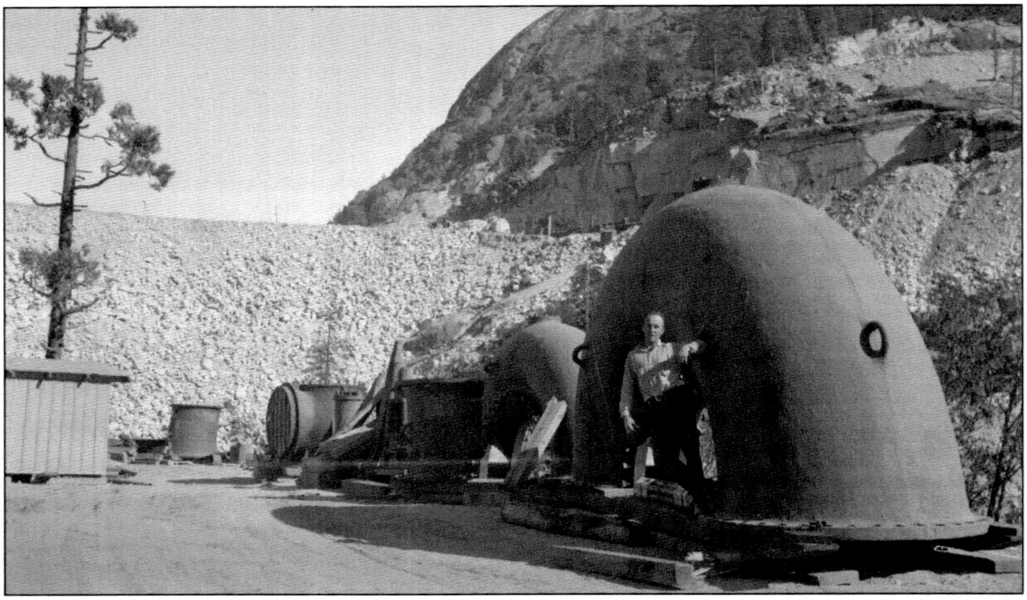

Much of the freight shipped by the Amador Central in the 1920s and 1930s was heavy machinery and building materials bound for the dams and powerhouses of the Mokelumne River Hydroelectric Project. In this photograph, a worker at the Salt Springs Reservoir project poses with large segments of pipe.

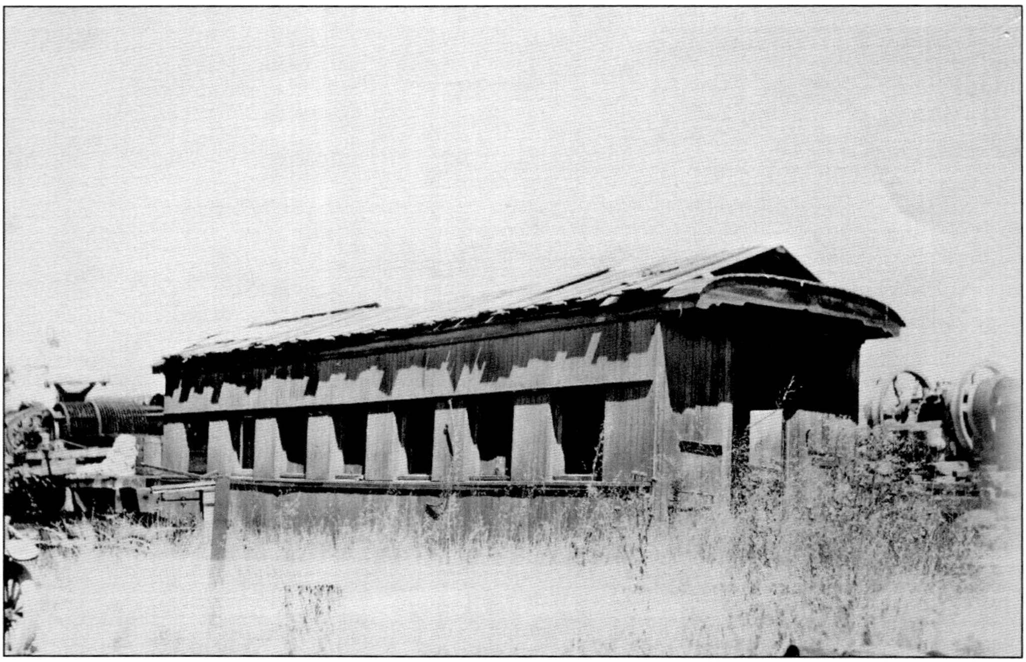

When the Great Depression hit, the Amador Central was not immune to its effects. Both freight and passenger service dropped off. In 1932, the Railroad Commission granted the line permission to suspend passenger service. In 1945, the California-Nevada Railroad Historical Society dismantled the interior of the Amador Central coaches to glean artifacts for preservation.

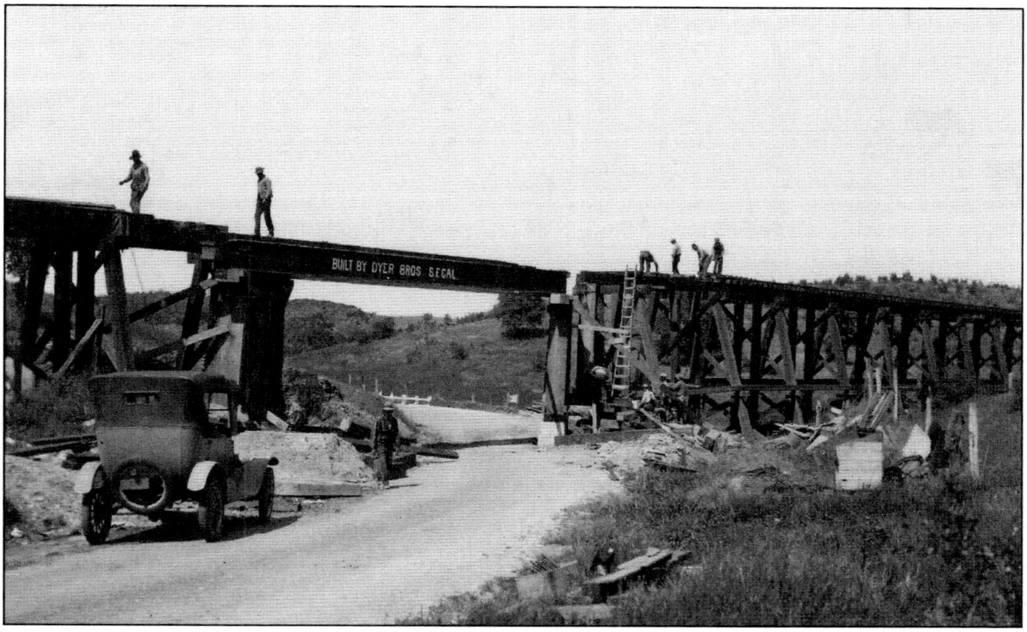

To the owners of the Amador Central, it seemed they were cursed during the Depression years. In addition to a loss of revenues, they experienced other setbacks. In 1935, the trestle that crossed the highway near Ranlett burned, leaving the railroad unable to move engines from Martell to Ione. At the time, the railroad was doing good business, shipping clay and bricks from the mines around Ione, and was now presented with the dilemma of how to move these products from the mines to the Ione depot for transfer to outbound Southern Pacific freights. To solve their problem, they loaded a small tank engine, No. 334, onto a flatbed trailer for transport and moved it to Ione (below). Above, crews work to rebuild the trestle across the highway.

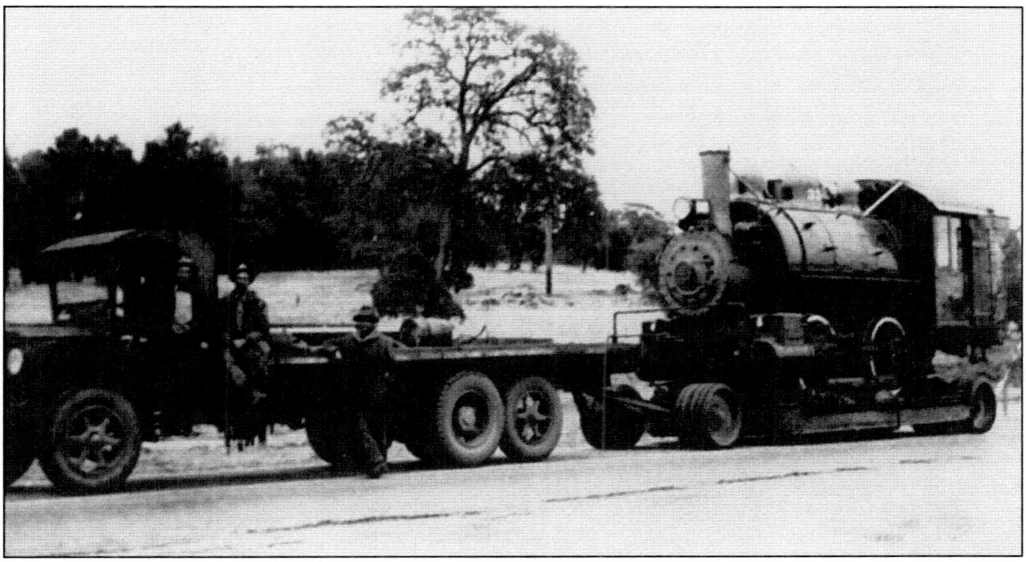

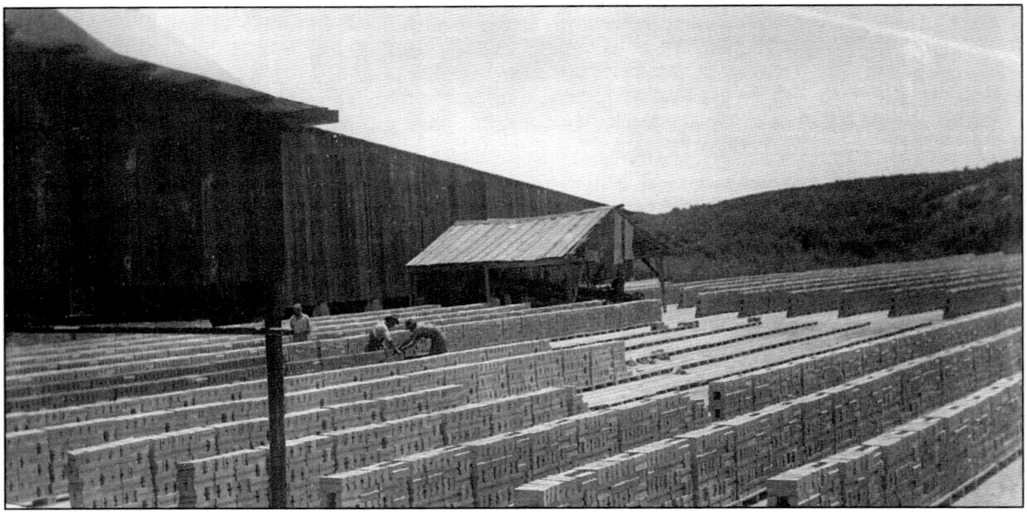

Fiscal instability plagued the Amador Central during the 1930s. Unable to fund operations, the company applied to abandon the line in 1938. The request was granted. Local businessmen then banded together and reorganized the railroad. The company now included the assets of the Ione Fire Brick Company and the Amador Lumber Company, both of which were doing a booming business. This is evident in the top photograph, taken at the firebrick plant, where millions of bricks sit drying in the sun before being loaded for shipment. A railroad siding was built to this site when the Ione & Eastern was constructed. The photograph below was taken at the Amador Lumber Company sawmill, located a short distance from the Martell depot.

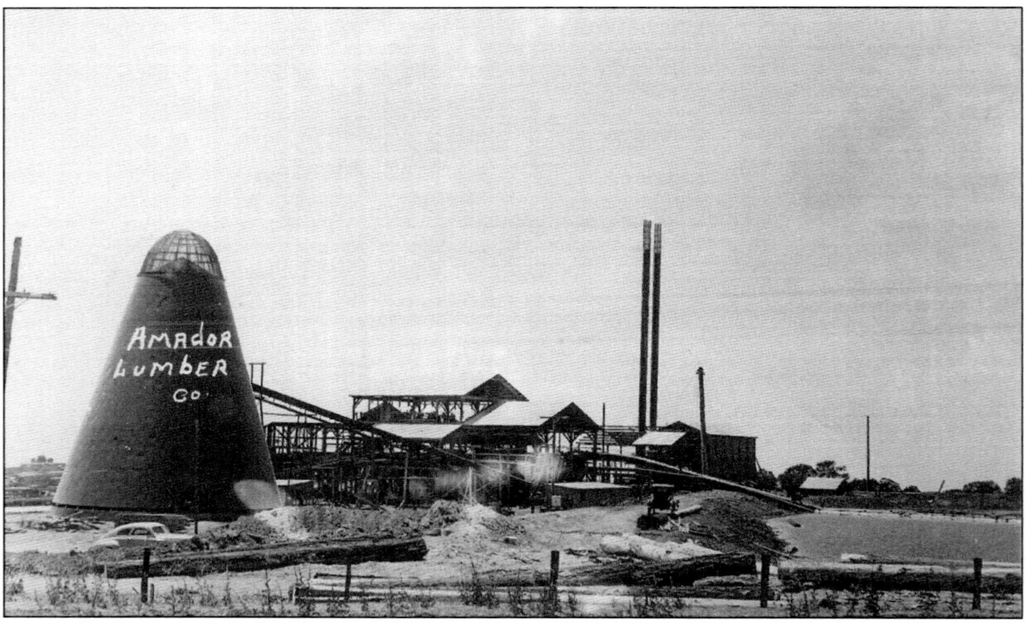

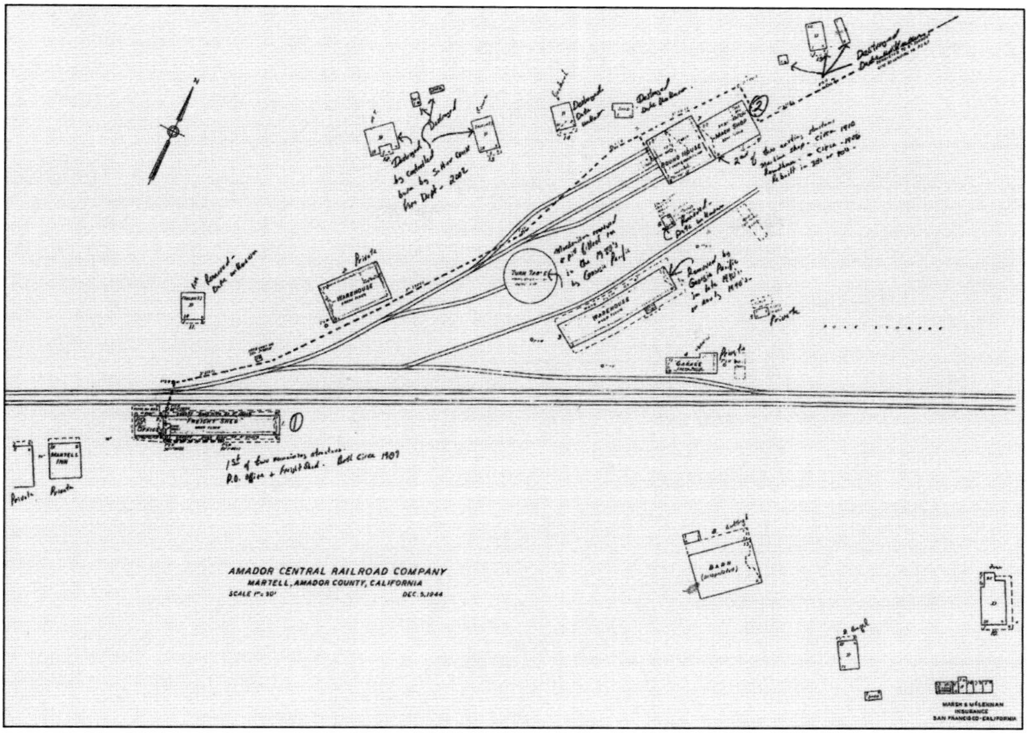

Under new ownership and the direction of general manager George Hark, the railroad set about making improvements. The roundhouse at the Martell site was refurbished, and a new car shop was built. Additionally, a regular maintenance program was established for all of the rolling stock. The map above shows the layout of buildings located at Martell. Below, engine No. 5 gets a good inspection by shop workers. The roundhouse shown in this photograph burned in 1939 and had to be replaced.

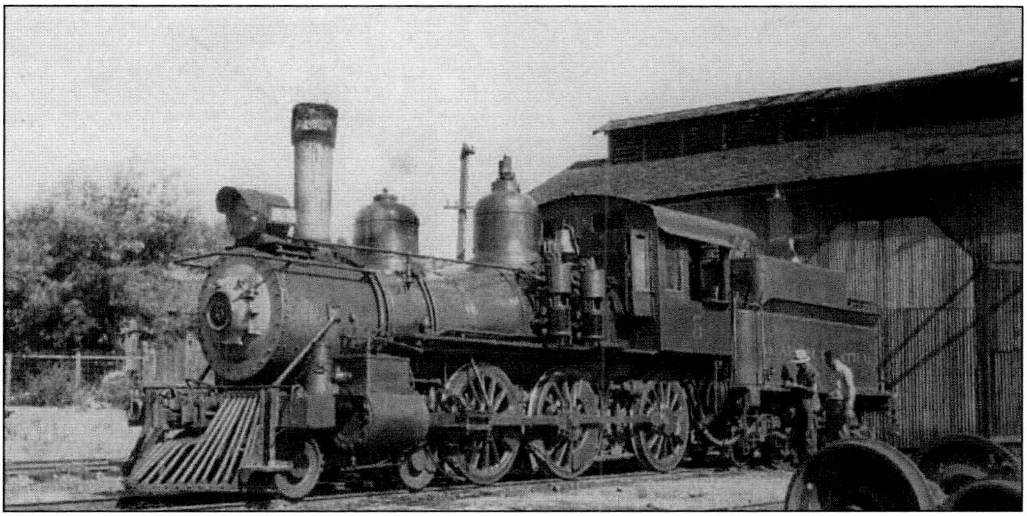

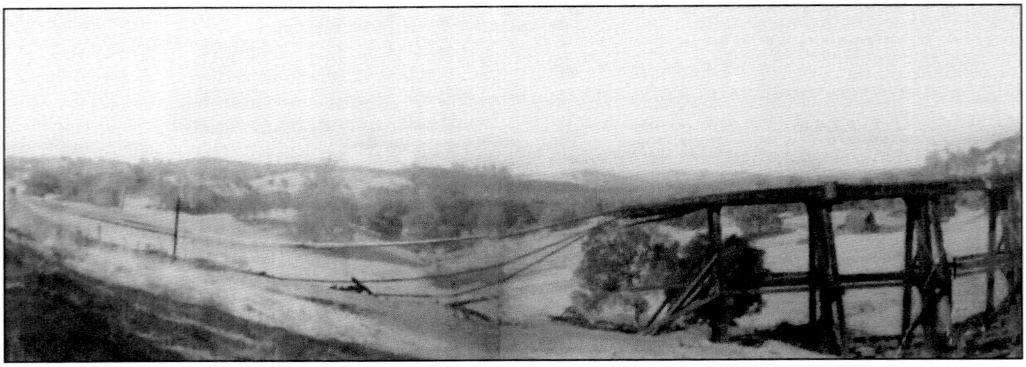

In 1939, within one month of the roundhouse at Martell catching on fire, two trestles on the Amador Central burned. The company employed a steam shovel and bulldozer to level ground, and new tracks were laid around the downed structures so trains were able to keep running. The photograph above was taken shortly after one of the fires.

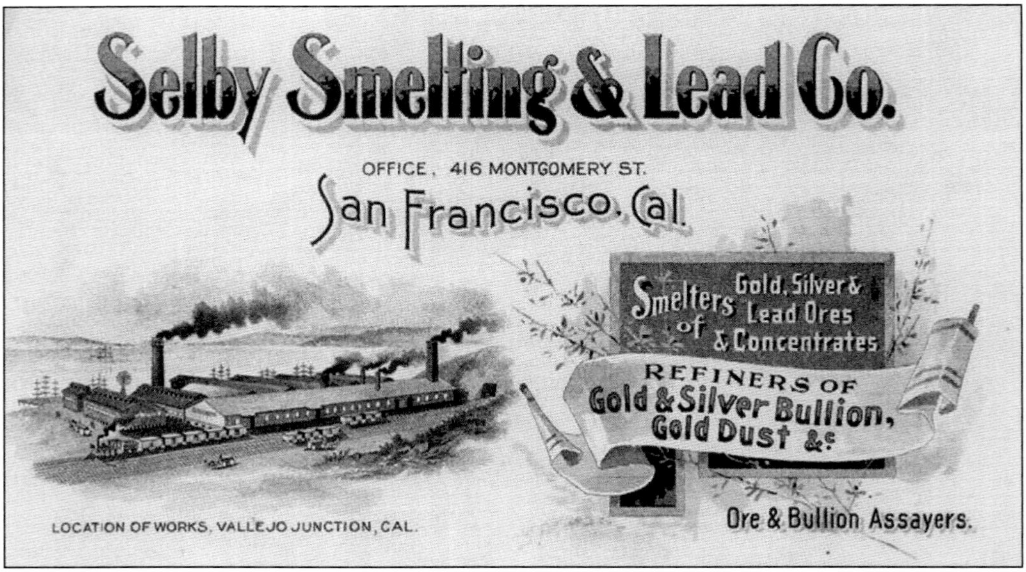

By 1940, business picked up for the railroad as many of the mines reopened; however, when World War II broke out, the railroad was hit hard. At the beginning of World War II, the trains moved as many as 20 cars of concentrates weekly to the Selby Smelting & Lead Company near Oakland. Then, when the War Production Board issued Limitation Order L-208, all of the mines shut down and the railroad was set back once again.

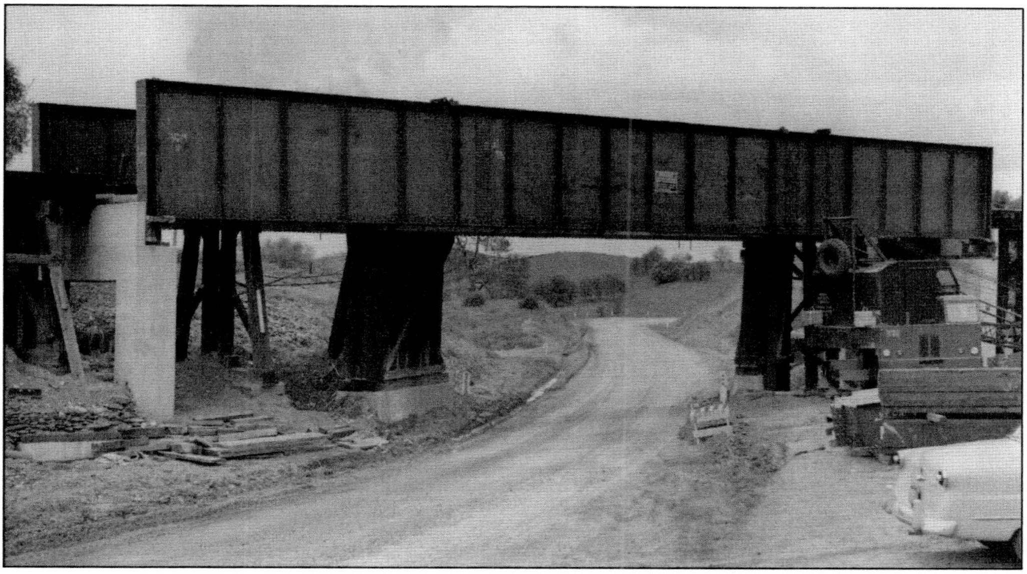

Despite financial hardships during the war, the Amador Central managed to keep its trains moving. In 1945, the Winton Lumber Company purchased the railroad and the Amador Lumber Company. The lumber business was booming in Amador County. Government contracts for lumber had been acquired during the war years and continued after the war. The new owners replaced nearly all of the 45-pound rails with heavier weights and completed much-needed bridge work along the line, including rebuilding the trestle over the highway near Ranlett. Winton also purchased engine No. 8 at this time, the first diesel to run on the line. Above, work is partially completed on the bridge replacement. The photograph of No. 8 (below) was taken at the Martell depot a few years after it was purchased.

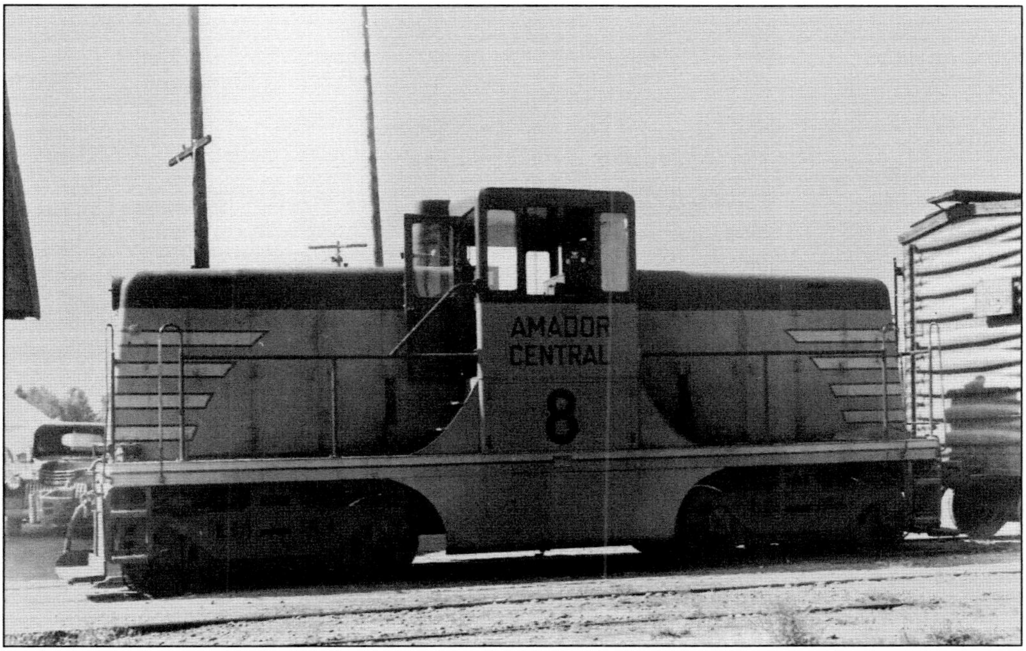

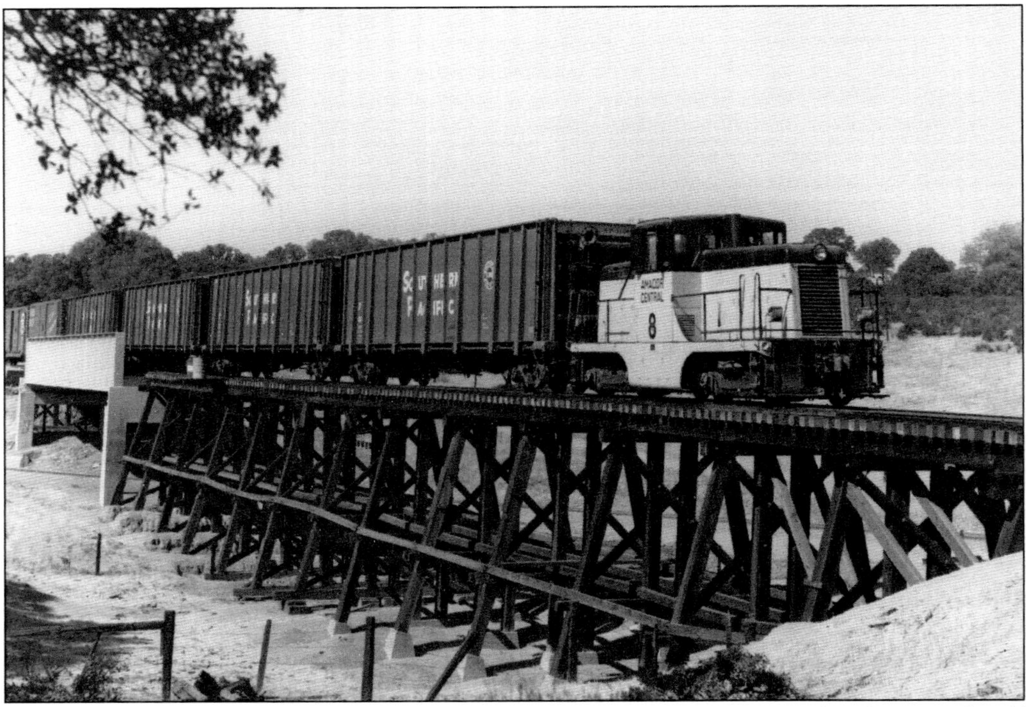

The lumber business continued to boom for the Amador Central. Logs arrived at the Martell mill by the truckload, and lumber was shipped out by the trainload. Over the next 59 years, ownership of the railroad and the lumber company would change three times. Principal operations of the Amador Central during this time were almost completely dependent on the lumber industry. In 1996, the lumber mill at Martell shut down, leaving only a particleboard plant in operation at the site. Then, in 2004, Sierra Pacific Industries applied for abandonment of the line. The top photograph shows engine No. 8 pulling a load to Ione in 1962. Below, engine No. 10 heads for Ione with mixed freight, including sawdust.

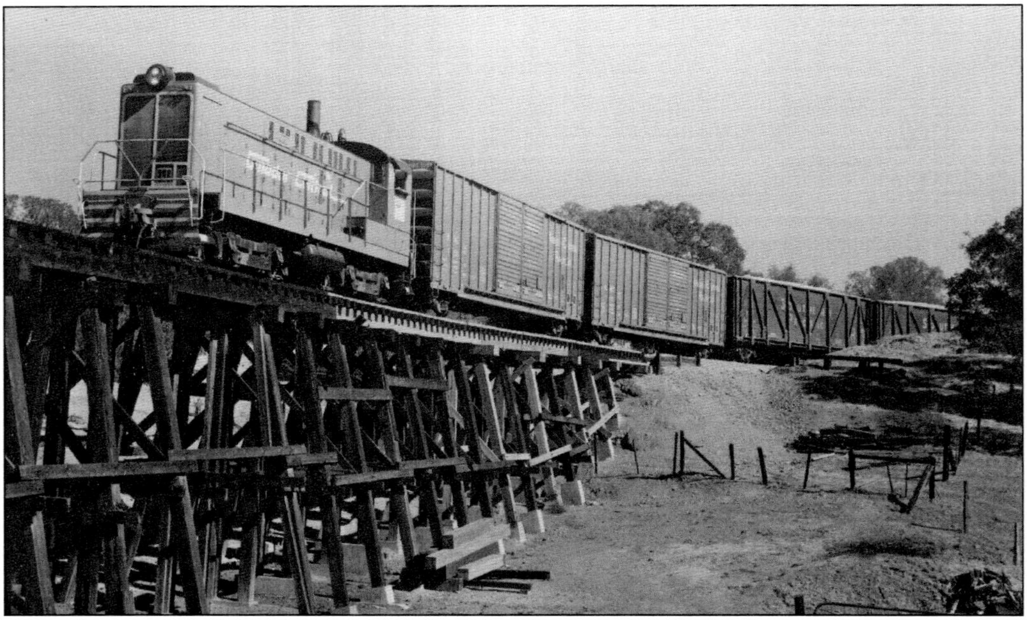

Seven

Hooray for the Timber!

The Amador Central seemed to be doomed from the start. Over its 100-year lifetime, it continually fell victim to mismanagement and economic trends. It changed hands a total of six times—twice because of financial failure. Passenger service came and went. Likewise, freight contracts with the mining industry went up and down. When the Mokelumne River Hydroelectric project was completed, the railroad lost a great deal of revenue. In its continuous battle to stay afloat, the one business that could be counted on was the lumber industry.

Many of the early promoters of building a railroad in Amador were lumbermen, eager to make money. Moving timber was one of the greatest challenges to logging companies. By the turn of the 20th century, many companies had constructed railroads in the Sierra to move timber from where it was felled to mountain sawmills. However, transport to markets far from mill sites still presented problems. One of the goals of the original builders of the Ione & Eastern was to extend the line into the mountains. As late as the 1940s, there was still talk of doing this. Hoping to build an extension from Martell to Pine Grove, the Amador Lumber Company actually had a route surveyed and maps prepared. Unfortunately, this never came to fruition; however, the company soon found it could do a booming business without the added track.

During World War II, lumber contracts were awarded to the Amador Lumber Company. When it sold out to Winton Lumber in 1945, the contracts continued, and the railroad reaped the benefits of the postwar building boom. Over the next four decades, under the ownership of some of the biggest corporations in the lumber business, wood products were the freight that kept the Amador Central running. However, by the 1990s, federal government policies that curbed logging in old-growth forests and endangered habitats impacted the lumber business. The mill at Martell closed down in 1997. A particleboard plant at the site continued to operate and haul products via the rail line until 2004, when the last run was made and the line was abandoned by Sierra Pacific Industries.

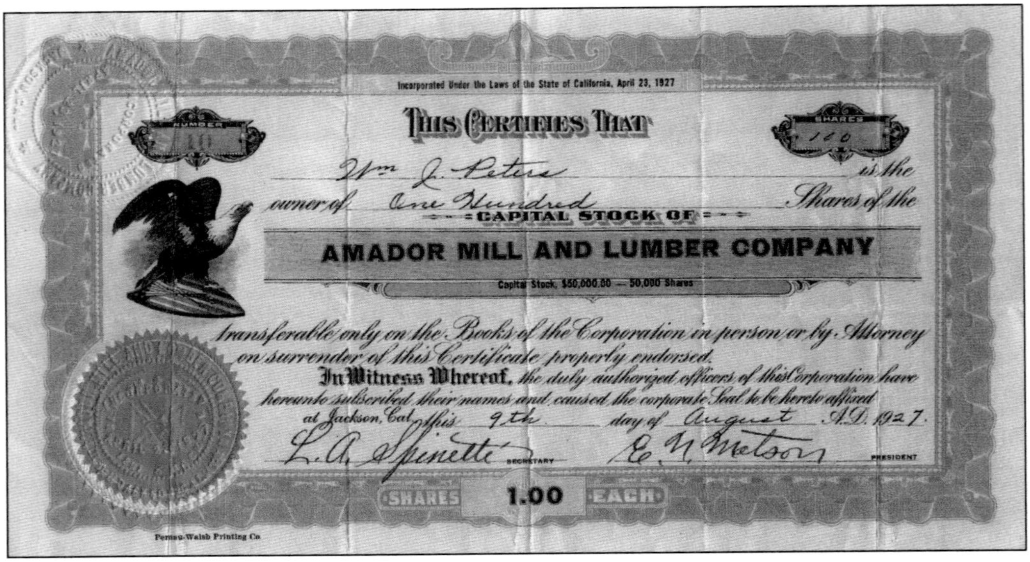

From the beginning, lumber companies had a vested interest in bringing a railroad into the center of Amador County. The Amador Lumber Company was one of the earliest organized in Amador. In 1879, it was a part of the larger conglomerate that included the Amador Canal and Mining Company and the Sutter and Amador Water Works. With the coming of the railroad, it hoped to expand its interests. During construction of the Ione & Eastern, local newspapers were littered with articles about extending the railroad into the timber country. The stock certificate shown above was one of many issued by the company, which went through several reorganizations over its lifetime. The map section below marks the route of a proposed rail extension into Pine Grove, commissioned by the Amador Lumber Company in about 1940.

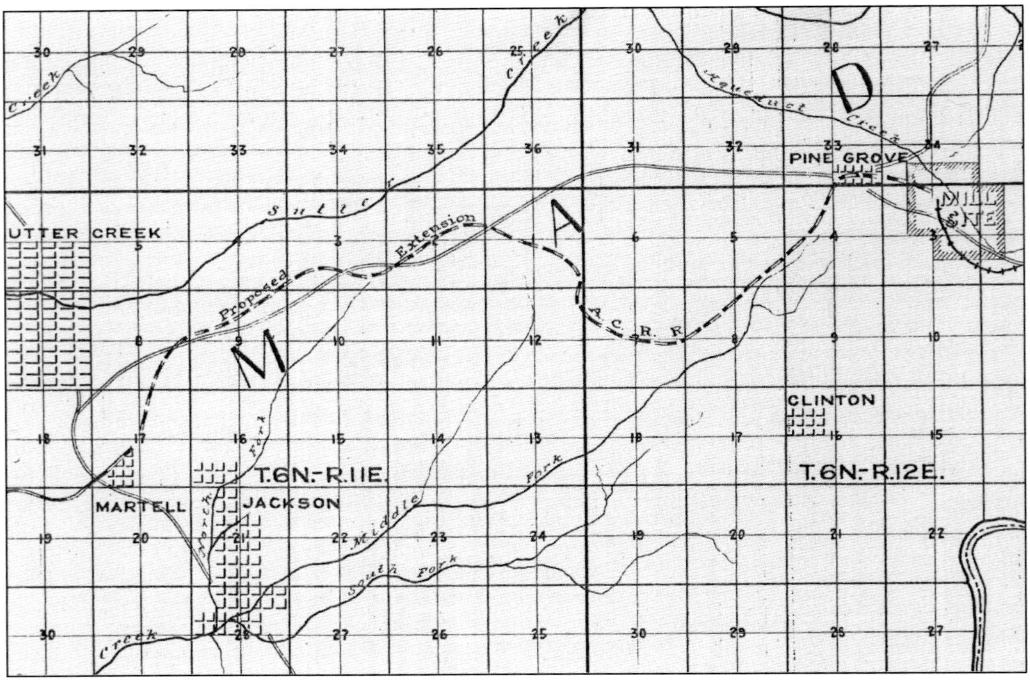

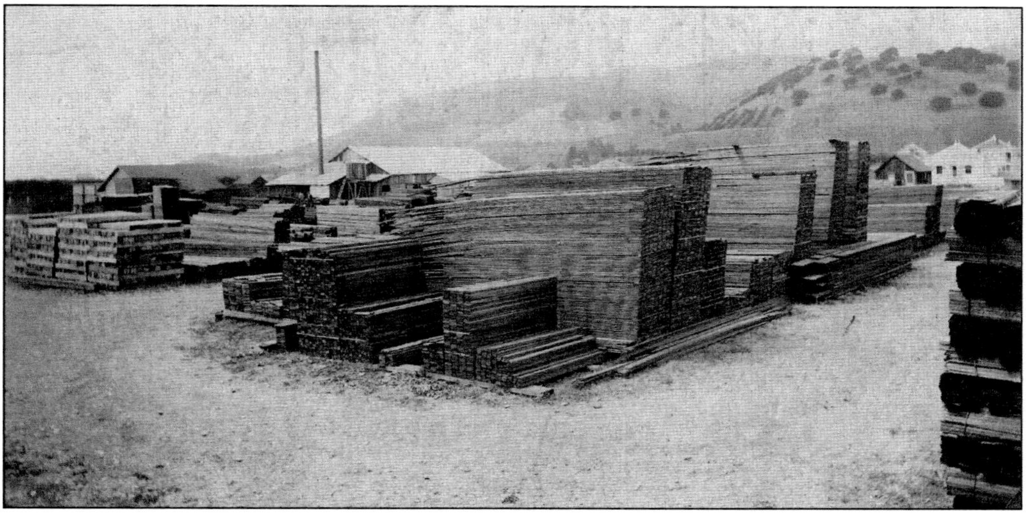

Another lumber interest that supported building an extension into the mountains was owned by Charles Edward Fournier. Fournier was the contractor who built the first two passenger coaches used on the Ione & Eastern (his photograph appears on page 74). Pictured here is a view of Fournier's mill and lumber yard, once located near Sutter Creek.

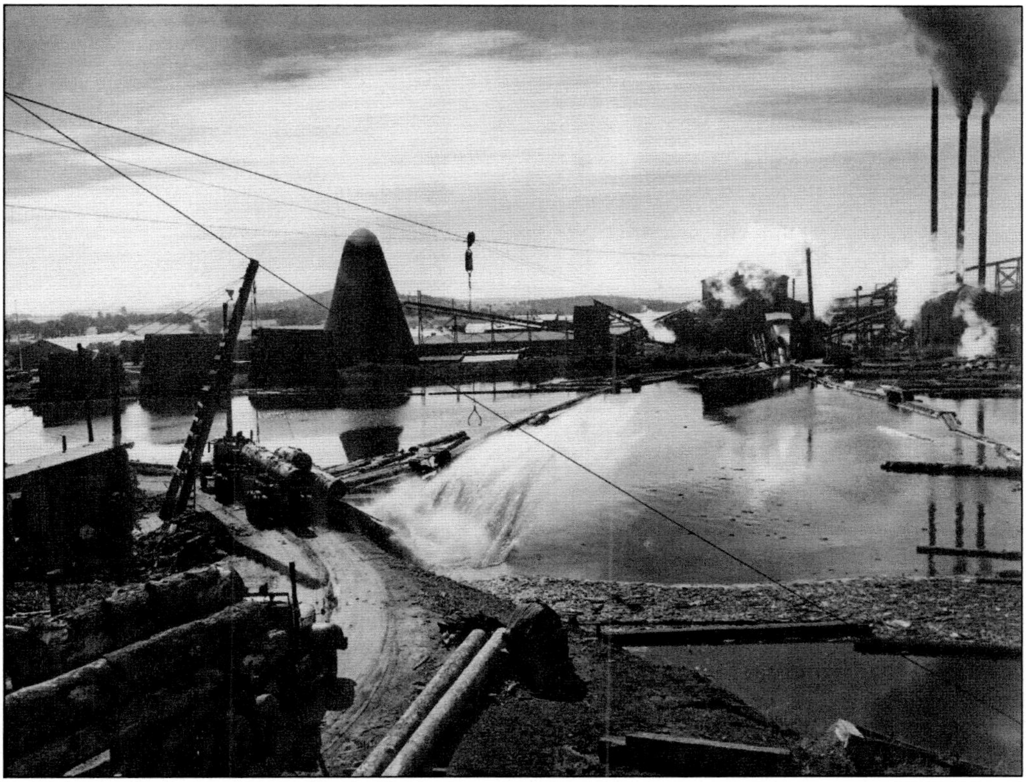

The railroad extension to the Sierra timber stands was never built; however, the lumber industry was determined to take advantage of transport via the Amador Central. In 1941, the Winton Lumber Company constructed a mill next to the rail line, just a short distance west of the Martell depot. In the photograph above, taken in about 1950, logs roll from a truck into the pond at the mill site.

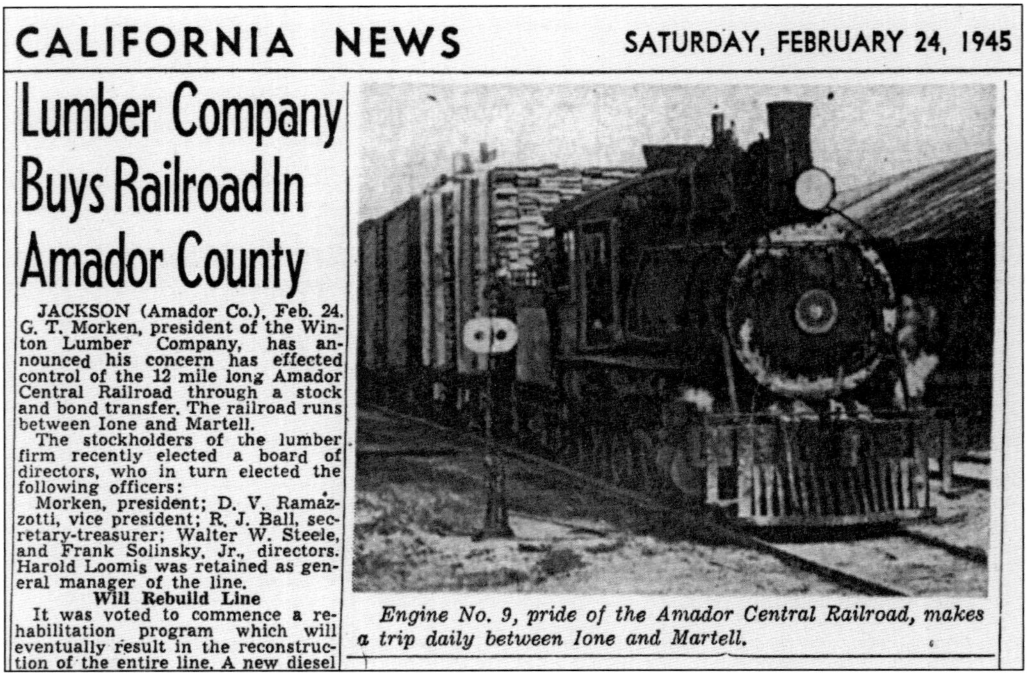

CALIFORNIA NEWS SATURDAY, FEBRUARY 24, 1945

Lumber Company Buys Railroad In Amador County

JACKSON (Amador Co.), Feb. 24. G. T. Morken, president of the Winton Lumber Company, has announced his concern has effected control of the 12 mile long Amador Central Railroad through a stock and bond transfer. The railroad runs between Ione and Martell.

The stockholders of the lumber firm recently elected a board of directors, who in turn elected the following officers:

Morken, president; D. V. Ramazzotti, vice president; R. J. Ball, secretary-treasurer; Walter W. Steele, and Frank Solinsky, Jr., directors. Harold Loomis was retained as general manager of the line.

Will Rebuild Line

It was voted to commence a rehabilitation program which will eventually result in the reconstruction of the entire line. A new diesel

Engine No. 9, pride of the Amador Central Railroad, makes a trip daily between Ione and Martell.

Through World War II, the Winton Lumber Company leased the Amador Central and kept the trains running. Large amounts of lumber were shipped for the war effort under government contracts. In 1945, it was announced that Winton had purchased the railroad through a stock and bond transfer. This article appeared in the *Sacramento Bee*.

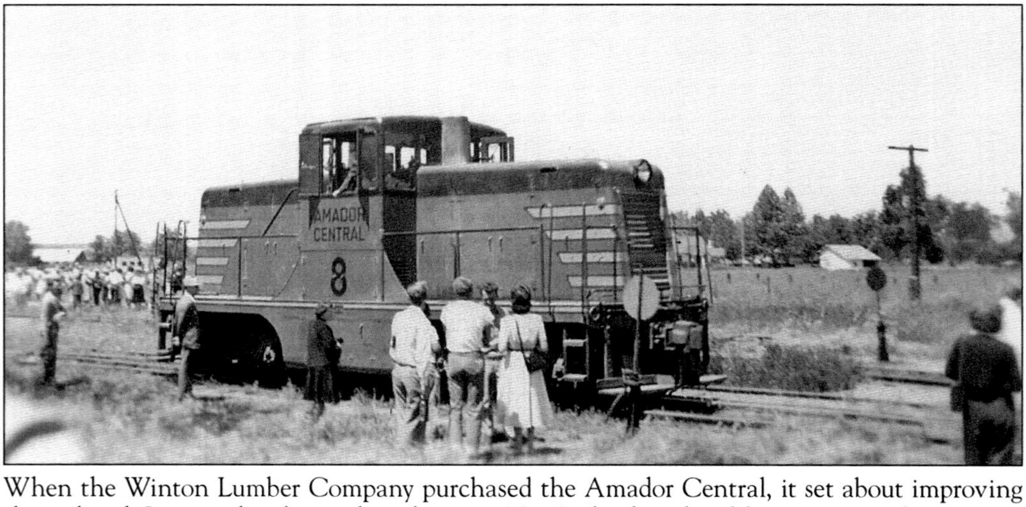

When the Winton Lumber Company purchased the Amador Central, it set about improving the railroad. It immediately purchased engine No. 8, the first diesel locomotive to be put into service on the line. In this photograph, spectators come out in number to see the new engine on its arrival in Ione.

From 1945 until 1964, Winton Lumber Company brought jobs—and a much needed postwar economic boost—to Amador County. With improvements in operations and equipment, it hauled thousands of feet of timber out of the Sierra. Employing a large fleet of trucks, such as the one pictured at right in about 1950, the company provided a constant supply of milled lumber to fill boxcars of the Amador Central. Soon after the arrival of No. 8 on the Amador Central, No. 7, known as Iron Ivan, was put to pasture. That the faithful old steam engine had become obsolete in the new age of diesel became evident when Iron Ivan needed the assistance of No. 8 to help him pull an excursion train from Ione to Martell in 1948. In the photograph below, Ivan awaits his fate at the Martell yard.

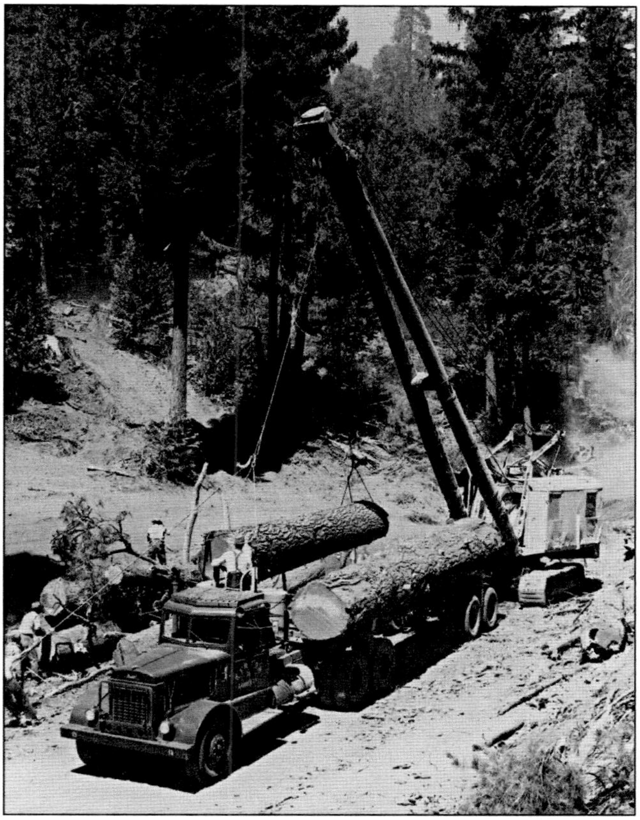

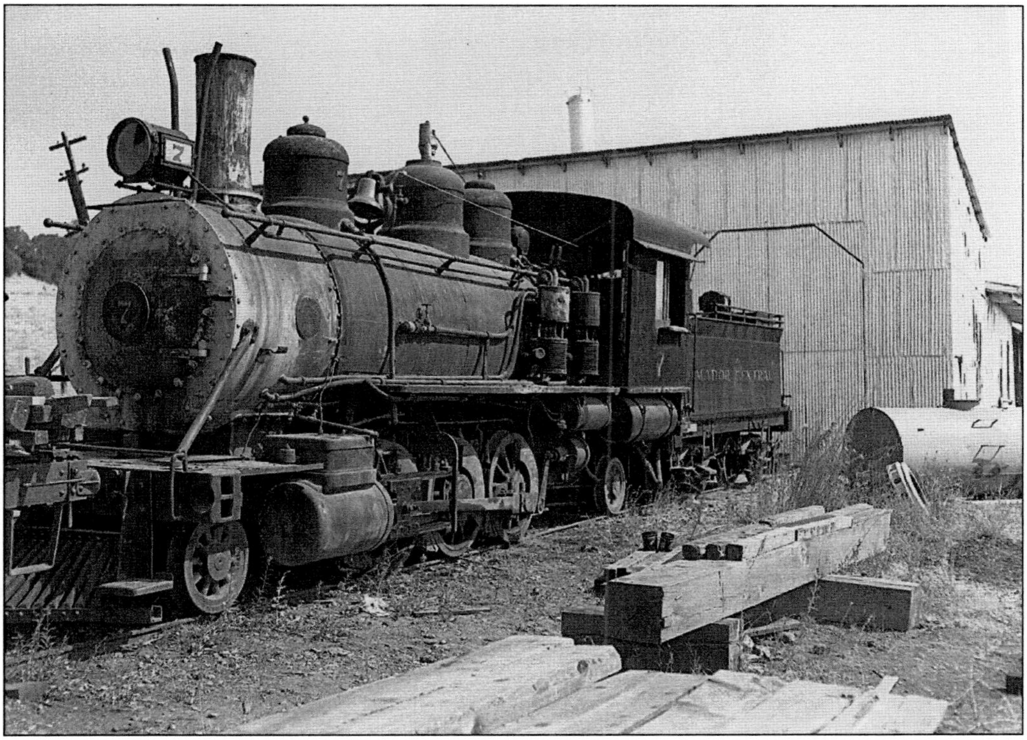

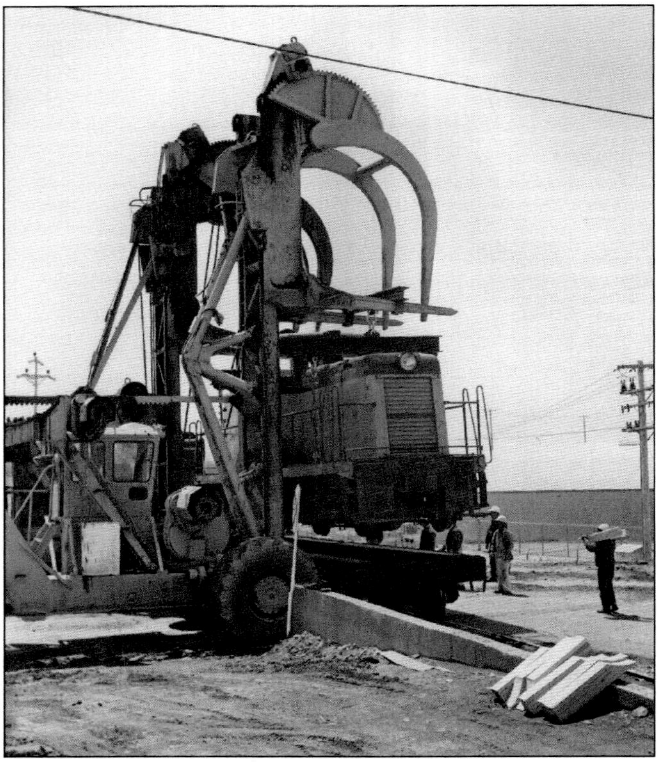

In 1964, American Forest Products purchased the assets of the Winton Lumber Company. By this time, many technological improvements had been made in both the railroading and the lumber business, including the ability to move locomotives without a turntable. At left, engine No. 8 is moved with the help of a log loader. Pictured below is an aerial view of the Martell lumber mill when owned by American Forest Products. The rail line came into the mill from the Martell depot, just behind the molding and trim mill, shown in the photograph as the long, narrow building oriented right to left near the top of the photograph, right of center. The Martell depot is the cluster of buildings at the top left.

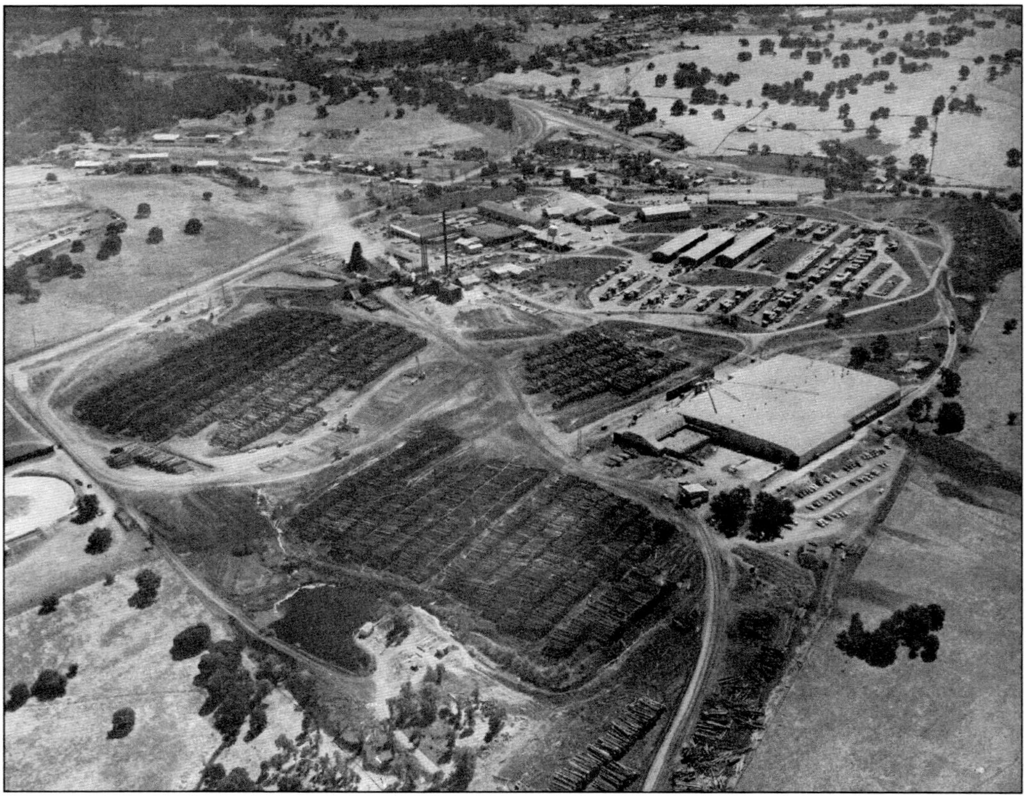

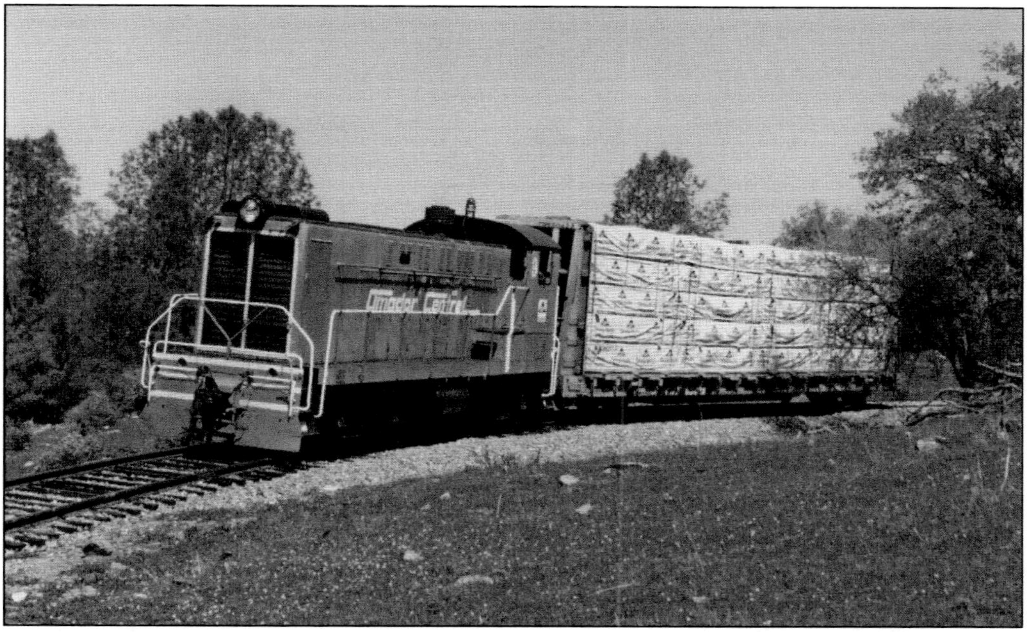

In 1988, the holdings of American Forest Products were sold to Georgia Pacific Industries. Shipments of wood products increased under the new ownership. In 1992, the Amador Central pulled 600 carloads of lumber products out of Martell. However, within four years, business fell off, and Georgia Pacific closed the mill in December 1996. In this 1993 photograph, engine No. 10 heads to Ione, pulling a flat car loaded with Georgia Pacific product.

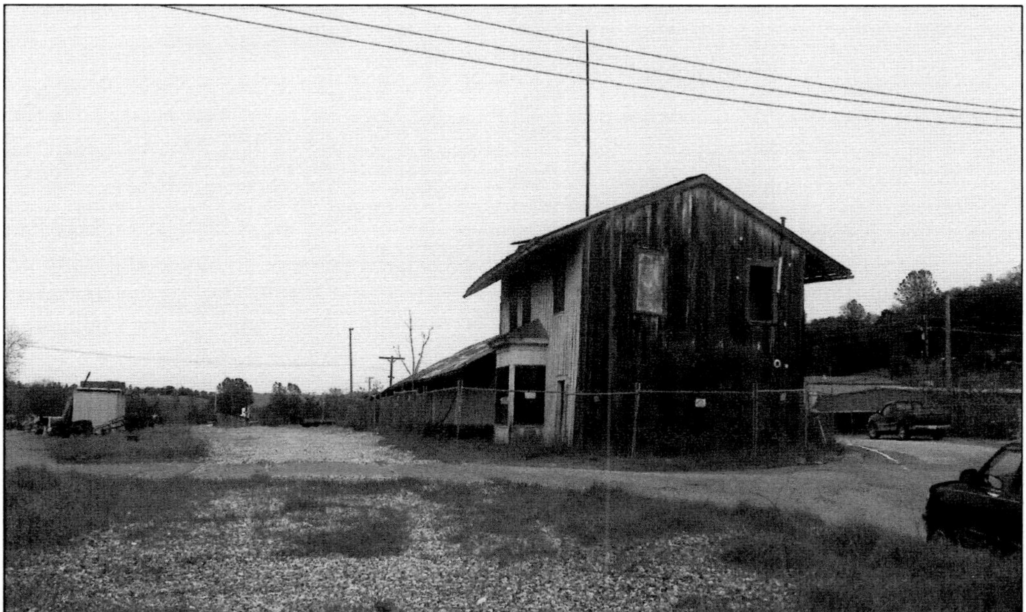

Under the ownership of Georgia Pacific, all of the freight shipped out of the Martell area originated at the mill site, leaving the Martell depot to fall into a state of decay. Today, the depot sits, ever so slightly listing, circled by a fence put up to keep out vandals. The wide avenue of gravel to the left of the building marks the route of the tracks that were removed in 2009.

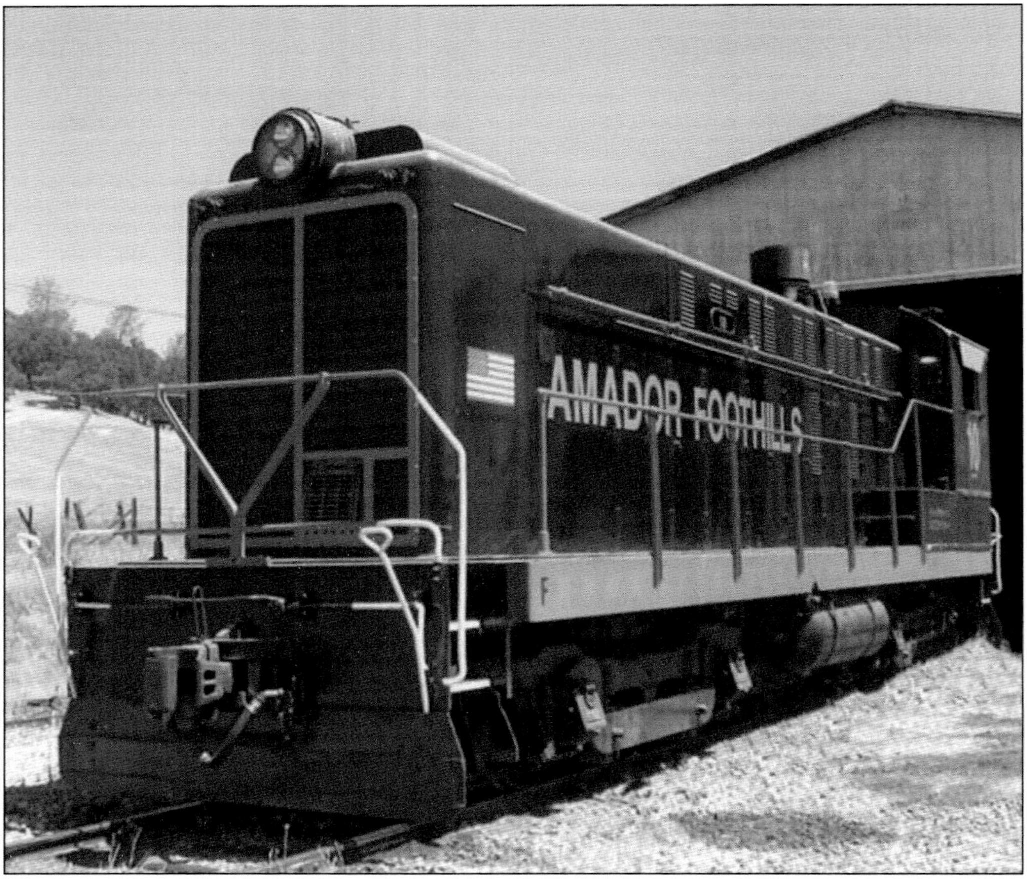

In 1997, the Amador Central once again came under new ownership when Sierra Pacific Industries bought out Georgia Pacific. In addition to the railroad, the sale included the Martell lumber mill and particleboard plant and 127,000 acres of timberland in Amador County. The following year, Sierra Pine purchased the particleboard plant and leased the railroad from Sierra Pacific. It was at this time that the name of the line was changed to the Amador Foothills Railroad. In 2004, Sierra Pine allowed its lease to lapse and on May 10, 2004, the last train to run on the line made the trip from Martell to Ione. Above, engine No. 10 sits at the Martell depot prior to making that last trip. The bottom photograph shows No. 10 pulling a line of cars over the State Route 88 trestle for the last time.

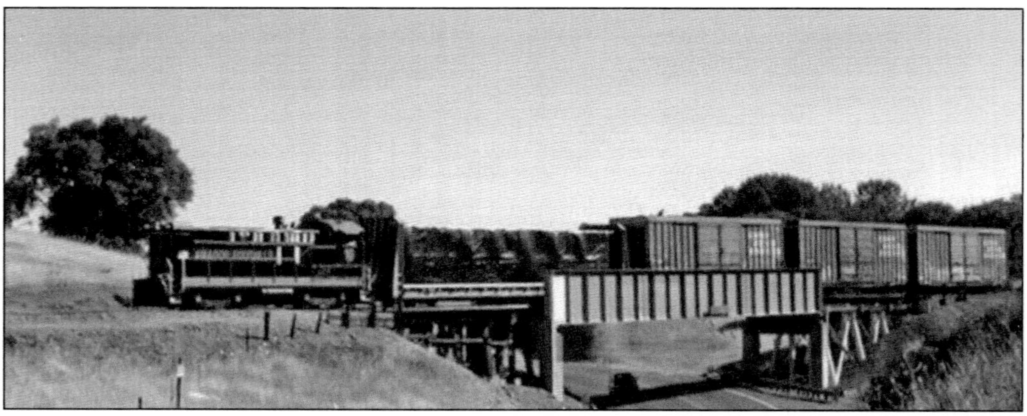

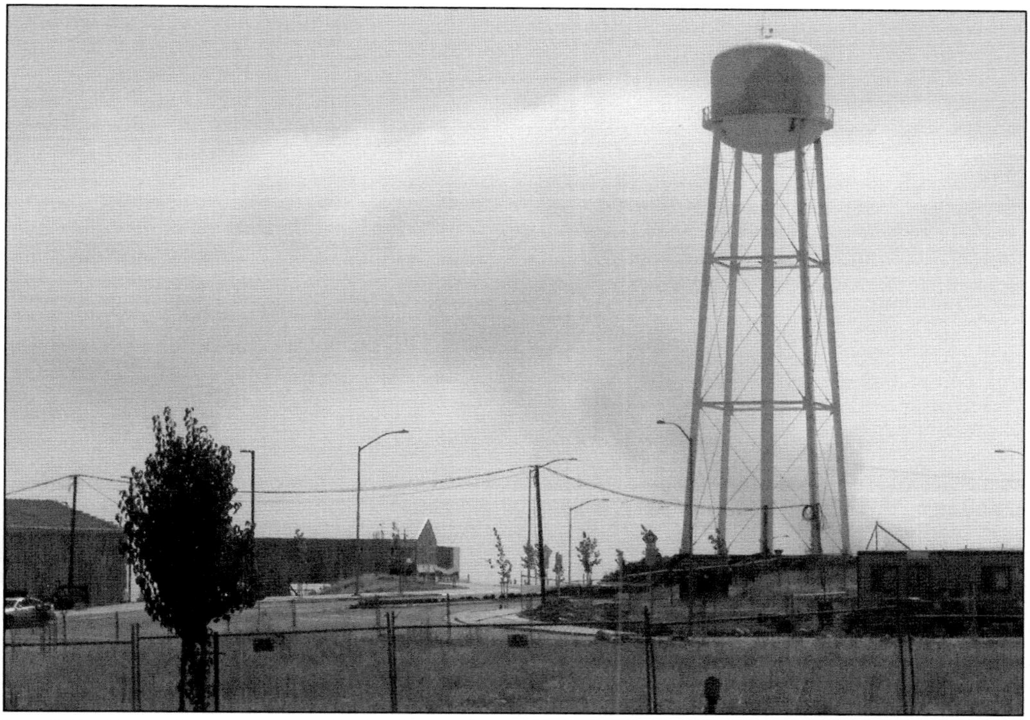

In 1998, Sierra Pine purchased the Martell particleboard plant from Sierra Pacific Industries and leased the railroad. The sawmill was not part of the sale. Within a few years, the mill was dismantled, the property sold, and a shopping center built at the site. All that remains of the mill is the water tower that now stands at the center of a roundabout at the shopping center.

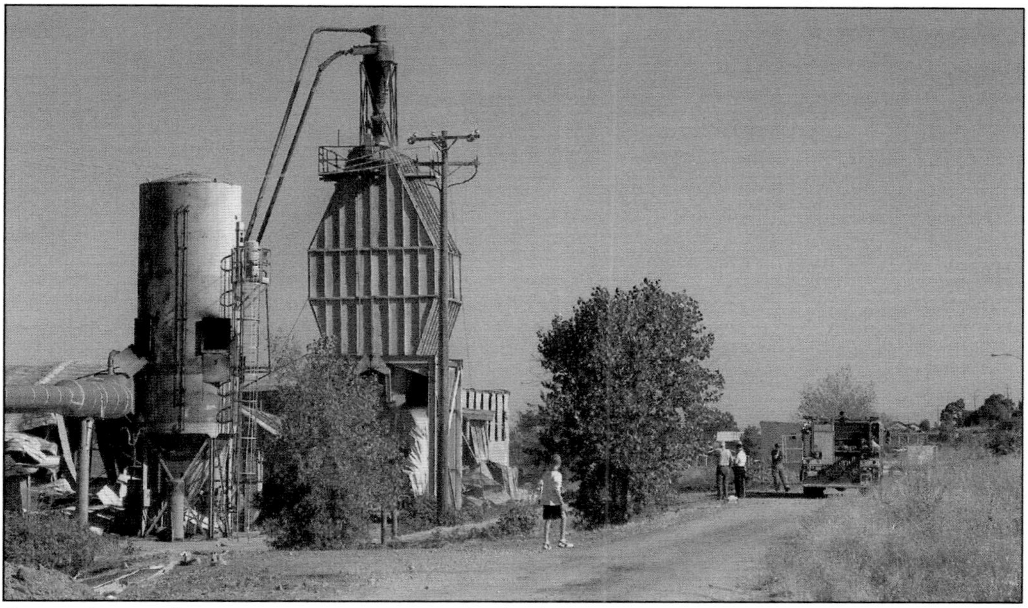

On an August day in 2007, at 1:00 a.m., a fire broke out in the cabinet making building at the Sierra Pine facility, further reducing the wood product industry in Amador County. It took about 50 firefighters nearly four hours to put down the blaze. This photograph was taken by the author on the day of the fire, while fire crews were still mopping up. (Author's collection.)

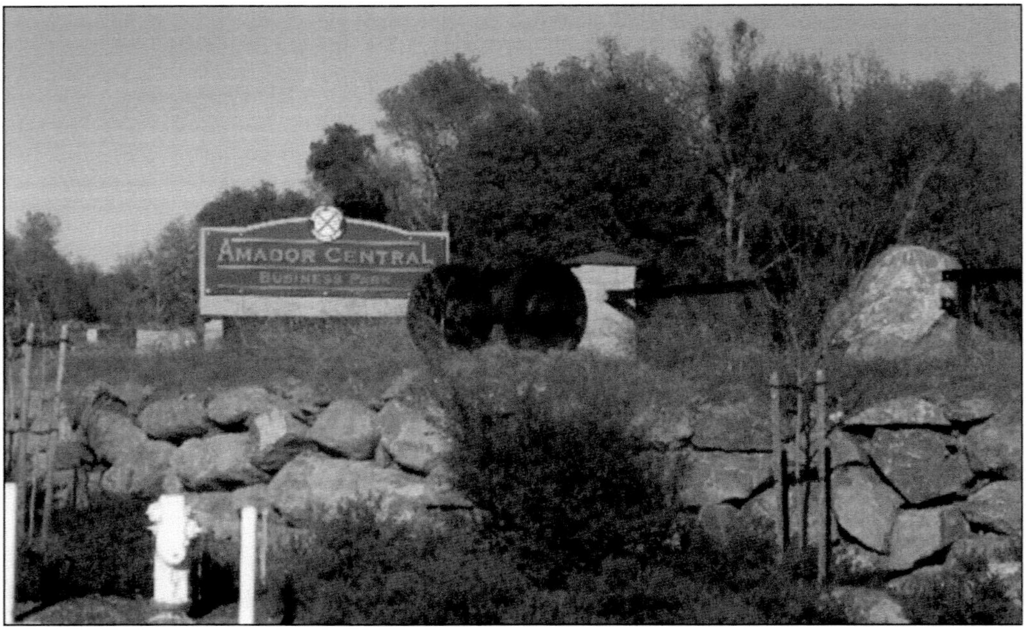

A large parcel to the west of the shopping center and the particleboard plant was set aside by Sierra Pacific Industries to develop a business park. The sign pictured here, commemorating the railroad, is one of several that are placed at various entrances to the site. To date, the only occupants of the site are county offices. (Author's collection.)

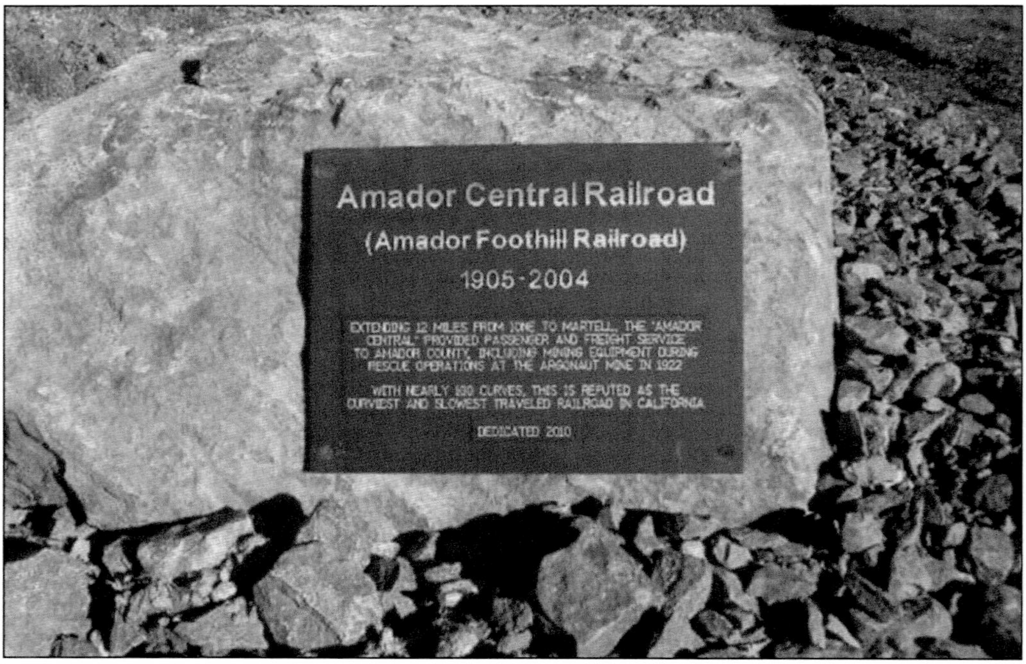

In 2009, Sierra Pacific Industries removed the tracks that were located within the business park property. Amador preservationists, who had hoped to preserve the railroad in its entirety, were disappointed—a 100-year era of railroading in Amador County had come to an end. In 2010, Sierra Pacific Industries placed a plaque on the Amador Central right-of-way within the business park. (Author's collection.)

Eight

Tracks to the Future

The first full run on the Amador Central Railroad between Ione and Martell occurred in 1905, and for the next 99 years, trains continued to make the trip back and forth. Less than a decade ago, a drive along State Route 88 might have offered the motorist a glimpse of a locomotive clacking along the tracks with cars in tow. That opportunity ended in 2004, when the tracks fell silent, engines were dismantled, sold, or parked, and the engine house and shops at the Martell depot were shut down. It seemed that the life of an old and familiar friend in Amador County had come to an end; however, through the efforts of preservationists and the generosity of Sierra Pacific Industries, it simply changed its countenance.

In September 2004, the author received a letter from Sierra Pacific, stating that the company had been granted abandonment of the line. The author replied with a letter informing their attorneys that the railroad was a historic resource and should be evaluated as such before abandonment. The Surface Transportation Board (STB) was also contacted. While local government expressed its concern about losing the transportation corridor, it would be the six-year-long efforts of the Amador County Historical Society (ACHS) and the Recreational Railroad Coalition (RRC) that would eventually save the Amador Central from destruction.

While the Amador County Historical Society became engaged in preservation discussions with Sierra Pacific, the Recreational Railroad Coalition acquired a lease to run its speeder cars over the line in 2005. The lease provided a bit of insurance that the rails would remain, but in 2010, the lease was terminated. The preservation cause was furthered when the author, as an archaeologist, along with archaeologist Shelly Davis-King and historian Judith Marvin, compiled a historic studies report and found the railroad eligible for the National Register of Historic Places. In 2009, a section of track was removed; however, through the perseverance of ACHS and the RRC, Sierra Pacific Industries recognized the significance of preserving the line. In August 2010, Sierra Pacific sold the railroad to the two groups for one dollar, and another chapter in the history of the Amador Central began.

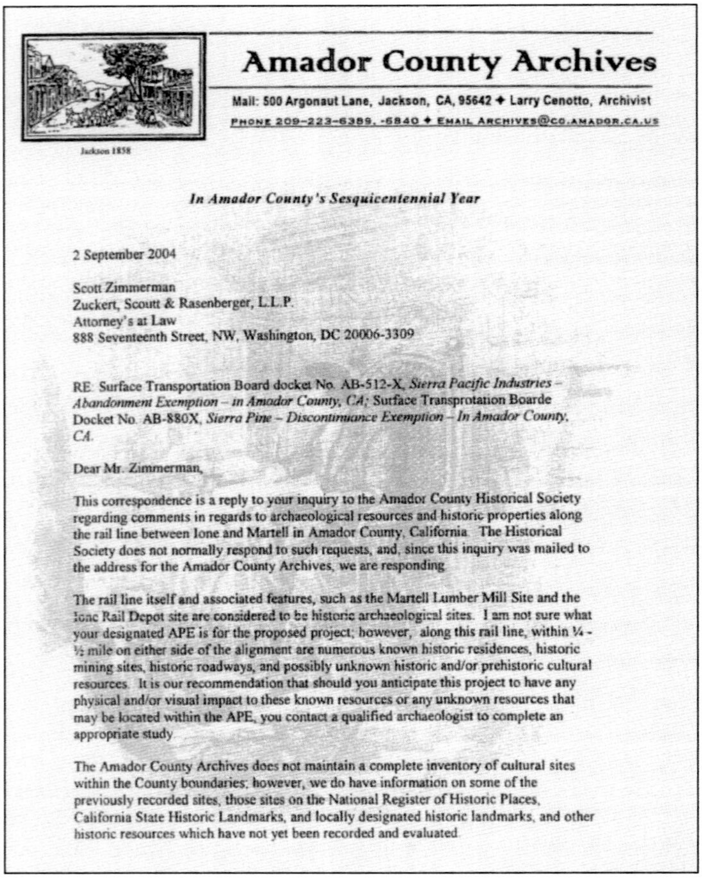

Amador County Archives

Mail: 500 Argonaut Lane, Jackson, CA, 95642 ✦ Larry Cenotto, Archivist
PHONE 209-223-6389, -6840 ✦ EMAIL ARCHIVES@CO.AMADOR.CA.US

Jackson 1858

In Amador County's Sesquicentennial Year

2 September 2004

Scott Zimmerman
Zuckert, Scoutt & Rasenberger, L.L.P.
Attorney's at Law
888 Seventeenth Street, NW, Washington, DC 20006-3309

RE: Surface Transportation Board docket No. AB-512-X, *Sierra Pacific Industries – Abandonment Exemption – in Amador County, CA;* Surface Transprotation Boarde Docket No. AB-880X, *Sierra Pine – Discontinuance Exemption – In Amador County, CA.*

Dear Mr. Zimmerman,

This correspondence is a reply to your inquiry to the Amador County Historical Society regarding comments in regards to archaeological resources and historic properties along the rail line between Ione and Martell in Amador County, California. The Historical Society does not normally respond to such requests, and, since this inquiry was mailed to the address for the Amador County Archives, we are responding.

The rail line itself and associated features, such as the Martell Lumber Mill Site and the Ione Rail Depot site are considered to be historic archaeological sites. I am not sure what your designated APE is for the proposed project; however, along this rail line, within ¼ - ½ mile on either side of the alignment are numerous known historic residences, historic mining sites, historic roadways, and possibly unknown historic and/or prehistoric cultural resources. It is our recommendation that should you anticipate this project to have any physical and/or visual impact to these known resources or any unknown resources that may be located within the APE, you contact a qualified archaeologist to complete an appropriate study.

The Amador County Archives does not maintain a complete inventory of cultural sites within the County boundaries; however, we do have information on some of the previously recorded sites, those sites on the National Register of Historic Places, California State Historic Landmarks, and locally designated historic landmarks, and other historic resources which have not yet been recorded and evaluated.

Pictured here is the first page of the 2004 letter sent to Sierra Pacific Industries attorneys by the author, while employed as an archivist by the County of Amador. It was sent in response to the announcement that Sierra Pacific had been granted abandonment of the Amador Central and that a historic evaluation of the line was not required. In 2005, the Recreational Railroad Coalition, under the leadership of former state assemblyman Larry Bowler, acquired a lease from Sierra Pacific Industries to run its recreational speeder cars on the Amador Central rails. In the photograph below, speeders are lined up for a run. Bowler can be seen walking next to the cars. (Both, author's collection.)

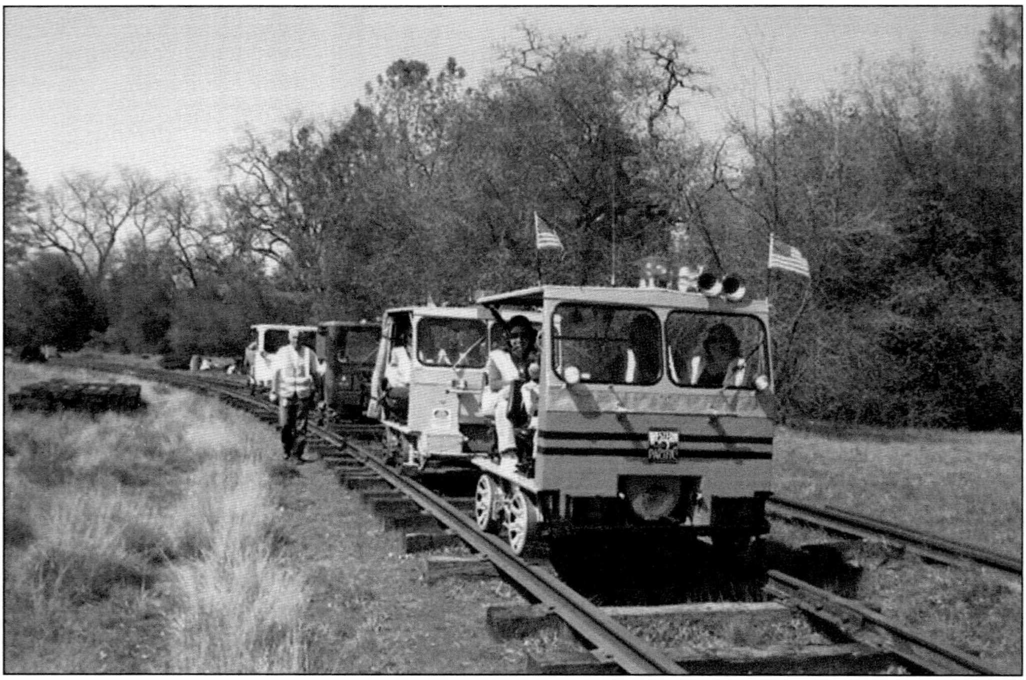

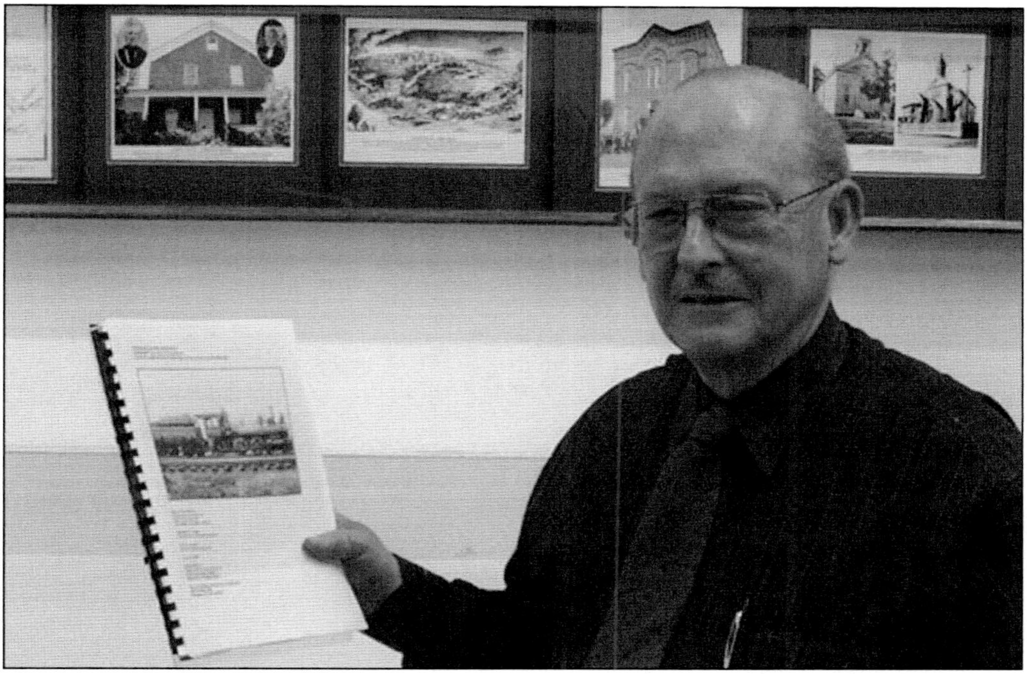

For nearly four years, during his tenure as president of the Amador County Historical Society, Dave Butow worked tirelessly in promoting and lobbying for preservation of the Amador Central. Through his efforts, the California Office of Historic Preservation became involved and contributed to the cause. Butow is pictured holding up the historic studies report that determined the railroad eligible for the National Register. (Author's collection.)

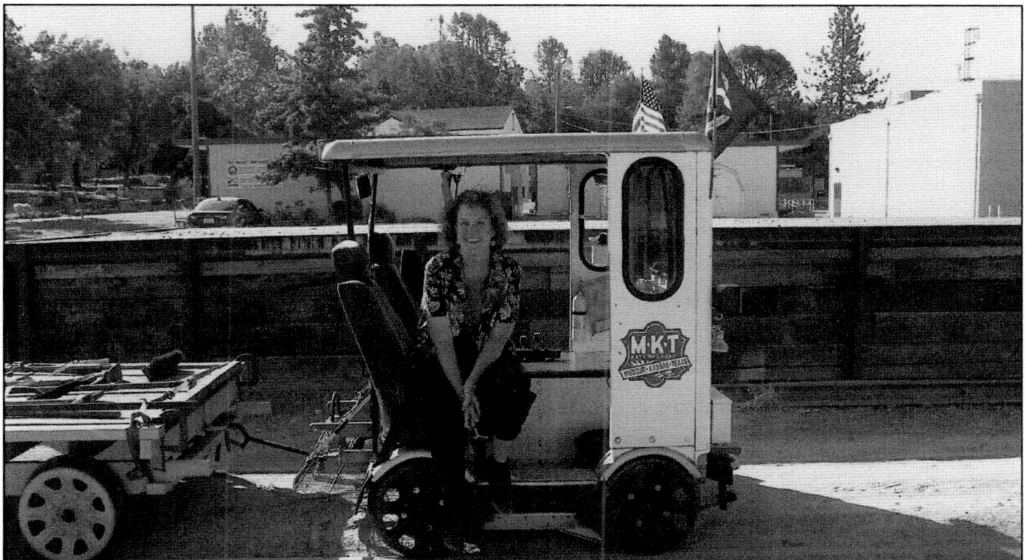

Archaeologist Shelly Davis-King poses inside a speeder car while waiting to take a run on the Amador Central. In 2007, King, along with the author, made the run to visually survey the railroad prior to compiling the historic studies report. Architectural historian Judith Marvin did not participate in the run, but provided important assessments of the buildings and other structural features at the Martell depot. (Author's collection.)

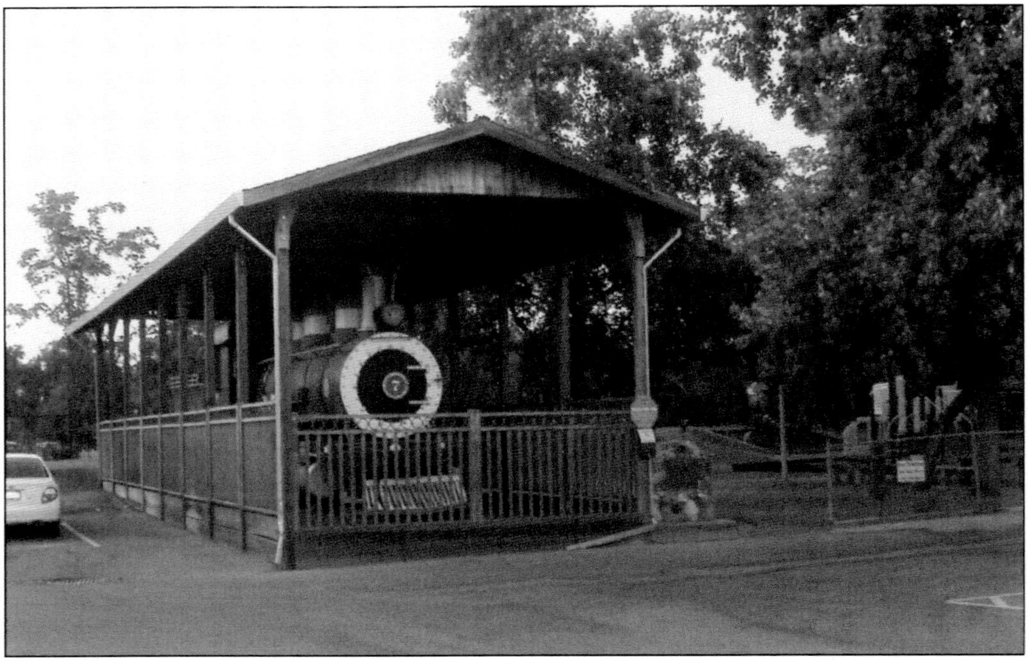

Since 1961, the City of Ione has played an important role in the preservation of Amador County's railroad heritage. Since that date, it has been the caretaker of old No. 7, Iron Ivan. From the time the locomotive was moved to the Ione City Park, the city has continually improved its conservation methods for the engine. (Author's collection.)

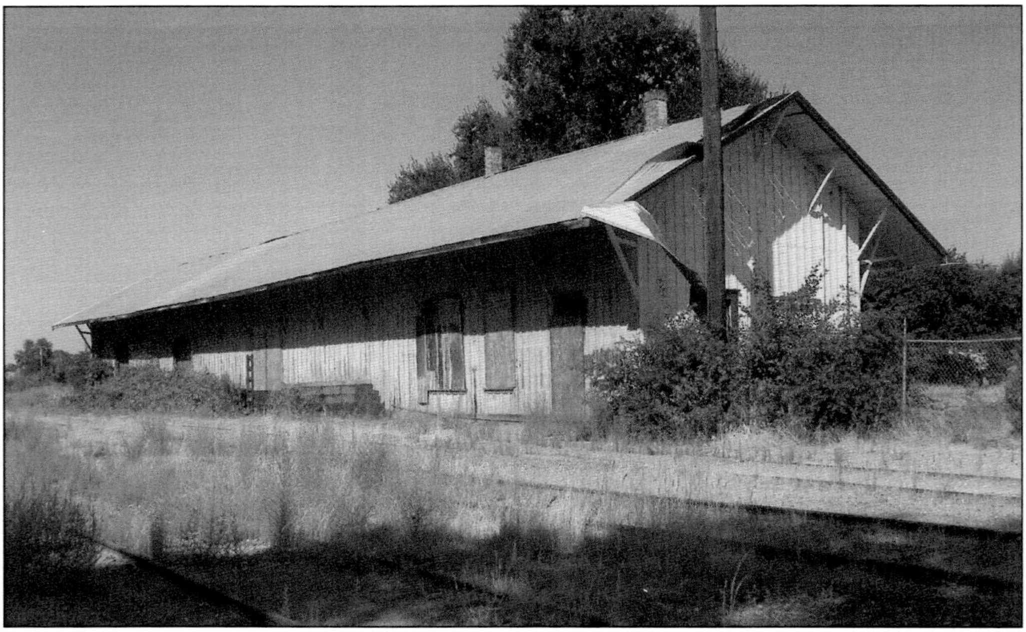

The Southern Pacific depot in Ione, which provided a home to Amador Central ticket offices, now stands in a state of disrepair; however, the City of Ione has taken up the cause of restoring the building. In 2010, current owner Union Pacific signed an agreement to donate the depot to the city, provided that the city restores the building. Efforts are currently underway to complete that work. (Author's collection.)

On October 27, 2010, the Amador County Historical Society and the Recreational Railroad Coalition Historical Society held a press conference at the Ione rail yard to announce that Sierra Pacific Industries had sold the railroad to the two nonprofit organizations for one dollar. In this photograph, Mark Luster, public relations officer for Sierra Pacific Industries, addresses the crowd that has gathered for this historic event. (Author's collection.)

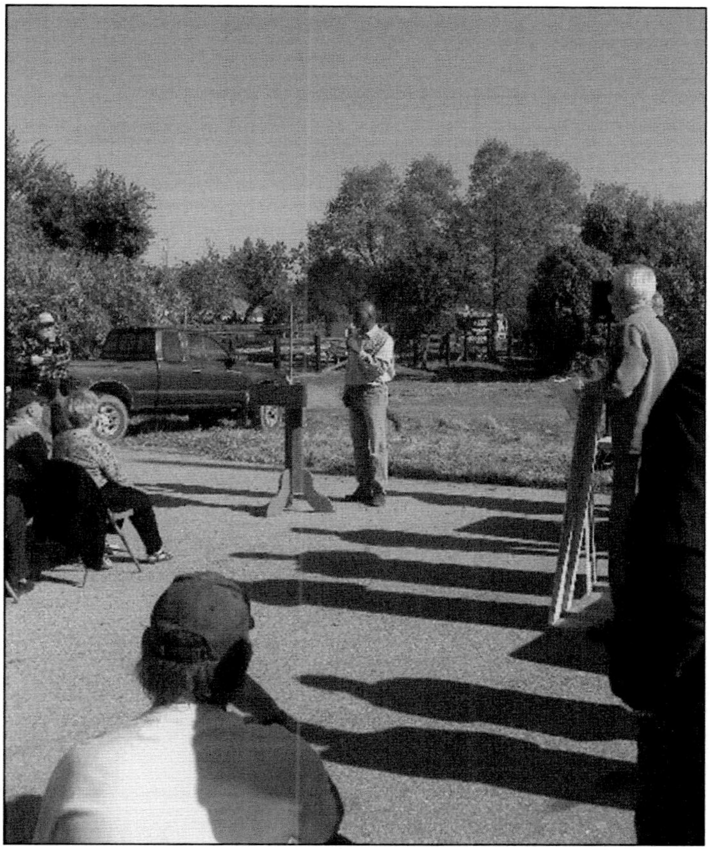

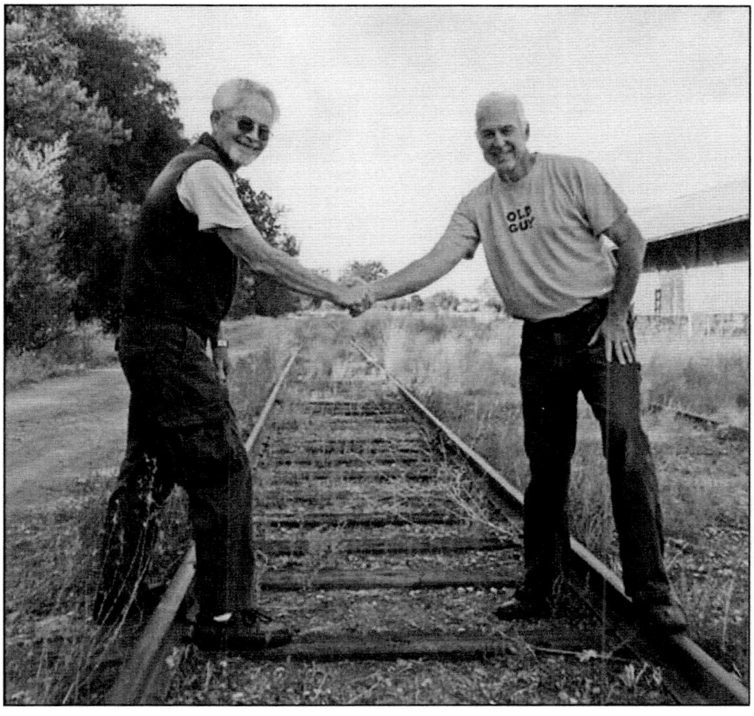

In a celebratory moment, Larry Cenotto (left), president of the Amador County Historical Society, and Larry Bowler, president of the Recreational Railroad Coalition Historical Society, shake hands while straddling the rails at the Ione rail yard. Both devoted a tremendous amount of effort to saving the Amador Central from destruction. (Courtesy Larry Cenotto.)

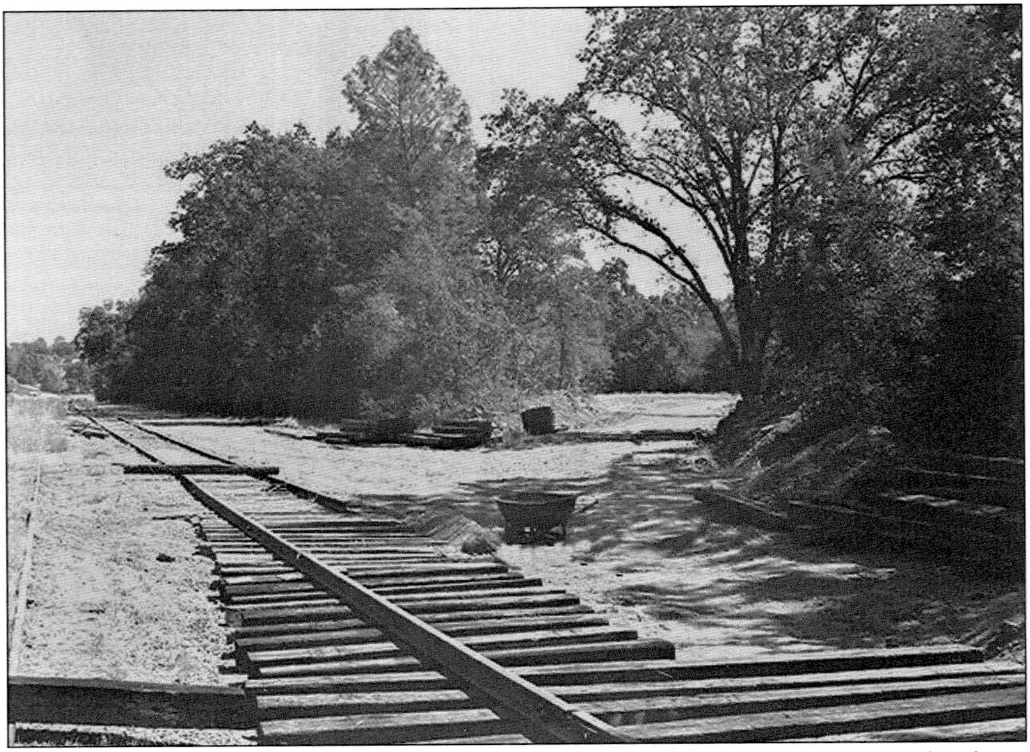

Since 2005, the Recreational Railroad Coalition has maintained the Amador Central right-of-way, including track maintenance and keeping the rails clear of vegetation and debris. This photograph was taken in 2009, during the reconstruction of the Ione's wye, a triangular layout of tracks used to divert trains from one track to another. The work was conducted by volunteers working one day a month over a two-and-a-half-year period. (Author's collection.)

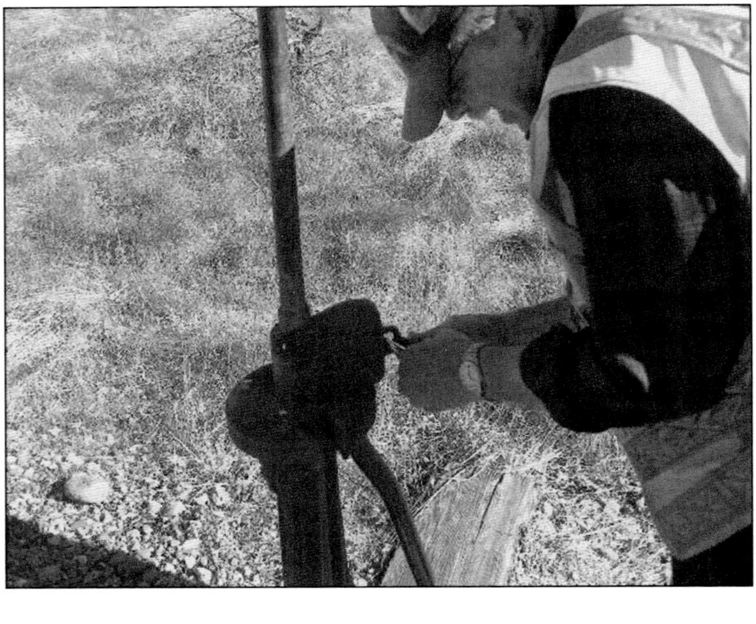

Maintenance of the railroad is not limited to taking care of the tracks. There are also switches and road crossing signals to be kept up. In this photograph, Grant Vogel, roadmaster for the Amador Central, replaces a padlock on one of the switches just outside of the Ione rail yard. (Author's collection.)

In addition to maintaining and preserving the Amador Central, it is the goal of the Amador County Historical Society and the Recreational Railroad Coalition Historical Society to provide the public with access to the railroad through events held on the line. The annual Ione Railfair and Motorfest has become a popular event for railroad buffs. Not only are speeders lined up to take participants for a ride over the railroad, displays of model trains and vintage vehicles are included. The Amador County Historical Society provides a forum for learning about the history of the Amador Central during the event. (Right, courtesy Amador Central Railroad Management Committee; below, author's collection.)

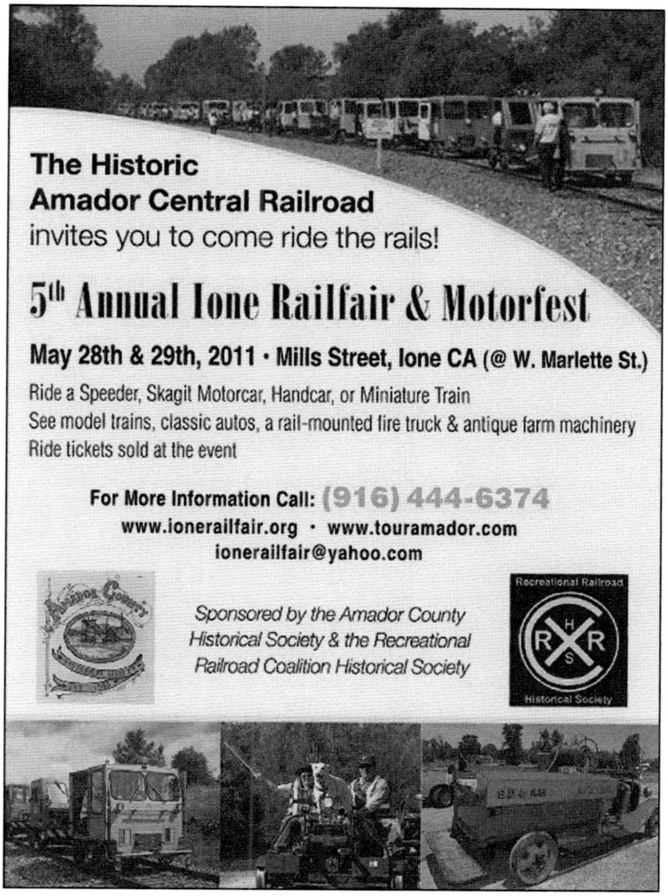

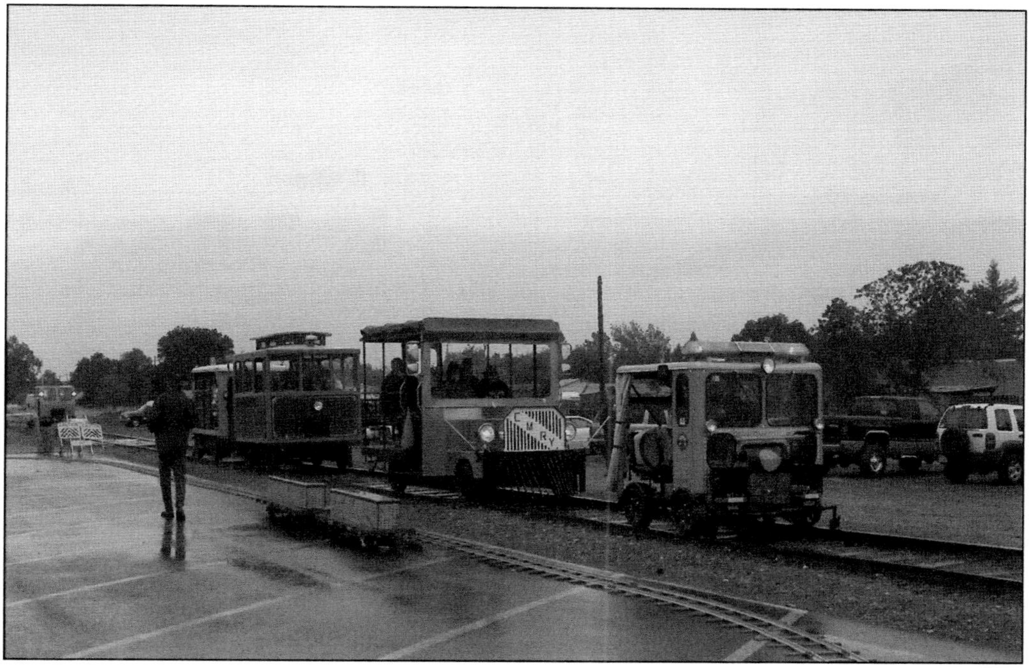

www.arcadiapublishing.com

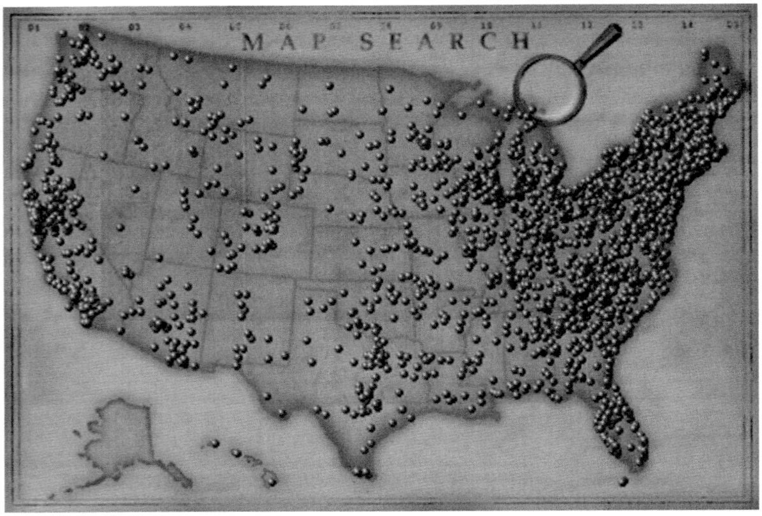

Discover books about the town where you grew up, the cities where your friends and families live, the town where your parents met, or even that retirement spot you've been dreaming about. Our Web site provides history lovers with exclusive deals, advanced notification about new titles, e-mail alerts of author events, and much more.

MADE IN THE USA

Arcadia Publishing, the leading local history publisher in the United States, is committed to making history accessible and meaningful through publishing books that celebrate and preserve the heritage of America's people and places. Consistent with our mission to preserve history on a local level, this book was printed in South Carolina on American-made paper and manufactured entirely in the United States.

This book carries the accredited Forest Stewardship Council (FSC) label and is printed on 100 percent FSC-certified paper. Products carrying the FSC label are independently certified to assure consumers that they come from forests that are managed to meet the social, economic, and ecological needs of present and future generations.

FSC
Mixed Sources
Product group from well-managed forests and other controlled sources

Cert no. SW-COC-001530
www.fsc.org

Find Your Place in History.